EVERYDAY TALK

The Guilford Communication Series

Recent Volumes

Everyday Talk: Building and Reflecting Identities
Karen Tracy

Women in Public Relations: How Gender Influences Practice
Larissa A. Grunig, Elizabeth Lance Toth, and Linda Childers Hon

Daily News, Eternal Stories: The Mythological Role of Journalism
Jack Lule

Perspectives on Organizational Communication:
Finding Common Ground
Steven R. Corman and Marshall Scott Poole, Editors

The Idea of Public Journalism
Theodore L. Glasser, Editor

Communicating Across Cultures
Stella Ting-Toomey

Communications Policy and the Public Interest:
The Telecommunications Act of 1996
Patricia Aufderheide

The Business of Children's Entertainment
Norma Odom Pecora

Case Studies in Organizational Communication 2:
Perspectives on Contemporary Work Life
Beverly Davenport Sypher, Editor

Regulating Media: The Licensing and Supervision
of Broadcasting in Six Countries
Wolfgang Hoffman-Riem

Communication Theory: Epistemological Foundations
James A. Anderson

Television and the Remote Control: Grazing on a Vast Wasteland
Robert V. Bellamy, Jr., and James R. Walker

Relating: Dialogues and Dialectics
Leslie A. Baxter and Barbara M. Montgomery

Doing Public Journalism
Arthur Charity

Everyday Talk

Building and Reflecting Identities

KAREN TRACY

THE GUILFORD PRESS
New York   London

© 2002 The Guilford Press
A Division of Guilford Publications, Inc.
72 Spring Street, New York, NY 10012
www.guilford.com

Printed in the United States of America

This book is printed on acid-free paper.

Last digit is print number: 9   8   7   6   5   4   3   2   1

Library of Congress Cataloging-in-Publication Data

Tracy, Karen
  Everyday talk : building and reflecting identities / by Karen Tracy.
    p. cm. — (The Guilford communication series)
Includes bibliographical references and index.
  ISBN 1-57230-789-7
  1. Oral communication. 2. Identity (psychology) 3. Ethnicity. 4.
Speech acts (Linguistics) 5. Social interaction. I. Title. II. Series.
P95 .T7 2002
302.2′242—dc21
                                                    2002005598

Contents

IV. The Conclusion

Preface

This book grew out of my own fascination with talk and my belief that knowing how to listen to and analyze talk is fundamental to understanding communication. Language has always been part of the study of communication, but language only partly overlaps with talk. Language is an abstract code; talk is a, if not the, focal activity of ordinary life. Talking is how we express who we are and who we want to be; it is how we make relationships as well as relational problems; it is the instrument that creates, exacerbates, and—not quite as often as we'd like—solves troubles. At work, in public meetings, and in everyday social occasions talk is what we do. The examples of everyday talk that I use in this book are taken from studies appearing in discourse-analytic journals and books, as well as from my own research and teaching materials. Whenever I could find suitable instances, I have used actually occurring instances of talk to illustrate the point being made; however, when I could not, I invented exchanges that seemed plausible. Introductory text to examples will make clear if an exchange is real or imagined.

One goal in writing the book was to move the findings of discourse analysis—a rich, interesting, and too often overlooked area of study—into the mainstream of communication coursework. I am assuming that college students will be the book's main audience. I am also assuming that some students will be reading the text with no prior coursework in communication. As such, core concepts are explained with key vocabulary highlighted, and each chapter has a preview and summary. In addition, references are used sparingly in the body of the text. Although the intended focal audience is undergraduate students, the book is designed to be useful to novice scholars (graduate students and academics new to discourse studies) as well. To facilitate scholarly engagement, there are extensive endnotes. Endnotes identify authors responsible for ideas, differences in terminology, current debates, and my position in the controversies. Also discussed are how I adapted or combined different viewpoints, my reasons for doing so, and likely criticisms of the choices.

My hope is that this book will be useful in a variety of teaching venues: in interpersonal and intercultural communication classes; in seminars exploring topics such as social interaction, language, discourse analysis, social influence, or vernacular rhetorics; and in introductory courses in communication departments or in communication classes that are required as part of business, education, or health science curricula. If the text were included as part of an interpersonal communication course, the issue of personal relationships could be foregrounded, emphasizing face and relational identities (Chapter 1), divorce mediation (Chapter 2), marital naming and marriage philosophy (Chapter 3), face-threatening speech acts (Chapter 4), indicating sexual interest (Chapter 5), directness style differences and interpersonal conflict (Chapter 8), and the relational work that narratives do (Chapter 9). If this book were part of an intercultural class, attention could be given to the diversity of speech communities considered, including (1) racial and ethnic groups, among them African American (Chapters 1, 5, 8), Latino/a (Chapters 3, 7), Native American (Chapters 2, 6), and European Americans (all chapters); (2) social class groups (middle class, all chapters; working Americans, Chapters 2, 6, 9); (3) gender (most chapters); and (4) different nationalities, among them Australia, Colombia, China, Denmark, the Dominican Republic, Germany, Greece, Israel, Japan, Kenya, New Zealand, North America, The Netherlands, and the United Kingdom.

Acknowledgments

Many people contributed to my writing of this book. First and foremost were the students in my communication and society classes at the University of Colorado. Over the last half-dozen years, their questions, comments, and collective reactions, made out of both interest and boredom, helped me determine the text's basic shape. A second important group was the doctoral students who served as teaching assistants in this course. Thanks to Rob Agne, Donald Anderson, Barry Liss, Julie Naughton, and Alena Sanusi for their many conversations with me about talk and identity.

On the conversation front, I especially want to thank four colleagues. Kristine Fitch challenged me to engage with culture more seriously, Curt LeBaron nudged me from a logocentric view of talk toward a more embodied one, James McDaniel helped me figure out what it means to be a rhetorical discourse analyst, and Bob Craig served as a favored and frequent sounding board as I worked out how best to put these ideas together. Comments on drafts of individual chapters or the entire book came from many people and were highly useful. Thanks to Brenda Allen, Richard Buttny, Kristine Fitch, Phil Glenn, Liz Grassi, Kristal Hawkins, Eliza Hines, Mariko Kotani, Sandra Metts, Yair Neuman, and several graduate classes and anonymous reviewers.

Finally, a big thanks goes to my husband, Bob, and my daughter, Jill. Along with our dog, Moogie, they kept me grounded. Besides serving as ongoing topics for my own talk, they were (and continue to be) my most valued conversational partners. They listened to what I had to say on topics big and small; they valued my doing the same for them; and they lived their involvement with me by disagreeing, criticizing, and arguing as occasions required.

The Argument

◈ Talk and Identity

You are sitting in a restaurant, waiting to meet a friend. To pass the time, you go into people-watching mode. Based on what you see and hear, you create ministories about the individuals in the restaurant. You decide who the people are, what they must be to each other, their purpose in meeting, what kinds of political commitments they must have, and so on. Then you begin to focus on the man in the booth across from you.

He looks Asian—you think maybe he's Japanese. He's drinking coffee and watching the door. After a few minutes an American-looking couple join him. The woman introduces herself and her companion. You hear the following conversation:

EXAMPLE 1.1 (9:06 A.M., Turley's Restaurant. JI = Jolene Incar, LY = Lee Yamda, RL = Robert Lester)

JI: Mr. Yamada? (Yamada nods) I'm Jolene Incar (offers her hand) and this is my husband, Robert Lester (thr two men shake hands). I'm sorry we're a little late. There was a car accident and we had to go the long way around. I hope you didn't have to wait long.

LY: No problem—I've only been here a minute myself. Please join me. The coffee is great.

RL: (As they slide into the booth) Jolene has been telling me about the difficulties your office has run into and I think we may be able to help you . . .

The woman's speech is accented; you conclude that your initial assumption about her being American was wrong. But the other two certainly sound American.[1] From this short exchange, you infer that (1) the men are American but the woman probably isn't; (2) the three had not met previously in person, although Ms. Incar and Mr. Yamada probably had spoken on the phone; (3) the husband and wife work together in a business; (4) the trio are meeting for business rather than for pleasure; (5) Jolene Incar cares about being perceived as a polite person; and (6) Jolene and Robert are not a traditional married couple.

In creating this story—in making these particular inferences—you have drawn upon extensive knowledge about how people in American culture talk to and about each other. Whether or not your inferences are accurate is something that would require you to question the three people. However, it is likely that many people would make the same inferences as you. This is the case because there are ways of talking that routinely go with being a certain kind of person, doing particular activities, and having certain relationships.

Most likely you are already aware of some features of the conversation that contribute to the inferences I have made; probably there are others that you would have a hard time naming. That both of the men are native-born Americans but that the woman probably is not is suggested by the way the three speak English, especially the dialect each person uses. That Jolene and Robert are married is cued rather obviously by Jolene's introduction, in which she refers to Robert as her husband. That they do not have a traditional marriage is suggested, although perhaps more ambiguously, by their differing last names and the fact that different last names for husband and wife are unconventional in American society. That the trio are business acquaintances is cued by Ms. Incar's formal term of address ("Mr. Yamada" rather than "Lee") and Robert's topical reference to Mr. Yamada's office. That they are first-time acquaintances seems probable because Jolene introduced herself, an act that would be quite strange if she and Mr. Yamada had met previously in person. In addition, the noticeable absence of pleasant inquiries ("How have you been since I last saw you?" or "How's your new system working out?") makes the most sense if the trio has had no prior relationship in which they had an opportunity to share information about each other. The impression that Jolene is a polite person can be tied to what she said and some specific features of the situation. Ms. Incar offered an apology for the couple's tardiness, a reasonable excuse for why it happened, and a statement that indicated her concern about inconveniencing Mr. Yamada. Given that it was only 5 or 6 minutes past the hour—a conventional time when appointments start—it seems likely that Jolene was no more than 5 minutes late. That Jolene did all this conversational work rather than offer a perfunctory apology creates a sense of her as a polite person.

My purpose in this book is to look at the myriad ways everyday talk reflects, sustains, builds, and challenges who people are. **Everyday talk** refers to the ordinary kinds of communicating people do in schools, workplaces, shops, and at public meetings, as well as when they are at home or with their friends. Who people are is what communication theorists call **identity**.[2] Identity includes the most personal aspects of people, what in ordinary life we refer to as a person's character (*honest, considerate, sleazy*) or personality (*overbearing, quiet and thoughtful*). It also includes characteristics we take to be relatively fixed, such as ethnic and racial background, age, sex, or nationality. In addition, identity includes the roles we take on with another in particular situations (e.g., supervisor–employee, friend–friend, coach–player, sister–brother, discussion leader–participant).

WHY IS UNDERSTANDING THE LINK BETWEEN EVERYDAY TALK AND IDENTITY SO IMPORTANT?

Since you have participated in family, school, and work life for many years, you already possess a wealth of experiential knowledge about links between different identities and communicative practices. Much of the knowledge you possess is tacit, that is, it is knowledge you routinely use to make sense of other people's actions and to inform your own communicative choices. But it is not a kind of knowledge you could articulate easily; it is hidden and below the surface.

That knowledge is tacit is unproblematic when exchanges between people go well. But when people have difficulties with each other, it is crucial that they are able to analyze explicitly what went wrong. Only by being able to accurately analyze the character of an interactional difficulty is it possible to create more effective ways of managing such difficulties in the future. The central purpose of this book is to help you transform your **tacit knowledge** about everyday talk into **explicit knowledge**. With explicit knowledge of how talk links to important identities, you should find yourself better able to be the kind of person you are seeking to be and to more satisfactorily manage the social, work, public, and intimate relationships about which you care. In addition, you will be better able to avoid the inevitable and serious danger of tacit knowledge: presuming that what you know is natural and universal, and that what you take for granted is the only way that a particular identity could be linked to a communicative practice.

In the remainder of this chapter I describe one particularly influential view of the purpose of conversation—to exchange information—and argue why this view is inadequate to understand what happens when people talk. Then I introduce four sets of ideas (interactional meaning, identity-work, identities, and discursive practices) that are crucial to the argument I make in this book.

THE LOGIC OF CONVERSATION: INFORMATION EXCHANGE?

One of the most influential views of conversation is the one articulated by the language philosopher Grice.[3] Conversation, he suggested, has many purposes, but its major one is the "effective exchange of information."[4] To accomplish this informational purpose communicators in their roles as speakers and listeners orient to the cooperative principle. The **cooperative principle** guides both how people talk and interpret, and it specifies that participants should "make their conversational contribution such as is required, at the stage at which it occurs, by the accepted purpose or direction of the talk exchange in which you are engaged."[5]

In describing conversation as "cooperative," Grice did not mean to say that conversation is only and always nice and pleasant. Conversation is a cooperative activity in much the same way that football is cooperative. For the game of football to work, players need to assume that other players will adhere to the basic logic of the game. Players, for instance, are expected to run toward a particular goal post, not toward the other one, nor up into the grandstands. Moreover, every move in football is to be interpreted by assuming that all players are adhering to this logic.

Conversation's cooperative principle, however, does not stand by itself; there are four maxims that give it meat. These maxims (i.e., rules) specify more particularly what it means to be cooperative. Speakers are expected to (1) say just the right amount (**quantity maxim**), (2) say what they believe to be true (**quality maxim**), (3) make their comments relevant (**relevance maxim**), and (4) be orderly and avoid ambiguous, obscure phrases (**manner maxim**). These rules, rather obviously, do not provide a straightforward description of how people talk. People, rather frequently, make irrelevant comments, say too much or too little, and assert things that are not literally true. If Grice's claim were simply "This is how people talk," he would have been wrong and his views would not have been very influential. However, his argument was subtler than this.

According to Grice, rather than straightforwardly describing conversational action, the cooperative principle with its maxims furnishes an interpretive logic for conversation. Thus, if a man upon walking outside into pouring rain comments, "Beautiful day, isn't it?," his partner will assume that he is cooperating to convey information but that he is ignoring the quality maxim. She most likely will hear his remark as giving information about how awful the weather is.

Blatantly ignoring (flouting) a maxim is a way conversational implicatures are generated. **Conversational implicatures** are meanings that differ from what a person said explicitly. For instance, assume that Len has applied for a job as manager of a small store. As part of the decision-making process his possible future employer telephones his past employer. She says, "Len is a great person. He's always on time." The new employer interprets this comment about Len as being less informative than would be expected for this type of job reference. The meaning she takes from the comment, since she assumes the past employer is following the cooperative principle, is that Len has some habits that might make him ineffective as a manager.

Grice's view of conversation is a powerful one. It begins to explain some of what happens in conversation. Yet, as I hope will be clear to you by the end of this book, information exchange is not the most important reason that people talk with each other.

INTERACTIONAL MEANINGS AND IDENTITY-WORK

Although people do talk with each other to give and receive information, other activities are always getting done. Most important for our purpose is the ongoing way talk is doing identity-work. **Identity-work** refers to the process through which talk makes available to participants and observers who the people doing the talking must be. There are two sides to identity-work:

1. Talk does identity-work. Through a person's choices about how to talk, identity-work is accomplished. That is, people's ways of talking construct pictures of who people must be.
2. People's preexisting identities (e.g., their nationality, age, profession, or social class) work to shape how they will talk.

I will explore this twofold process in detail in subsequent chapters. At this beginning point, however, I need to say a few things about the meaning-making process.

Utterance Content versus Interactional Meaning

In talk, the smallest meaningful unit is the **utterance**.[6] Utterances, what a speaker utters, may be as short as a single word or phrase or as long as a couple of sentences. But unlike sentences—the basic unit for writing—utterances are situated, occurring at particular times and places, and directed toward particular someones. For instance, in Example 1.2 there are four utterances.

EXCERPT 1.2

Yvonne is walking toward Jared and they catch each other's gaze.

1   Y: Hello, how are you?

2   J: Not bad, you?

3   Y: Good.

4   J: Goo::d. Got time to go get coffee?

Utterances are responses to other utterances (Jared's "Not bad, you?" is a response to Yvonne's greeting) or to events in a local environment (Yvonne's "Hello, how are you?" is a response to catching Jared's eye). The audience for any utterance is particular. Jared and Yvonne were addressing each other. Because utterances are units of social life, as well as linguistic expressions (words, phrases, and sentences), they will always have two levels of meaning.

The **content** of an utterance, the first level, is the conventional meaning of the words or phrases that were said. It is the literal or dictionary-level meaning that exists apart from any particular context. For instance, the conventional meaning of the word *hello* is a greeting, a friendly token one person uses in meeting another. But *hello* also has other meanings. If a person says "hello" in the middle of a telephone call, its interactional meaning may be to check that the other person is still on the line. If "hello" is said in the midst of a face-to-face conversation, particularly if the syllables of the word are elongated ("he:h-lo:h"), it may be intended as criticism for making an unreasonable remark. The **interactional meaning** of an utterance is its meaning for the participants in the situation in which the utterance (or more usually, a sequence of utterances) occurred. Interactional meaning arises from and depends on the context, and may be given or given off.

Communicators may consciously work to create a certain impression or may do so inadvertently. Goffman[7] describes this as the difference between meanings that are intentionally **given** and those that are

given off. For instance, a person speaking to a group may work to present herself as relaxed and confident and do so by smiling, gazing at everyone present, telling a joke to get started, speaking extemporaneously rather than reading, and so on. However, if in speaking her voice cracks or she pauses after just a few words, members of the audience might see her as being a bit more nervous than she is trying to show. The cracked voice and the inappropriate pause would be meanings that were given off, that is, not intentionally planned by a communicator but revealing nonetheless. In considering the relationship between everyday talk and identities, we will be interested in both kinds of meaning.

Linking Content and Interactional Meaning

Every utterance, then, can be analyzed in terms of its literal meaning (the content) and its meaning in context (interactional meaning). Of importance is the linkage between the levels. For the most part, the content level is relatively straightforward and unambiguous. If people share a common language and the physical communicative situation is not noisy, it is pretty easy to agree on what the content of an utterance was. In contrast, its interactional meaning not only is dependent on what was said, but is considerably more ambiguous.

Arriving at the interactional meaning of a sequence of utterances requires examining what was said (the words) in light of how it was said, the people who said it, the situation, and what had previously been uttered. Put another way, the interactional meaning of an utterance arises from the content of a message in combination with the context. **Context**, then, references all the background kinds of information that shape how interactional meanings get assigned to what is said.

For instance, imagine you are in the park on a hot summer day. A jogger comes up to you as you are picnicking and asks, "Could I have some water?" Given the heat of the day and the jogger's dripping sweat, you probably take the question as a straightforward request for water that arises because the person is thirsty. But imagine you are a parent who has just put your child to bed after the usual nightly bathroom and story-reading rituals. As you are getting ready to turn off the light, your child asks, "Could I have some water?" The content of the child's utterance is the same as the jogger's, but the context is different. In the situation with the child, you may interpret the utterance as something other than a genuine request for water by someone who is thirsty. You might, for instance, reply, "No—no more stalling. It's time for bed."

Thus the particular setting and identities of the participants, as well as a person's tone of voice, facial expression, the order in which parts of the message are sequenced, and so on will shape the situated meaning of an utterance. Those factors that are included in the utterance itself, but especially the tone of voice, are what Gumperz[8] refers to as **contextualization cues**. Contextualization cues, then, reference those features of talk that people use to arrive at the interactional meanings of what is being said. Figure 1.3 portrays the relationships among utterance content, context, and meaning.

When people use the same contextualization cues—a likely state when people come from the same sociocultural background—a speaker's intended meaning is more likely to be in alignment with the one that a listener assigns. But if people do not share contextualization cues, a problem can arise. For instance, in American English a central way that speakers convey interest in a person or enthusiasm about an issue is through their tone of voice. Thus, if a speaker in responding to an invitation said in a monotone voice, "Thank you for asking, perhaps another time," a different meaning would be attached to her utterance than if she emphasized the phrase "Thank you" and had a strong upward vocal inflection at the end of the phrase "another time." In the former case, the American English-speaking listener is likely to infer that the person is trying to be polite but does not really want to spend time with him. In the latter case, the listener may infer that the other person really does want to get to know him but cannot accept his invitation at this particular time. The use of voice inflection to signal attitude is a contextualization cue. But voice inflection, as well as other contextualization cues, is not universal. Consequently, if speakers come from communities that use different contextualization cues, they may very well misinterpret each other.

Gumperz[9] describes a number of problems that have arisen between Indian English speakers and British English speakers because of just such different contextualization conventions. For instance, Indian English-speaking women working in a cafeteria were getting complaints from British English-speaking patrons about their rudeness. In looking at their

FIGURE 1.1. Relationship between content and meaning (interactional).

conversational action, Gumperz discovered that the British English patrons were attributing rudeness to the staff because of the workers' intonation patterns when they offered services. Instead of saying "Gravy?" with a rising intonation, as British English speakers would to offer a service and be polite, the Indian English speakers were saying "Gravy" with a falling intonation. For British English speakers, this conveyed an identity message that suggested *you're not important, so just take it or leave it.* This was unintended by the Indian English speakers whose communicative practices did not include using intonation to convey these relational attitudes.

So far I have discussed interactional meaning as if it were a single thing, but this is not the case. Interactional meaning is best thought of in the plural: interactional meanings.

The Multiple Layers and Kinds of Interactional Meanings[10]

In every communicative situation there are at least two versions of interactional meaning: (1) the meaning intended by the first person speaking, and (2) the meaning assigned by the conversational partner. Put another way, interactional meanings are positioned and likely to differ across participants. When communication goes smoothly, we tend to think about meaning as unitary and seamless—what a listener understood is what a speaker meant.[11] But, to be able to manage communication well, it is important to recognize that there are always two views of what an interaction meant. Often the two views are similar enough that the difference can be ignored. Nonetheless, they are always there. Differences in interactional meanings quite frequently lead to awkward moments or small confusions, but sometimes they lead to serious conflicts. Consider how these differences might occur and become apparent in the most ordinary of situations.

Imagine that a woman (Melinda) has asked her roommate (Susan) for permission to get something from the refrigerator. Susan may understand the content of Melinda's utterance (her question) but nonetheless be puzzled about what she actually meant. Susan is likely to feel puzzled because she regards herself as having an equal roommate relationship with Melinda: in her mind, she has no special authority over the refrigerator. Because asking permission is more often done in unequal relationships where the higher status person is the person who gets to grant permission and the lower status person is the one expected to ask for permission, Susan may be confused about why Melinda is asking her permission. The following exchange might well result.

EXAMPLE 1.3

S: Why are you asking me? It's your refrigerator too.

M: But yesterday you told me you were going to defrost and I didn't want to get in the way.

S: Oooh, I forgot I was going to do that.

In Example 1.3, Melinda makes visible her meaning for asking permission. In this case, it had nothing to do with her seeing herself as in a lower status than Susan. Rather, her asking permission was meant as a conversational device to show courtesy to someone in the middle of a task.

Not only is interactional meaning positioned and shaped by each participant, it also involves layers. These layers can be thought of as answers to questions about the meaning of an interaction. A first question to ask is, "What act is being performed by uttering a particular set of words?" If a speaker says, "Excuse me," is the action apologizing or reprimanding? **Speech acts** name utterances in terms of their purpose. Is what a person saying (1) giving information, (2) making an offer, (3) complimenting, (4) criticizing, (5) requesting a favor, (6) ordering another to do something, (7) apologizing, or (8) something else? I will have more to say about speech acts and how they do identity-work in Chapter 4.

A second layer of interactional meaning is the situation **frame**. How should the kind of occasion that is happening be labeled? Frames are broader than speech acts; they are the everyday names we give to speech occasions, such as a therapy session, two friends chatting, an interview, a lecture, an advising session, a prayer group, a team meeting, a coffee break, and so on. Frames typically go unnamed, seeming self-evident to participants.[12] It would be quite strange indeed for a college teacher to begin a class by announcing: "The situation we're in is a lecture. This means I'm going to do most of the talking and you get to do most of the listening. If you want to make a comment or ask a question, raise your hand."

Frames are inferred from the physical situation and change through the ways people talk with each other. For instance, imagine a group of eight people in a room. There's a large rectangular table with chairs around it, and off to the side is a small table with coffee and sweet rolls. At one point in time people are standing up, sipping coffee, milling around the room, and chatting in small groups of two to three about such topics as their baseball team's recent loss, a good movie that someone saw, and a coworker's recent engagement. At a later point, all eight people are sitting around the large table, one person is speaking at a time, and the person at one end of the table is directing the talk of the others with phrases such as "The next item on our agenda is . . . " or "Does anyone have anything else to propose?" The frame for the first kind of interaction is a coffee break; the frame for the second is a work meeting. The coffee-break frame changes to the meeting frame when participants purposefully change how they talk with each other. In a college lecture, if a group of students stood up, shouted at the instructor, held up placards, and shook their fists, the understood frame would change from a lecture to a student protest.

Most often communicators assume the same frame as their partner, but this is not always so. For instance, if one person set up a meeting with a colleague to talk about a joint project, the expected frame is likely to be a work meeting. However, if in the course of the meeting the person commented positively about the colleague's appearance, touched the colleague's hand a couple times, asked about the colleague's past weekend, and held the colleague's gaze for slightly longer than is normal, the colleague might wonder if the other is flirting. Frames are suggested by the physical context (meeting in a teacher's office vs. meeting in a coffee shop) but are modified and redefined through ways of talking.

A final set of questions we could pose about the meaning of an interaction focuses directly on the people doing the talking. What kind of person is each communicator? How does each one regard the other? What kind of relationship do the two have? **Identity-work** refers to this kind of interactional meaning; it is how a segment of talk implicates who the people must be. Consider a segment of talk that Erickson[13] taped between a physician (an intern) and his supervisor (a senior physician). The situation frame was a "patient presentation," a talk occasion in which one physician (or physician in training, i.e., medical student) presents information to another physician about a patient and gives his or her tentative diagnosis as to what is the patient's likely medical problem. Consider what the intern initially said (Example 1.4), as well as one exchange (Example 1.5) with his supervisor.

EXCERPT 1.4

This is Ned Nagon, a twenty-nine year old black male. He was referred from emergency room with complaints of lower abdominal discomfort, super-pubic discomfort. It's sorta hard to get a clear history. I'll sorta go from the top (*the intern goes on to say that the patient had normal health until two months ago. Then he had a swelling in the right eye—he has a prosthesis in the right eye from a gunshot*

*wound—no neurological damage from that wound. He went first to
the eye clinic "eye," and to the ear, nose and throat clinic "ENT." He
was treated five to seven days with "Amox"*—amoxcillin. Intern notes
how patient had had a new sex partner and had recently been tested
for sexually transmitted diseases by another doctor.

At one point in giving the patient's history, the intern begins to describe medications and the following exchange occurs:

EXCERPT 1.5

I: → Let's see, medications. He doesn't take anything. He hasn't taken
anything over the counter. No home remedies. He doesn't smoke.
He does do, he does smoke some marijuana, thirty dollars a
week.

S: (smiles) how much is that?

I: (no smile) I have no idea

S: (smiles) it used to be an ounce (smiles)

I: (smiles) It's probably a little more depending on where you live
(serious face). NO IVDA, no cocaine. He, he's had multiple episodes of sexually transmitted diseases.

S: he's straight or gay?

I: he's straight. He has a girlfriend but sounds like he has other partners as well. His support is, he's on SSI for the gunshot wound

S: any history of colonic cancer?

The first thing to be said about this presentation and exchange is that
the talk reflects and constructs the two as medical personnel, either both
doctors or a doctor and a medical student. These identities are constructed through the accurate use of acronyms and medical jargon
(Amox, ENT, IVDA [intravenous drug administration]) as well as vocabulary related to social services and funding that are common in urban
hospital settings (e.g., SSI). In addition to the jargon another aspect of
the talk that reflects that they are doctors is the patient presentation
frame in which they are participating.

This type of impersonal style for describing a patient in which age
and race are mentioned first, followed by a general category description
of the person's complaint, imply not only that the speaker is a doctor (or
doctor in training), but also that the addressed other is. This is not the
style doctors would use in talking with a patient's family to tell family
members what was wrong with their relative. In the language of identity-
work, we could say that this segment of talk presents the speaker (I) as a

physician and altercasts his conversational partner (treats the person he is talking with) as also a doctor. Anyone with familiarity with this kind of talk could rather easily guess which party is the supervisor and which is the junior doctor. By and large, it is medical students and junior physicians who present patient cases to senior physicians. Thus, in this situation, the amount and content of I's talk is doing identity-work that cues that he is junior to S.

There are other more subtle identities at stake in this interaction. Case presentations are a major site in which medical students, interns (beginning doctors), and residents (a doctor with several years of experience) seek to present self as medically competent for their level. In case presentations, medical students are quickly corrected by their seniors for errors. They are expected to use, and thereby display that they have command of, the vast array of medical terms. But as interns gain experience their style of doing case presentations takes on a different flavor. The sign of an experienced physician is the ability to switch back and forth between technical medical terminology and casual everyday vocabulary. "Part of what the intern in residency needs to learn and practice is how NOT to appear as a beginning medical student performing a hypercorrect, stilted version of a case presentation."[14] In Example 1.5, then, through the way the intern mixes the everyday and the technical vocabulary—the phrase "eye clinic" rather than opthamology in one breath, and in the next "ENT" rather than ear, nose, and throat—he enacts himself as a relatively advanced doctor.

Finally, I must comment about the most subtle level of identity-work that occurs in the exchange. The intern is an African American man about the same age as the presenting patient; the supervisor is a white middle-aged man. Both men hail from middle-class family backgrounds and have had similar professional experiences (20+ years of school). The patient who is being presented is African American. Given the history of race in the United States, even recognizing the major changes that have occurred in the last 40–50 years, there is often a degree of tension in encounters between persons of different races. This is especially likely to happen when an upper-middle-class African American professional is in the position of speaking for an underclass African American to a senior professional who is white. Erickson puts it this way:

> The African-American professional may feel a special obligation for advocacy on behalf of the less powerful racial co-member or may feel an obligation to take the position of an institutional officer/professional (the vast majority of whom are white) and distance him- or herself from the racial co-member. Whichever side of this tension the African-American professional chooses to play in a given situation there is the potential for face threat.[15]

Face is the view of self each person seeks to uphold in an interaction. **Face-threat** is the challenge a person experiences in a particular situation to upholding a facet of identity that he or she cares about. I will say more about these concepts later. In this exchange, the intern experienced a face-threat related to his racial and professional identities. Erickson works through a detailed analysis of how this happens. Suffice it to say that in Example 1.5 the intern could have used the casual everyday terms ("pot" rather than "marijuana," "shooting up" rather than "IVDA") along with the medical ones, thereby displaying the terminology mix that is the sign of an advanced intern. He did not do this.

Interestingly, though, the intern appeared to be going to use the informal forms. When people change what they are saying in midstream it is often possible to infer what they started to say but decided against. Consider how the intern began to describe the patient's marijuana use: "He doesn't smoke. He does do, he does smoke some marijuana." It appears, then, that the intern was about to say that the patient "does do *pot,*" but rejected this word choice and used the more formal term. In essence, the intern's choice to use a formal term at this juncture made him sound more like a medical student than like an advanced physician. Why might he have edited his talk toward the more formal style? Why was he willing to let his talk imply that he was more of a novice than he actually was? There is no way to know for sure, but one consequence of using the informal drug names is that it could be seen as somewhat dismissive or unsympathetic to a fellow racial member. Or he may have edited what he was saying to avoid displaying the kind of familiarity with street drug usage that could be negatively linked to being African American.

What identity-work was accomplished by the white supervising physician in making the casual remark about the "price of an ounce?" One possibility is that the white physician may have been involved in a moment of stereotyping, presuming the intern's knowledge of street drugs because he was African American. Or the remark may have had nothing to do with race. It may have been meant as a small gesture of bonding, a recognition of similarity between the two men. From this perspective, the supervising physician's remark about the cost of an ounce was an identity-work move that referenced both men's college experiences in which knowledge of marijuana could be presumed commonplace. We do not know what either doctor intended or interpreted, but we do see that the conversation displayed a moment of interactional discomfort. As Erickson concludes, "It is through just such subtleties—the attribution of a whiff of a hint, whether intended by the other party or not—that interaction can become racialized in collegial interaction in the helping professions in the United States."[16]

Talk both reflects who people are and is the instrument through which people build who they want to be. While talk does identity-work and identities work to shape talk, the process is by no means straightforward and certain (if a person says X, it means that he or she is a Y kind of person; or Y kinds of people will always talk in an X kind of way). Identity-work is an inherently uncertain process. It is a cueing procedure that involves guesswork, a bit like a detective working to figure out the most likely culprit for a crime. As clues begin to add up and point in the same direction, an interpreter can have greater confidence in the conclusion that is being pointed to. Identity-work, then, is the glue linking identity with ways of talking. Let's examine the concepts that are glued together.

WHAT DOES "IDENTITY" MEAN?

Identity is a term rich with meaning. On the one hand, identity refers to core aspects of selfhood; identity is something each person possesses; it is stable and fixed. People who are confused about who they are are having an "identity crisis." Identity also reflects the boxes societies use to categorize their members. It is the descriptive stuff that is treated as informative and necessary when people fill out forms. Disputes that occur between groups of people who would check off different boxes—racial and ethnic-language groups, social class (cued by income), marital status, men and women, the young and the old—are the workings of "identity politics." Still yet another meaning of identity is reflected in its use by a group of contemporary scholars called postmodernists. Postmodernists see identity as fragmented and in flux. Identity is an accomplishment, not a thing. Moreover, people change identities to suit the needs of the moment.[17] To treat people as if they are fixed, stable entities may be politically useful, but it is not the way things are.

All of these meanings—some of which are contradictory—are part of what identity means. Moreover, these multiple and contradictory meanings are part of what make the concept so useful. In an interesting book about the nature of everyday thought, Billig[18] argues for the importance of recognizing how contradictory impulses are not only typical but are a virtue of ordinary thinking. Common sense, as he puts it, "is not unitary but is composed of contradictory aspects."[19] Analytically useful concepts, I would argue, will also have the ability to encompass competing impulses.

Identities, then, are best thought of as stable features of persons that exist prior to any particular situation, *and* are dynamic and situated accomplishments, enacted through talk, changing from one occasion to the next. Similarly, identities are social categories *and* are personal and unique. When we take these two competing impulses seriously, four kinds of identities become visible.

The first kind, **master identities**, references those aspects of personhood that are presumed to be relatively stable and unchanging: gender, ethnicity, age, national and regional origins. Any particular person is male or female; Hispanic, European, or African American; 20, 40, or 60 years of age; and so on. Master identities do not change from situation to situation. But while master identities are fixed and preinteractionally given in one sense, in another they are not. That is, what it means to be young, middle-aged, or old, or an American, a Colombian, or an Egyptian person shifts across time and interactions among people. Through the ways people with different master identities deal with each other, the meanings of particular identities are established. Meanings can, and do, change over time and across situations. Of note is the fact that master identities frequently are conceived as **contrastive sets**. The meaning of being male is deeply bound up with the meaning of being female; each gender category informs and contrastively defines the other. Similarly, what it means to be a southerner is understood in terms of the visible ways it contrasts with being a midwesterner, a northerner, or a westerner.

A second kind of identity is a person's **interactional identity**. Interactional identities refer to specific roles that people take on in a communicative context with regard to specific other people. For instance, Jason may be a friend in one context, an employee of Pizza-Plus in another, a college student, a hospital volunteer, a son, or a husband in yet others. Interactional identities are situation- and relationship-specific. Interactional identities are distinct from master identities but are not independent of them. In American society, for instance, the interactional identities of elementary school teacher, secretary, or nurse are expected to go with the master identity of being female, whereas the interactional identities of surgeon, engineer, or manager are expected to go with the master identity of male. To the degree an interactional identity is strongly associated with a master identity, whether it is gender, race, or age, that interactional identity takes on some of the broader master identity features with which it is associated. One consequence of society's deep-seated expectations about what identities are natural partners is that persons who take on identities that are not seen as going together (e.g., a male nurse, a female judge) will experience some communicative difficulties in enacting both identities satisfactorily.

A third kind of identity is what in ordinary life we talk about as personality, attitudes, and character. This third kind of identity, **personal identities,** is expected to be relatively stable and unique. When people are characterized in terms of their attitude about a local issue (e.g., in a western U.S. city, people may be seen as pro-growth or anti-growth, a

Buffs football fan or not-a-sports-kind-of-person), a personal kind of identity is being invoked. Personal identities also include those aspects of personhood that reference ways people talk and routinely conduct themselves with others (hotheaded, honest and forthright, reasonable, fair, a gossiper, a brown-noser). In contrast to master and interactional identities, personal identities are frequently contested. Others do not automatically grant a person's claims to be honest, reasonable, thoughtful, and so on. They may imply or even directly challenge whether those qualities apply ("That was inconsiderate" or "You're the most inconsiderate person I've ever known.").

Personal identities are bound up with master and interactional identities in two ways. First, other people hold expectations regarding what kind of personal identities are likely depending on existing master and interactional identities. Cultural beliefs about these links are the strongest for gender but operate for other facets of identity as well. In American culture Hispanics, for instance, are usually expected to be more *emotionally expressive* than Anglos. *Arrogance* is more likely to be attributed to a doctor or a person in some other high-status profession who disagrees with another person. Being *cantankerous* or *spry* are identities assigned to older people much more often than to 20-year-olds.

Second, what counts as expression of a personal identity is going to depend on a communicator's master and interactional identities. For example, although being *fair* may be valued across situations, the communicative actions that realize fairness will shift across interactional identities. Being a fair judge is going to be different than being a fair friend or a fair group member for a school project. Moreover, what a culture may count as adequately enacting a personal identity may depend on one's master identity. The judgment that a person is *supportive* or *aggressive*, for instance, rests not only upon the person's communicative actions, but also upon whether that person is male or female.

A final kind of identity, **relational identities**, refers to the kind of relationship that a person enacts with a particular conversational partner in a specific situation. Relational identities reference the interactional qualities of the parties. Are the people equal? Near equal? Is one party superior? Which one? Are the parties friendly or hostile, distant or close, trusting or wary with each other? Relational identities are negotiated from moment to moment and are highly variable. They are what people monitor most to see if a relationship is improving or disintegrating. As with the other types of identities, relational identities do not exist apart from other kinds of identities. Persons in an employee–supervisor relationship, for example, would be expected to enact an unequal relationship at least part of the time. However, there may be other occasions— having coffee in the morning, drinking beers after work—in which the relational identities enacted between the two become equal. For many Americans, having equal (or near-equal) relations with a superior on at least some occasions is the mark of a good work relationship.

In everyday talk situations, then, communicators have multiple identities. Some of these identities are visible, are brought to interaction, and shape how people talk; others are built up in the interaction through the particular ways each person expresses self and treats the other. Figure 1.2 diagrams the competing features and different kinds of identity that are lurking within every communicative encounter.[20]

Face and Facework

Closely related to the concept of identity is the notion of face. **Face**, a term initially popularized by Goffman,[21] refers to the positive image of self that is desired in a particular situation. In communicative exchanges the face that each person achieves will depend on what the partner does. This means that face is an accomplishment; it is constructed in an interaction through self's and others' conversational moves. The kinds of face people seek to construct relate to their desires to be liked and appreciated (solidarity face), to their desires to be seen as competent (competence face), and to their desire to avoid having others imposing upon them (autonomy face), or stated positively, to be treated with respect.[22]

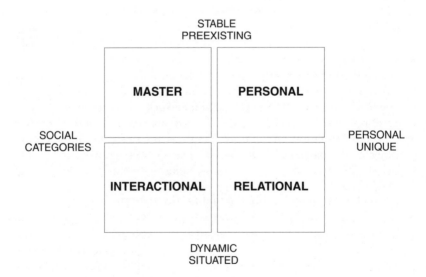

FIGURE 1.2. Conceptualizing identities.

The concept of face, then, relates most strongly to personal and relational identities. When I am highlighting the relational and personal kinds of identity, I will often use the word *face* (rather than personal or relational identities) and refer to the communicative activity as *facework*.

WHAT ARE DISCURSIVE PRACTICES?

Scholars who write about everyday talk most commonly refer to talk as "discourse,"[23] where **discourse** means nothing more than a multi-utterance unit of talk. Interpreting and analyzing a conversation, a meeting, or a speech, such as was done in the conversation between the two doctors, is the doing of discourse analysis.[24] The concept discursive practices links to discourse but puts an emphasis on the communicators performing the practice. **Discursive practices** are talk activities that people do. The reason we use the label *discursive practices* rather than *talk* is that it leads us to see talking not just as a single thing but as an activity that has many different parts and kinds.

A discursive practice may refer to a small piece of talk (person-referencing practices) or it may focus on a large one (narratives); it may focus on single features that may be named and pointed to (speech acts) or it may reference sets of features (dialect, stance). Discursive practices may focus on something done by an individual (directness style) or they may refer to actions that require more than one party (interaction structures). Figure 1.5 offers a beginning definition of the discursive practices with which you will be familiar by the end of this book.

LINKING DISCURSIVE PRACTICES AND IDENTITIES

The relationship between discursive practices and identities is a reciprocal one. The identities a person brings to an interaction influence how that person communicates. At the same time, the specific discursive practices a person chooses will shape who he or she is taken to be, and who the partner is taken to be. Table 1.3 presents a visual display of this reciprocal relationship.

Thus far, I have primarily focused on the self-presentational dimensions of talk. It is also the case that a person's talk, his or her selected discursive practices, will shape who the conversational partner is taken to be. Identity-work (or facework) always has two sides, a self-presentational side and a partner-directed one. For example, imagine you are sitting outside someplace on a university campus. You hear two people ask for directions to the communication department's main office.

TABLE 1.1. Kinds of Discursive Practices

Discursive practices	Description
Talk's building blocks	
Person-referencing practices	Words used to address others and to refer to self/others
Speech acts	Social acts performed through talk: includes criticizing, informing, praising, directing
Sounds of speech	Dialect and accent; ways of using one's voice (loudness, rate, pitch quality)
Language selection	The meaning of choosing one language, another, or a combination in talking (e.g., English, Spanish, Vietnamese)
Complex discourse practices	
Interaction structures	Expected ways to pair utterances, rules about taking turns
Directness style	The relative directness or indirectness with which a speaker expresses self
Narratives	Structure, content, and style of stories
Stance indicators	The linguistic, vocal, and gestural means of conveying an attitude toward a topic or the conversational partner

---

EXAMPLE 1.6

Go to the UMC, on the fountain side, across from the door where all the student organization tables are. Across from that door is the university museum and next to it is Hellems. Go in that door on the ground floor and you'll be right by the communication office.

EXAMPLE 1.7

Go straight up this street. You can see you're going west because it's toward the mountains. Follow this path, you'll have to go around several buildings until you come to the University Memorial Center, that's the student union. On the northwest side of the building, you'll see a fountain area, although the fountain probably won't be filled or on. Kitty-corner to the fountain area, you'll see Hellems. It's right next to

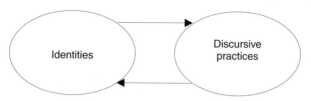

FIGURE 1.3. The reciprocal relationship.

the university museum. Go in the door on the ground floor and you'll be right by the communication office.

In Examples 1.6 and 1.7, the speaker's talk altercasts the recipient of the asked-for directions differently; that is, the speaker's directions create or suggest a picture of who the person must be. In the first case, the directions altercast the recipient as a regular member of the university community, a fellow college student, a faculty member, or staff member. That the direction asker is taken to be a university insider is implied in the first set of directions (Example 1.6) by the use of an acronym to identify a major campus building ("UMC" rather than "University Memorial Center"), the reference to a door where certain activities occur (student organization tables), which presupposes familiarity with the setup of the UMC, and the less detailed style. All of these features contrast with the directions in Example 1.7. As such, the second set of directions altercasts the asker as a visitor, a stranger to the university who is unlikely to be familiar with its landmarks.

That a speaker's talk altercasts a partner to a certain identity does not mean that the partner has to accept that identity. Conversational partners can respond in ways that reject or seek to modify the identity that a speaker implies. In the first case, then, if the direction asker was actually a visitor, she might interrupt the direction giver to say, "What does UMC stand for?" In the second case, if the direction asker was a member of the university community, he might interrupt to say, "Yeah, I know where the UMC is." Thus, while the identities that get constructed are negotiable, each exchange simultaneously offers a picture of who the self is and who the other is taken to be.

Altercasting, then, references the work a person's talk does to maintain, support, or challenge the conversational partner's identities. Altercasting, a term developed by several social psychologists,[25] highlights how the way we talk to and act toward others (alters) puts them in roles (casts them). Sometimes altercasting is done explicitly. When people talk about how they see each other (e.g., "I see you as someone who takes deadlines seriously and will put in whatever time you have in order to get a job done well" or "You're a warm, sensitive person who sometimes tries too hard to please others"). Most often, however, altercasting is done implicitly. Through the ways, for instance, a man talks with a woman we can infer whether he regards her as his equal, his superior, or his subordinate, as boring or fun, as having reasonable or outrageous opinions. His altercasting also informs us as to whether he is aware of or oblivious to her being a female, a Hispanic, or a young person.

SUMMARY

A crucial part of the meaning of everyday interaction has to do with the views of self and other that are being built up and reflected in talk. Talk does identity-work; it presents who people are and it altercasts the partner. Talk includes a variety of discursive practices, some quite simple, easy to see, and label, and others more complicated, bigger units created though pairing and patterns among the simpler units. As we will explore in the next chapter, a focus on the way preexisting identities shape discursive practices is taking a cultural perspective; a focus on the way discursive practices shape people's situated identities is taking a rhetorical perspective.

◈ Two Perspectives

TYPICAL COMMENTS PEOPLE MAKE ABOUT OTHERS

1. (One teacher to another) "Lee never disagrees in class because Koreans think it is important to show respect to their teachers."

2. (One middle-aged woman to another) "The group next to ours at the fireworks was a bunch of college boys. They were acting like jerks, but what would you expect? 'Wow,' 'Big deal, huh?' The kept using the F-word—Loud and obnoxious after every display."

3. (One student to another) "Tim makes it a point to ask a few questions in class discussion period so that the teacher will see him as serious. Seems to work, doesn't it?"

4. (One coworker to another) "You can count on Randy to interrupt and change the topic. She wants everyone to think she's important but she's only rude and obnoxious."

The above comments exemplify the routine kinds of remarks people make about each other. In all four comments, a discursive practice is linked to a facet of identity; however, the analytic perspective taken in (1) and (2) differs from the one adopted in (3) and (4). In comment (1), Lee's not disagreeing is explained by a single master identity (he is Korean); in (2) the group's loud talking and use of obscenity are explained by a combination of master and interactional identities (being young, male, and college students). In contrast, remarks (3) and (4) explain the talked-about person's communicative action (asking questions, interrupting and topic changing) in terms of what each speaker is seeking to achieve. Tim asks questions to be (and be seen as) a serious student. Randy interrupts and changes topics in order to establish herself as *im-*

portant, even though, by the speaker's estimation, these actions lead to her being (and being seen as) *rude and obnoxious*. The last two comments, then, tie Tim's and Randy's communicative choices to particular personal identities each is presumed to be seeking.

These remarks are an everyday version of the explanatory perspectives that will be developed in this text. The first two comments illustrate a cultural perspective, the second set a rhetorical one. I begin this chapter by describing the rhetorical perspective—the main approach I take to understanding how talk and identities link. Then I describe the cultural perspective, arguing why it is necessary to have both viewpoints rather than just a single one.

THE RHETORICAL PERSPECTIVE

In the media, as well as in much informal talk, the term *rhetoric* has negative connotations. Politicians are described as spouting empty rhetoric. A boss's avowal that "everyone will receive a fair shot" may be described by employees as "mere rhetoric." These uses of the term do capture a part of its meaning, but the comments do not do justice to the term's full meaning. To be rhetorical is a virtue. A *rhetorical* person is thoughtful and reflective about how to act; she considers others and the occasion in making choices about how to talk.

Rhetoric is an important tradition in the field of communication, having deep historical roots. In the fourth century B.C., Aristotle defined **rhetoric** as the art of discovering the available means of persuasion in a given case.[1] As an area of academic focus, rhetoric has been most interested in exceptional and nonordinary communication, events such as speeches of presidents or other political leaders. Nonetheless, a rhetorical perspective can be taken toward everyday talk. In an introduction to rhetorical study, Hauser highlights this fact. He defines rhetoric as "finding things to say that will advance our own purpose with an audience"[2] and as "the management of symbols in order to coordinate social action."[3] Theorists such as Sanders and Duck have applied a rhetorical perspective to studying close relationships such as marriage.[4] In this book, I will be showing how and why a rhetorical approach to everyday talk and identity is useful.

Key Features

A rhetorical perspective assumes that people talk in particular ways in order to accomplish desired identities (or avoid disvalued ones). Talk is presumed to be instrumental and goal-oriented, and people are presumed to be strategic and purposeful. Communicators select one way of talking rather than another in order to present themselves and altercast others in particular ways. But people do not just talk; they talk to specific others on particular occasions for specific purposes. In attempting to accomplish certain goals (and avoid others), an individual's smallest communicative actions are often consequential: every word he uses can make a difference. Billig, analyzing a report about President Reagan's decision to go into Grenada, made this comment about the use of the word "invasion":

> Such is the rhetorical force of language that the very choice of terms implies a position. In consequence, it becomes impossible to talk about an invasion without implicitly or explicitly signalling a stance. Even a choice of ostentatiously neutral terms would indicate a position, for neutrality in the midst of conflict is every bit as much as position—and a controversial one at that—as is partisanship.[5]

Analyzing discourse rhetorically foregrounds three things. First, it highlights individual agency. People are not cultural dopes, merely enacting scripts. They are choice-making, planning agents, tailoring their communication for particular settings. Conceiving of people as choosing how to talk is likely to seem natural for some situations—for example, job interviews, giving a presentation, a first date—but, as I will show, the perspective can also be applied to the most ordinary exchange. One qualification is needed. In saying that people are *choosing*, it should not be assumed that they are always highly conscious about their choices.[6] But referring to a particular way of talking as a *choice* makes visible the hidden truth that some other way of talking could have been selected. That is, using the language of choice is part of how an action becomes a choice.

Second, a rhetorical perspective is a normative and evaluative one. If an action is an expression of some natural (or cultural) order, then a suitable response is to try and understand it; it is not something to be evaluated as "good" or "bad." However, if actions are choices, then moral and/or practical evaluation is appropriate. There are better and worse choices to make, and people are responsible for what they choose. This means that some ways of talking will be judged as evidencing positive personal identities—for example, *reasonable, moral and trustworthy,* and *competent*—while others will be judged in negative ways—for example, *self-important, out to impress, dishonest, obnoxious.* A rhetorical perspective, then, emphasizes how choices about how to talk build people's identities as desirable or problematic.

Finally, a rhetorical perspective is problem-centered, or, to put it more strongly, attentive to the dilemmas of social life. In many communicative situations participants' interests will not be fully aligned. If one party accomplishes her desired identity goals, it is quite possible that her conversational partner may not. Differences between people, and hence some amount of interactional tension, is part of the business of talking. In institutional encounters between doctors and patients, students and teachers, reporters and public figures, clerks and patrons, and so on, parties can be expected to have at least slightly different aims. This does not mean that people in these roles cannot enjoy and have satisfying encounters—they often do—but it is to mark this outcome as an accomplishment.

Dilemmas and Interactional Identities: The Example of Academic Advisors

Complicating this even more is the fact that the ideals for many interactional identities provide their own dilemmas: they contain contrary beliefs about the best way to talk. Take the example of college advising. Academic advisors are first and foremost gatekeepers for society and the institutions they represent. As institutional gatekeepers, they have the authority to make decisions that affect the future of the people they serve. In a college advising situation, advisors "decide" if a student's past work will count for institutional credit; if a person's credits match the graduation requirements; if her grade point average meets the entrance requirements for certain majors, and so on. Advisors also guide students toward (or away from) certain majors, jobs, or graduate schools. In opening or closing the gate, advisors are expected to use objective criteria and treat all students fairly. Merit, not personal connections, should guide their decisions about individuals' futures.

At the same time, an academic advisor is expected to be a person who looks out for the individual welfare of each student; a good advisor is expected to be a friendly helper. A good advisor is someone who genuinely cares about the students he serves. The difficulty with this two-part ideal—(1) being a fair gatekeeper and (2) being a friendly helper—is that the communicative actions that ensure one is attending to the first part of the ideal are just the communicative actions that endanger the second part of the ideal.

Evidence of this dilemma is nicely displayed in Erickson and Shultz's study of academic advisors in a 2-year community college.[7] They tape-recorded advisors talking with students in regular once-a-semester meetings that lasted about 15 minutes. In these meetings a student and advisor planned the student's upcoming schedule, recorded the previous semester's grades, and, more generally, planned the student's academic future. In these sessions, the primary way advisors worked to establish themselves as friendly helpers was by showing interest in a student. In the opening moments through the small talk both parties engaged in, advisors worked to create a personal link with students. Through such discourse moves as noticing a person's home address and inquiring if a student knew someone or some place (e.g., a neighborhood restaurant) in that area of the city, or commenting favorably on a sports team displayed on a student's T-shirt, advisors sought to build common ground. When an advisor's comments and inquiries succeeded in building common ground, students were likely to experience the advising session as one in which they had rapport. But advisors could not always find commonalties with the students. This was particularly likely to happen when students came from ethnic and racial backgrounds different than the advisors'. In such cases the likelihood of discovering that one shared the same neighborhood, church, or other kinds of interests or connections dropped dramatically. Thus, advisors were most likely to establish rapport with students whose social/ethnic backgrounds were similar to their own.

That individuals will be more successful in their friendliness attempts with some people is a fact of interpersonal life. Not all advisor efforts to be friendly will be equally successful. One might argue that it is a good thing for advisors to pursue friendliness even if they cannot achieve it fully with all the students they advise. This would be a reasonable position if friendliness attempts did not affect the fairness of the institutional gatekeeping. Unfortunately, Erickson and Shultz found that it did. It was particularly in sensitive situations—for instance, where a student might be failing out of school—that the authors found differences in how the students with whom advisors had created rapport were treated. With students with whom the advisor had created rapport, advisors were much more likely to give strong caring messages that oriented to wanting the student to succeed; advisors also gave these students more advice and suggestions. When rapport had not been created, advisors were much less likely to give advice. Thus, in seeking to be friendly, advisors created situations where not all students were treated in the same way. Some students were given more encouragement, advice, and attention than others.

In a nutshell, the dilemma academic advisors face is this: to be a fair gatekeeper, treating all students similarly, it is best to use a distanced, impersonal, formal style. This can be achieved with everyone. In contrast, to be a friendly helper is best enacted by using an interest-showing style that seeks to build rapport. The more an advisor uses the impersonal style to ensure fairness, the less he will succeed as a friendly helper. The more a person seeks to build rapport and to be interpersonally friendly, the less likely she is to be a consistently fair gatekeeper. Thus the ideal of a "good" academic advisor involves a pair of contradictory beliefs. Being fair and being friendly sound like reasonable expectations for advisors but may actually be quite difficult to accomplish. A rhetorical perspective would encourage communicators to be creative, to consider if there are conversational actions that might enable fudging this apparent contradiction.

To summarize, a rhetorical perspective toward talk is one that highlights talk as strategic, seeing discursive practices as chosen in order to accomplish some ends and to avoid others. It presumes that some choices will be difficult, because there are conflicts between self and others' wants, or an interactional identity may implicitly pit one desired personal identity against another. A rhetorical approach emphasizes that talk constructs identities. Through the moment-to-moment choices people make about how to talk, self and others' identities get built. Let us examine this process for the communicative situation of divorce mediation.

Divorce Mediation: A Rhetorical View

Mediation, and divorce mediation in particular, is a relatively new communicative process that has developed to help disputing parties settle their disagreements. As an alternative to the legal system, divorce mediation offers husbands and wives a method by which they can work out disagreements about child custody, finances, and property settlement in a way that is expected to be less costly in terms of money, time, and emotion.[8] While offering some distinct advantages over the legal system, divorce mediators do not have formal power, as a judge has, to force a settlement. To the degree mediators are successful, and are granted authority to shape dispute settlements, their success derives from the effectiveness of the conversational strategies each mediator uses to show self to be expert, fair, and deserving to influence the settlement outcome.

In 1989 the Academy of Family Mediators prepared two 90-minute tapes to help train future divorce mediators.[9] The tapes involved simulations: four sets of experienced mediators worked with a divorcing couple (information about Keith and Jane is provided in Table 2.1). The purpose of the videotapes was twofold: (1) to exemplify the actions of experienced mediators and (2) to illustrate the range of good styles of mediating. In a study Anna Spradlin and I did, we transcribed and analyzed these tapes in order to identify the communicative practices common to experienced mediators. We also sought to identify which practices contributed to different mediator personas, or, in the terminology of this text, distinctive personal and relational identities.

TABLE 2.1. Background on Jane and Keith's Marriage

1. Keith and Jane had been married for 22 years. Keith is a medical doctor and a professor at a medical school. Jane had been a homemaker most of her life but has recently completed a master's degree in counseling.

2. The couple has two children: Samantha is 20-years-old and away at college; Geoff is 17-years-old and a senior in high school.

3. Keith had initiated the divorce and wanted to complete it as quickly as possible. Jane was ambivalent about the divorce, preferring to stay married until Geoff finished high school.

In the opening of the mediation session all four mediators did conversational work to display themselves as fair. As noted above, that a mediator be fair and unbiased, not privileging one party's interest over another, is essential to a mediator's ability to work with two disputing parties. Of note is the fact that none of the mediators did this by straightforwardly announcing that he or she was *fair*. As we wrote, "There are reasons to proceed in more subtle ways. It is often the case in everyday interaction that self-labeling occurs [I am a fair person] when a person feels threatened. Thus to label self as fair makes relevant that others would see self differently."[10] Rather than explicitly self-labeling, then, experienced mediators displayed self as fair by engaging in conversational actions associated with fairness.

In particular, experienced mediators used three types of conversational moves. A first kind of activity was to imply self's fairness. By describing a desired outcome of mediation, a mediator could imply his or her fairness.

EXAMPLE 2.1

And I'm trying to help you emerge from this room with a detailed written agreement that you can say as you look at it. I understand what it means. I understand what we did. Ah, feels fair.

To help others create a fair agreement does not necessarily entail that a mediator is fair but it is strongly implied. Another way mediators implied their fairness was to display equal attention to both parties. One mediator explained how mediation would be working to understand what was important to each party ("try to understand what's important to you [gaze directed at Jane] and what's important to you [gaze directed at Keith]"). By verbally enacting self as someone who would give each party a turn, the mediator creates a sense of her fairness.

A second type of conversational strategy was to use referee-like conversational moves. As in a game of football, mediators "called" disputants for "fouls," that is, for talking in ways that violated the rules of mediation—in particular, for interrupting the partner or speaking for the other. Again, while it is possible to be perceived as an unfair referee, the mere act of refereeing is a significant way that a mediator seeks to establish fairness.

A final way that mediators established their fairness was to reframe face-threats. As Jacobs and his colleagues found,[11] back-and-forth blaming and faultfinding often become the central conversational activities of divorcing spouses. In this context a central way mediators establish their fairness is by taking one party's negative comment directed at the partner and rewording it in a way that diffuses the negativity. Example 2.2 illustrates this practice.

EXAMPLE 2.2

K: We could probably work it out and try to resolve it but Jane is always emotional every time we sit down to discuss it.

M: Oh all right but hang on there.

K: And therefore that's why we're taking this route [going to mediation].

J: Of course I'm emotional. I don't want you making me into the,

M: You both are emotional. Nobody goes through a divorce without both of you being emotional.

Although similar communicative practices are used by all experienced mediators to establish their fairness and expertise, mediators differed from each other in three striking ways: language use, topic management, and interaction structuring. The management of these three issues was central to displaying which of two philosophies of mediation a mediator was seeking to perform. Consider how this worked.

Mediators' language use varied in two observable ways. A first difference is seen in the language they used to describe mediation. Some mediators used language that implied mediation was a relatively objective decision-making process where a fair decision could be arrived at by considering all the "facts." Other mediators used language that portrayed mediation as a more complex, indeterminate process (mediation as clear-cut vs. complex and ambiguous). From the complex perspective, it is assumed that people often do not know what they need at the outset, and that such knowledge comes through serious reflection on data in which partners eventually arrive at a proposal that will work and be judged fair by both parties.

A second way language use varied was in the root metaphors used to talk about mediation. A **root metaphor** portrays one domain in terms of another.[12] Mediators used two different root metaphors for mediation. The first was mediation as a business. In talking about mediation as business, mediators drew upon economic metaphors to describe the activity of mediation. Attention was drawn to time and cost, relationships were described using organizational charts, and the decision to select mediation as an option was presented in a sales-oriented manner ("Now here's your choice and here's what mediation is all about, quick and simple"). In contrast, other mediators used therapy as the root metaphor. Mediators using a therapeutic root metaphor emphasized longer term interactional consequences, and spoke more about listening, reflecting, and feelings.

A second kind of conversational difference surfaced with regard to **topic management**. As Spradlin and I noted, "Mediators are information gatekeepers, deciding what is or is not an acceptable topic of talk."[13] Mediators differed considerably in their responses to emotional topics. Some mediators marked emotional topics as inappropriate for mediation; other mediators legitimated feelings, framing emotions as cues of each party's deeper interests that could be used productively to arrive at good settlements.

A final difference that distinguished mediators was their approach to **structuring interaction**. A mediation session could be presented as a kind of communicative exchange that had a relatively fixed structure, as would be cued by previewing the specific steps to be followed at the beginning of a session, or mediation could be framed as an occasion whose structure would emerge as mediator and couple talked. In this second approach a mediator would note at the outset that he or she would need to hear the couple talk about issues before he or she would be able to identify what ways to structure the session. Through these interactional choices mediators constructed themselves as either bargaining mediators or therapeutic mediators. Table 2.2 summarizes the discursive practices that contributed to these different mediator identities.

In sum, this study of divorce mediators illustrates a rhetorical approach to identity and communicative practices. As the analysis showed, particular ways of talking were systematically used to accomplish desired identities (being a fair mediator). In addition, a mediator's use of specific practices was found to be a key part of enacting his or her philosophy of mediation, what we could think of as a combined interactional-personal identity. Consider, now, an alternative way to analyze talk and identity.

TABLE 2.2. Mediator Identities

Bargaining	Therapeutic

1. Language use
   a. Clear-cut
   b. Business root metaphor
	1. Language use
	   a. Complex and ambiguous
	   b. Therapy root metaphor

2. Emotional talk considered off-topic	2. Emotional talk acceptable to explore issues
3. Interactional structure is preestablished	3. Interactional structure is emergent

THE CULTURAL PERSPECTIVE

In looking at how the interactional-personal identities of bargaining and therapeutic mediators were enacted, the rhetorical perspective downplayed the cultural frame within which the mediators' choices came to have meaning. All the mediators, as well as the divorcing couple, were middle-class Americans; their conversational actions—the manner in which they were seeking to manage this conflict—were typically Western, and particularly American. That is, mediation, like all communicative practices, is culturally inflected. Mediation, as it is practiced in the United States, arose from Americans' tendency to privilege individual expression and equality over other values. In societies that privilege harmony in interaction, and do not assume that everyone should be treated equally, there is a limited need for professional mediators. High-status others, such as a village elder or a boss, tell disputing parties what must be done and the parties then change what they are doing. A rhetorical perspective, then, tends to ignore, or at least to downplay, how communicative choices are deeply cultural. Individual communicators may be agents making choices, but they are bound agents. Communicators are acting within larger systems of meaning, social structures that are not of their own making. It is important to take account of the structural constraints that shape the categories of choice, and, to a certain degree, the choices themselves. A cultural perspective helps us do this.[14]

Culture, as defined by Fitch,[15] is an invisible system of symbolic resources that shapes people's daily interactional practices. To adopt a cultural perspective on everyday talk is to foreground the fact that groups of people will speak and interpret the actions of those around them in patterned ways. To understand talk, we need to recognize how groups channel communicative action.

Key Features

To understand why people talk as they do, it is important to look at the groups in which people have spent large amounts of time. The groups in which people live, first as children and later as adults, Hymes[16] calls **speech communities**; professional, school, work, and recreational groups other scholars have labeled "discourse communities,"[17] or "communities of practices."[18] In these different kinds of communities individuals acquire beliefs about appropriate ways to speak and interpret. The system of beliefs that one person in a community has is not going to be idiosyncratic but will be shared by other members of that same community.

Speech communities share ways of talking—**speech codes**—and ways of making sense (interpersonal ideologies).[19] These two are deeply bound together where the ideology furnishes the logic behind a code. **Interpersonal ideologies** are communities' beliefs about interpersonal issues: people, relationships, and communicative action. In particular, an interpersonal ideology includes beliefs about (1) the values people should pursue in intimate, work, and public relationships (e.g., establishing closeness between people, respecting individual autonomy, validating people's basic equality, respecting status and social rank differences); (2) what communicative acts count as being reasonable, fair, friendly, and so on, and why they count as such; and (3) what are appropriate communicative practices for persons of different master and interactional identities. Interpersonal ideologies are answers to the question of how people should resolve the myriad dilemmas that confront them in everyday interaction. In that regard, speech communities can be seen as developing distinctive ways of prioritizing among desirable but competing values.

Similar to political ideologies, then, interpersonal ideologies are as much about what they devalue as they are about what they esteem. In this sense, both the rhetorical and the cultural perspectives attend to dilemmas. In the cultural perspective, however, the societal dilemma gets transformed into a community-linked distinctive conversational style. This style is the community group's resolution to whatever competing values are at stake. Let us consider two analyses of identity and talk conducted from a cultural perspective.

Ethnic Identities: Athabaskan/English

A first example of a cultural perspective is seen in Scollon and Scollon's study in which they compare Native Americans who are Athabaskan to English (i.e., European Americans) communicators. As the authors note,

[b]y "Athabaskan" we mean anyone who has been socialized to a set of communicative patterns which have their root in the Athabaskan languages. These people are ethnically Athabaskan but may not speak any Athabaskan language. We mean by "speakers of English" anyone whose communicative patterns are those of the dominant mainstream American and Canadian English-speaking population.[20]

The Athabaskan and English speech communities have quite different interpersonal ideologies and communicative practices. Some of the most notable differences revolve around self-presentation styles. If one were observing an initial conversation between an English speaker and an Athabaskan speaker, a likely occurrence would be a talkative English speaker and a quiet, or taciturn, Athabaskan. Among English speakers, if two people do not know each other well, the best and natural way to manage that lack of knowledge is to talk. So at a typical party English speakers will ask each other lots of questions about their background (What do you do? Where are you from?) and attitudes (What do you think about the school board issue? Do you favor environmental controls?). Talk, within an English speaker's interpersonal ideology, is regarded as the way to build friendly connections to another. It is a necessary activity when people are strangers.

On the other hand, Athabaskan Indians see this kind of initial exchange situation very differently. It is when people do not know each other well that relationships are particularly easy to rupture. Conversation has the potential to uncover differences that may threaten people's abilities to be appreciative and respectful of each other. For this reason, Athabaskans regard it as generally preferable to be reserved and relatively quiet at the start of a relationship. However, when two Athabaskians know each other well, they can be very talkative. In a relationship that is strong, the differences that talk may uncover are unthreatening. In close relationships it is easy to talk.

For English speakers, it is only in situations where people know each other well that it is appropriate not to talk. In close relationships, quietness in the presence of another is a relational sign of comfort and intimacy. Thus we see that the relational meaning of talkativeness and taciturnity are virtually opposite for the Athabaskan and English speakers. For Athabaskans, taciturnity is expected in initial acquaintance and talkativeness is seen as a sign of intimacy. For English speakers, the reverse is true. Talkativeness goes with initial acquaintance and low intimacy, and interactional quietness is a positive expression of intimacy.

A second difference between these two speech communities concerns the ways each community conceives of the relationship between appropriate ways to display self in relationships of unequal status, as might be seen in parent–child or teacher–student relationships. Among English speakers, the person in the higher or dominant position is often the spectator whereas the subordinate person is the exhibitionist.[21] This means that in the presence of parent or teachers, children are expected to display what they know and to show off their skills while the dominant parties watch and encourage.

Athabaskans understand this relationship differently. As Scollon and Scollon note, "Children are not expected to show off for adults. Adults as either parents or teachers are supposed to display abilities or qualities for the child to learn."[22] Thus, in contrast to English speakers, Athabaskans see exhibitionism as going with the dominant role and spectatorship with the subordinate role. An upshot of these differences is the likelihood of problems for Athabaskan Indian children when they are in mainstream American classrooms:

> For the English-speaking teacher an Athabaskan child will either seem unduly reserved because he is spectating or unduly aggressive if the child has assumed the superordinate role that he feels is consistent with display or exhibitionism. For the Athabaskan child the teacher will either seem incompetent because he is not exhibiting his abilities, or unduly bossy because in spite of not exhibiting he is taking the superordinate role.[23]

In addition to these rather prominent self-presentational differences, there are subtle differences between the two communities in the way moment-to-moment talk gets managed. In any conversation one person has to start the conversation. In an exchange between an English speaker and an Athabaskan, the first speaker will usually be the English person. This is so because Athabaskans regard it as important to have a feel for the relationship before beginning to talk, and English speakers believe that talk is the best way to get to know others. That Athabaskans rarely start a conversation has an interactional consequence. Whoever starts a conversation is usually the person who gets to propose what conversational topic will be discussed. Thus, not only are English speakers likely to speak first, but their interactional position makes it quite likely that they will define what is to be talked about.

These interactional differences in how a conversation gets set up are further compounded by a difference between the two communities in what is regarded as a reasonable pause between speaker's turns. When two people talk to each other, they try to avoid interrupting each other. One key to accomplishing this task successfully involves reading the turn-taking signals that indicate that one's conversational partner is finished. Across speech communities, pausing is one of the major ways speakers signal that they are at the end of a turn. However, the length of a pause that is used to signal "I'm done talking" versus "I'm in the middle of a thought" is not universal. By and large, the kind of short pause that English speakers would understand as a signal meaning "I'm done talking" within the Athabaskan community would be understood as a signal meaning "I'm in the middle of a thought." The upshot of this is that from the Athabaskan point of view, English speakers seem to be constantly interrupting a speaker when he or she is talking. From the English speaker's point of view, Athabaskans are overly slow in talking. The differences described here are not the only ones that distinguish the two speech communities, but they do begin to suggest why communication between Athabaskan and English speakers so frequently is experienced as problematic. Consider a second example of a cultural perspective.

Class-Linked Communities: Teamsterville/Nacirema

A second example of a cultural perspective on the relationship between identity and talk is evidenced in Philipsen's[24] studies of Teamsterville and Nacirema. "Teamsterville" is the name Philipsen gave to a particular blue-collar Chicago neighborhood in which whites of a variety of ethnic groups lived. Nacirema[25] is the name Philipsen gave to the speech community of middle-class Americans. As the second name suggests, the Nacirema speech community is a geographically broader community than Teamsterville. The speech practices of Nacirema are what are considered mainstream and typical in U.S. society; Nacerimans, as I will discuss in Chapter 10, are those Americans who are spoken about without hyphens. "Nacirema" is another way of naming the speech community that Scollon and Scollon called English speakers.[26]

One belief about communication that distinguishes among speech communities is the value they place on talk itself. As Philipsen notes, "Talk is not everywhere valued equally." "Each community has its cultural values about speaking and these are linked to judgments of situational appropriateness."[27] The central question that Philipsen explored in his study of Teamsterville was what it meant to *talk like a man*. For the men in this community, interactive situations were divided into three kinds. A first type of situation was one where a man was in a symmetrical or equal relationship. Symmetrical relationships were ones where a man shared similar master and interactional identities, that is, the other was also male, in the same age range, had the same ethnicity and occupational status, and lived in the same neighborhood. In symmetrical relationships, there was lots of talk. Talk was perceived to be the vehicle for building solidarity and affirming each man's connections with other men.

A second kind of situation was one in which the participants were not equal and the Teamsterville male was superior. Situations of this type included relationships with wives and girlfriends, as well as with children. In these kinds of asymmetrical relationships, self-presentational strategies other than talk were expected. For instance, in situations that posed a potential threat to the honor of women or the well-being of children to whom one was connected, Teamsterville men were expected to do more than just talk. Difficulties with another were to be met with a display of one's willingness to fight. Thus in dealing with a misbehaving youth, the valued response was not talking through a problem, as one would be more likely to do in the Nacirema community, but the use of physical discipline. To avoid using discipline in such situations not only implied a man's lack of manliness, but generated increased disrespect and verbal abusiveness from the youth.

A third kind of situation was one in which there was asymmetry and the Teamsterville man was in the subordinate position. Talking with persons in institutional authority roles in the larger society is an example of this kind of relationship. As Philipsen notes, "Most of the Teamsterville man's necessary contacts with 'outsiders' is mediated through a local precinct captain, Catholic parish priest, or union steward."[28] Thus, priests, political block captains, and so on acted as intermediaries for the Teamsterville men, making a case for what they needed to the outside world. This pattern of using an intermediary was a widespread one in the European countries from which many Teamsterville men originated, but it stands in contrast to the practice of middle-class Americans in which individuals are expected to speak for themselves.

Teamsterville's interpersonal ideology gives weight to the master and interactional identities of one's conversational partner in determining what are appropriate ways to communicate. Communication in this community draws upon an **ideology of honor** in which persons are valued because they enact and further promote the values of hierarchy and community. The ideology of members of this group stands in sharp contrast to the one dominant in Nacirema in which persons are recognized first and foremost in terms of their individual uniqueness. Within middle-class American culture, "society is built up from the acts of autonomous individuals and itself is of value only to the degree it enhances the individual."[29] Valuing social equality and each individual's pursuit of self-expression, a middle-class American ideology privileges individual dignity above all else.

To sum it up, a cultural approach to everyday talk highlights how people's preexisting identities (but especially their ethnicity, race, gender, nationality, age, and social class) constrain how they will talk. Because of each person's membership in some communities (and not others), people acquire identifiable ways of speaking and interpreting. Since most speech communities are formed around master identities, and to a lesser degree interactional identities, identities that exist prior to any particular situation will shape how people will talk. To state it a bit differently, I could say that the cultural perspective highlights how everyday talk reflects identities.

THE RELATIONSHIP BETWEEN THE RHETORICAL AND THE CULTURAL PERSPECTIVES

In terms of adequately understanding how discursive practices and identities are linked, the cultural and the rhetorical perspectives provide complementary views. Each perspective highlights one part of the process and downplays the other. Each is the counterpoint for the other. The cultural perspective draws our attention to the ways in which people's ways of speaking are shaped by preexisting identities; the rhetorical perspective causes us to focus on how people's choices about how to talk will shape who they become. The cultural perspective makes visible the influence of social practices and structures that are outside of any individual's choosing; the rhetorical perspective highlights individuals as choice-making agents. Each of the perspectives is essential. Each is also problematic when taken alone.

The rhetorical perspective draws attention to how the discursive actions people choose realize the self as one kind of person rather than another. As such, the rhetorical perspective makes salient the uniqueness of individuals and the ways in which each person is a master of his or her destiny. However, in highlighting people's abilities to choose, the rhetorical perspective fails to recognize that choice is given meaning within a cultural frame. Moreover, in highlighting choice, the ways in which the communicative playing field is unequal are often ignored. A person's lack of success in attaining valued interactional and personal identities may be because of bad choices (ineffectiveness), but that outcome may also be because particular kinds of communicators face dilemmas that others need not confront. The invisibility of women, ethnic minorities, and working-class people in high-status positions is not merely because these categories of individuals chose not to pursue valued interactional identities, or did so in ineffectual ways. There are systematic and subtle institutional practices that make achievement of desired interactional, personal, and relational identities difficult, if not impossible, for persons of certain master identities. In ignoring how cultural group membership shapes individuals' sense-making practices, as well as the implicit interactional rights that will be given to some and withheld from others, the rhetorical perspective distorts the picture of how communication and identities are linked.

The cultural perspective helps right this imbalance. It reminds us that ways of talking are patterned and culturally rooted. At the same time, descriptions of cultural patterns—what can be called **cultural generalizations**—can and often are used inappropriately. They can become stereotypes that get used interactively to blame and to keep people in undesirable places. Assuming a cultural generalization is accurate—for example, more people in Speech Community *A* act in *X* way than people in Speech Community *B*—it is always necessary to problematize the scope of a generalization. To what sets of people does a generalization apply? In what local circumstances? At what points in time? For instance, from Philipsen's Teamsterville study we concluded that Teamsterville men are more likely to use an intermediary in dealing with authorities than would be seen in middle-class America. Other studies[30] suggest that the communicative practices identified in Teamsterville are not unique to this one Chicago neighborhood. But to what other communities should this generalization be taken as applying? All American working-class communities? Only white, ethnic, working-class communities? Only white, ethnic, working-class, urban communities? Only those that existed in the United States in the late 1960s and early 1970s?

Of note is the fact that generalizations are always problematic with regard to individuals. As Scollon and Scollon note, "Cultures do not talk to each other; individuals do."[31] Thus the cultural perspective, by highlighting the similarities among people of particular backgrounds, downplays the diversity that will exist within all cultural groups. The dictionary[32] treats generalizations and stereotypes as different kinds of things. Generalizations are necessary reasonable tools for sense making; stereotypes are either (1) a conventional oversimplified belief or opinion, or (2) when a person is thought to typify or conform to an unvarying pattern and is lacking any individuality. Cultural generalizations are not the same as stereotyping; nonetheless, generalizations can easily feed stereotypes. Cultural generalizations link categories of persons to specific discursive actions. Statements that highlight similarities among members of a group implicitly promote seeing and understanding people as products of their nationality, race, ethnicity, gender, age, social class, and so on. The cultural perspective captures a truth, but it also distorts the truth. It suggests that there is a greater degree of uniformity among people of some identity than ever actually occurs. To minimize the cultural perspective's limitation, we need a rhetorical one.

To understand everyday talk we need to keep both perspectives in mind. Whichever analytic lens is dominant at any one moment, the other should be no further than in the next room. In the next two parts—

Talk's Building Blocks and Complex Discourse Practices—I will be showing how different discursive practices do identity-work, as well as identifying the kinds each practice does. In addition, I will consider how some set of preexisting identities works to shape the unfolding of the focal practice. My starting point for reflection and analysis is middle-class American culture.[33] This is my home culture, the one I know the most about, as well as one that has been studied extensively. After unpacking the rhetorical consequences of discursive choices among middle-class American speakers, I describe how the focal practice varies in other communities.

SUMMARY

This chapter introduced the two perspectives on everyday talk that will be adopted and developed in the book: the rhetorical and the cultural perspectives. Drawing upon divorce mediation and academic advising, we saw how the rhetorical perspective treated talk as strategic action, and communicators as choice makers whose actions could be assessed for practical effectiveness and moral reasonableness. The second perspective, the cultural viewpoint, highlighted how people live in speech communities, such as ethnic or social class enclaves, in which they learn how to talk and interpret others' talk. It is in these communities that individuals develop distinctive and relatively fixed beliefs about what are reasonable ways to treat others (their interpersonal ideology) and ways of doing so. Both the cultural and rhetorical perspectives express important truths. At the same time, when used in isolation from the other, each distorts how everyday talk works.

PART II

◈ Talk's Building Blocks

3

◈ Person-Referencing Practices

During the spring of 2000 an unusual naming dispute erupted in Boulder, Colorado. The controversy concerned the label to use for people who had pets. Should people in the community continue to be referred to as "pet owners," the existing designation in city regulations, or should official documents be changed to refer to people as "pet guardians"? Over several months citizens of the community and staff at the local newspaper weighed in. "Names make a difference," advocates of the change argued; the label "guardian" conveys more respect for nonhuman species and better recognizes the importance of the relationship between dogs and their human families. Opponents of the change decried it as silly and stupid—dogs aren't going to care—and as having no legal consequences. As with most controversies, this one did not appear out of thin air. A dog had died because its owner had chained it outside, where it was unable to move out of the sun. Although the pet owner had been tried and convicted of animal cruelty, many members of the Boulder community wanted to prevent future occurrences of this kind. Changing the label for pets' people seemed one small way the city could encourage others to treat their animals better. In this controversy, the pro-arguments triumphed; Boulder is now a city that has "pet guardians" rather than "pet owners."

Was this particular name change silly or sensible? How would we decide? In what ways do reference terms for self and others have implications for speakers and their targets? In this chapter, I examine an array of person-referencing practices, considering how terms vary culturally, what different choices accomplish rhetorically, and several societal controversies. The chapter focuses upon marital names, personal address, and group-level terms that refer to ethnicity and gender. In the conclusion, I show how Harvey Sacks's membership categorization device (MCD) is an especially helpful concept for understanding the importance of person-referencing practices.

MARITAL NAMES

When people marry, they need to decide what names they will adopt or retain. Should each person keep his or her birth name? Should one or both parties change their names? If so, which party and to what? Traditionally in U.S. culture, it has been expected that upon marrying a woman would take her husband's last name. As a wife of more than 30 years noted, "Back then, we just assumed that the married name would be the husband's last name. Nobody challenged that idea."[1] Thus Sally Frand would marry Mark Ellis and subsequently she would refer to herself as "Sally Ellis," "Mrs. Sally Ellis," or "Mrs. Mark Ellis." Mark Ellis would continue using the same name he had before marriage.

In the last 25 years, though, social commentators have criticized this conventional practice. Arliss, for instance, described women who upon marriage adopt their husband's name as taking "the coward's way" and losing "more than a little of themselves in the process."[2] Maggio describes the practice as "one of the most sexist maneuvers in the language."[3] Many other scholars, while recognizing that marital name selection is no longer a no-choice issue, are less critical, seeing considerable complexity in the potential meanings associated with marital name selection. As Carbaugh[4] notes, names are cultural resources used to say something about one's personal identity against a backdrop of the more and the less typical choices. In the United States name selection has become a rhetorical choice. Let's consider the personal values and commitments that the three marital naming practices used most often in American society reinforce.

The American Options

The traditional option, indeed the one selected by the vast majority of Americans of all ages and educational levels,[5] is for the husband to retain his birth name (e.g., Mark Ellis) and the wife to change her surname to that of her husband (e.g., from Sally Frand to Sally Ellis). In discussing the significance of taking her husband's name a wife said, "It is my identity. It's my connectiveness to my husband. . . . The whole purpose of taking your husband's last name is to become identified with your husband."[6]

Considerably less usual as a choice is what Carbaugh labeled as the "modern option" where the wife retains her birth name (e.g., Sally Frand and Mark Ellis). A woman whom Carbaugh interviewed who had selected the modern option explained her choice this way:

> [It reflects] a certain view that I have about being married, that I am still my own person, that my life is not just created by my husband, that I am a person with my own profession, my own friends, and my own values, and all that stays. So, while in some ways it reflects that, I'm not really making that statement. Mostly I just feel like I don't know why you would change your name unless you were [pause]. It just doesn't make sense to me, which is mostly why I did it [kept my birth name] . . . but I do think it reflects a certain kind of marital relationship when I am fairly independent from my husband although we're interdependent with each other.[7]

This interviewee went on to comment about how she remembered her mother sending notes to school for her and signing them "Mrs. Steve Jones." She concluded, "I always thought that was real bizarre because it was like she had no identity of her own. . . . I possess my name and my identity, not my husband's."[8]

But couples adopting the modern option face a choice that traditionals can avoid: What name should they give to their children? Most commonly, such couples give their children a hyphenated last name that combines the wife's and the husband's names (e.g., Lee Frand-Ellis) or they give the father's name, but perhaps use the mother's surname as the child's middle name. Traditionals often see the hyphenated name combinations used by moderns for their children as silly and cumbersome.

A final choice, labeled "integrative" or "combiners",[9] involves a woman keeping her birth name as her middle name or changing her last name so that it is a hyphenated combination (e.g., Sally Frand-Ellis). Although it is possible for a man to adopt the same hyphenated name, it is quite rare. The more typical move is for the man to make no change to his birth name. A woman who opted to retain her surname as a middle name and to take her husband's last name explained the marital name's meaning in this way: "[it] says I am a person, the same person that I've been since I was born. I'm also a married person. . . . I am a part of a family that I've chosen and, uhm, but I'm still the person that I always was."[10]

Each of these name choices (traditional, modern, and integrative) conveys a distinctive interpersonal ideology. For couples selecting the traditional option, their joint name conveys a valuing of conventionality and a strong sense of identity as a connected couple rather than as separate individuals. In addition, especially for the woman, it conveys a conciliatory, noncritical stance toward existing social practices. Wives and husbands who select the modern option are paying greater attention to the independence and equality of each member of the couple. In addition, this choice signals that the woman is taking a more assertive stance that includes being critical of traditional social expectations related to men, women, and marriage. Finally, for wives and husbands that combine their names in some fashion, the conveyed meaning is a hybrid, more attentive to social change than the traditionals and more conventional than the moderns.

The reasons wives (and husbands) give for marital name choices involved factors other than the above-noted value commitments. People chose to keep or change names because of identification with their family of origin or ethnic group (e.g., Jewish, Irish), their professional identity, or for practical reasons such as how a particular name combination would sound. In addition, although these three practices are the most common, husbands and wives make other choices such as naming themselves after a long-deceased ancestor or selecting a name that captures a commitment that they both share (e.g., peace, gaia).

Other Cultures' Options

The "choice" in American society that is regarded as challenging convention—giving a child a surname that includes the wife's as well as the husband's last name—is the conventional option in many other societies. In Colombia[11] and other Spanish-speaking countries, children receive both parents' surnames at birth with the father's name first. Women typically keep their father's last name and drop their mother's name, replacing it with "de" (of) and their husband's last name upon marriage. "Teresa Pérez López would thus become Teresa Pérez de Torres (wife of Torres) upon marrying Juan Torres. When identifying herself or signing her name, however, she could choose to do so as either Teresa Pérez or Teresa de Torres."[12] As Fitch[13] notes, although there has been some discussion about naming practices in Colombia, by and large there is much less tension about this issue than in the United States. In Colombia, because husbands and wives routinely have different last names, a wife who has a last name different than her husband's is not regarded as a woman taking a stand for women's rights or against patriarchy.

In the United States and other English-speaking societies, marital naming tends to be thought of as a "women's issue"—men may have strong feelings about what their wives should do but it's not something that affects them directly. But in some other countries, like Japan, for instance, this is not the case; under certain circumstances a man who marries has to decide if he should take his wife's name.[14] The most common practice, as is the case in the United States, is for women to take their husbands' names. But, if a wife comes from a household that owns a small business, her family has no son, and her husband comes from a family of limited means, the wife's family may "adopt" the man. "Adoption" occurs at the time of marriage and involves the bridegroom taking the wife's last name while the wife retains her birth name. In so doing, the man becomes a son of the household and a potential successor to the family business.

In sum, when viewed culturally, we are led to see that societies vary regarding naming practices at marriage, what aspects are taken to be choices, and who has to make them. Once a cultural practice is criticized, as happened in the United States for women taking husbands' names, some people begin to do things differently. When the number of people becomes a visible minority, what had been a convention (i.e., no one did anything differently and it required no thought) becomes a rhetorically informative choice. Rejecting the convention becomes a way to present self as unconventional, uncomfortable with, or challenging of traditional assumptions about marriage. Similarly, choosing the conventional naming practice conveys that, at least in this instance, one is a person who sees no need to question what has been done traditionally.

PERSONAL ADDRESS

That married couples in the United States do not all use the same naming practice means that when people meet for the first time, there may be moments of tension. For instance, at an office party if you address your female coworker's husband as "Mr. Silver" because her name is "Mary Silver," you may be calling him by his wife's last name and not by his own. Moments of discomfort may occur related to other forms of address as well. The discomfort arises because address choices convey how speakers see themselves in relation to the other. When a person initially meets his or her significant other's parents, to address them jointly as "Tom and Lisa" conveys a different sense of the speaker's relationship than calling them "Mr. and Mrs. Broadfoot." This discomfort occurs in public encounters too. In a department store when a clerk takes a woman's credit card that has her full name printed on it (e.g., "Jessica Traut") the clerk could thank "Mrs. Traut," "Ms. Traut," "Miss Traut," or "Jessica" for her purchase. Any of the choices may be reasonable yet could be responded to with irritation. These moments of tension arise because decisions about forms of personal address are interactionally consequential. As several scholars have noted,[15] people are hardly ever indifferent to what they are called.

Personal address is the label we give to terms used to refer to a person in his or her presence. They include five main types.[16] The first and broadest type is versions of proper names including a person's first name (FN) (e.g., Timothy, Susan), last name (LN) (Reston, Frand-Ellis), and informal or diminutive versions of a first name (e.g., Timmy, Suz).

A second form is kinship terms. These include the different names given to mothers (e.g., Mother, Mama, Mom), fathers, grandparents, aunts, uncles, and so on. In addition, in many groups, kinship terms get used as forms of address with nonbiologically linked others. Close family friends, for instance, might be addressed as "Auntie" or "Uncle" by younger family members. Among Malaysian speakers, in fact, kinship terms such as "Big Sister" and "Little Sister" are the preferred forms, used more often than proper names or pronouns (e.g., "What does Little Sister want?" rather than "What do you want?").[17]

A third form of address is titles. In English, the most common titles for men are "Mister," usually combined with a last name, or "Sir." Typical title terms used for women distinguish whether a woman is single or married ("Miss" or "Mrs."), although "Ms." now makes it possible to avoid making this distinction. If a woman's name is unknown the titles "Miss" or "Ma'am" are common, with the speaker's selection depending on the woman's age. Other titles are occupationally tied. Religious leaders might be addressed as "Rabbi," "Father," or "Pastor," either alone or in conjunction with a first or last name. "Mayor," "Professor," and "Doctor" are other common titles. In the United States, although the title "Dr." is usually reserved for people who have a medical degree, a PhD, or the equivalent, in Colombia, "Doctor/a denoting male and female forms of 'doctor,' traditionally designated any person with a college degree. Nowadays, it is extended to any adult of middle to high social status, especially by members of the working class."[18]

A fourth form of personal address includes nicknames and endearments. While there are certain terms that are used by many people within a culture (e.g., "sweetie," "honey," "Junior" for a son with the same first name as his father), many are idiosyncratic to persons and relationships. "Bean," for instance, is a term of endearment among a number of members of my family. "Face," in contrast, is a nickname for my sister-in-law that is used only by my brother (her husband). Nicknames often have a cultural flavor. A study of American usage found names such as "Boo," "Kok," "Toots," "Tarpot," "Snugglebug," and "Duke," whereas British speakers use terms like "Fluffy," "Higgly," "Bobo," "Pippy," "Podge," and "Biff."[19]

A final form of address, actually not significant in English but consequential in most languages, is the choice of second-person pronouns. In English, "you" is the only option. In German ("du," "Sie"), Italian ("du," "Lie"), French ("tu," "vous"), and most other languages a speaker has to chose a pronoun that fits the situation and the relationship. Use of one of the pronouns frames the situation as unequal or informal, possibly altercasting the other as intimate. Usage of the other form positions the recipient as being in a distant relationship or the participants as being in a formal situation. Selections that a recipient does not see as reasonable will lead to negative evaluations—for instance, that a speaker is disrespectful, overly chummy, arrogant, or patronizing.[20]

Identity Implications of Address

Although many aspects of identity can be important, two facets of a relationship are usually of prime concern: (1) the degree of closeness or distance between people, and (2) whether the parties are equal or not. In a nonequal relationship, it also matters which of the parties is more powerful, of higher rank, or deserving of more polite regard or respect. By the forms people select to address others and refer to self, they present their view of the existing relational identities. Within American English, address forms can be arrayed in a rough continuum of formality. Anchoring the informal and close end are nicknames and endearments, titles are at the formal end, and use of first names or last names falls somewhere in the middle.

The choices noted in Figure 3.1 by no means exhaust address possibilities. Communicators are rhetorically skillful and are able to generate hybrid forms (e.g., title + FN ["Dr. Bob"] creates a respectful informality) that draw upon the meaning of common choices but put them together in novel ways for new relational meanings.

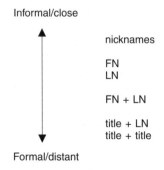

FIGURE 3.1. Distance continuum and likely address forms.

The second key dimension, equality, is marked in relationships through the use of reciprocal terms of address. If both parties use FN, or both use title + LN, they are framing their relationship as a roughly equal one. In contrast, when one speaker uses the other's first name (e.g., "Jeffery") and the other addresses the first person by title (e.g., "Ms. Gruning"), they are enacting a nonequal relationship where the person being addressed with the more formal term is being treated as the higher ranking individual. The likelihood of selecting any particular address form is shaped by a person's nationality. In contrast to British speakers, for instance, Americans are known for informality and friendliness (also for inappropriate chumminess). Part of this reputation derives from the widespread use of FN–FN address.[21]

Personal address is one important piece of the way people attend to each other's face. As I noted above, the dominant logic within mainstream American culture is to pursue mutual solidarity. In many other cultures, including Native American groups and most Asian ones, the dominant face logic is one that favors the giving of mutual deference and respect. These different impulses—to be friendly or to be politely respectful—create problems when persons from these different cultures come together. Moreover, as Scollon and Scollon[22] note, the difference invariably disadvantages the communicator who assumes the importance of granting autonomy and showing respect. If there is not mutuality in the selected face system (i.e., solidarity vs. autonomy face), then the identity enacted by the person using the more formal selection to address the other is that of being lower status. For this reason, Scollon and Scollon argue, it is a culturally more sensitive practice to use formal address terms and strategies that display respect to others when meeting strangers.

ETHNICITY- AND RACE-LINKED REFERENCES

When a citizen calls the police to report a problem involving a person, whether it be for loitering, fighting, or something more serious, one of the first requests from the police call-taker will be to describe the person's race: "Was she black, white, or Hispanic?"[23] Put simply, "labeling" is an inescapable requirement of everyday talk. Situations in daily life require us to refer to another person, and to do so in a way that distinguishes that person from others. Although there are many ways to refer to a person—describing him or her in terms of size, assumed age, smell, dress, and so on—racial and ethnic labels are a key part of our vocabulary for describing persons in public life. Of interest is the fact that the labels, whether they are used in a police call or on forms for employment or the census, are **social constructions,** ways of categorizing people that in different situations and at different times have been different.

Historically, in the United States, race has been a central category affecting decision making. Since the United States was born, not being a white person has had negative consequences. To determine how many congressional representatives a state should receive, people had to be counted. Although since amended, the Constitution initially had a counting principle in which a white counted as one person and a black equaled three-fifths of a person.[24] In addition, who could be counted as white has varied across time. In the early 1900s, for instance, Irish Catholic immigrants were treated as a category different from white.[25]

The social constructive aspect of categories is especially visible in the changing categories used to reference persons that the Census Bureau now refers to as "Hispanic." Not until the late 1970s did the label "Hispanic" become a popular one. According to Gomez,[26] the emergence of Hispanic as the preferred category arose from influential Mexican American groups' criticism of the undercounting of their people that occurred in the 1970 census. As a result, an advisory committee was formed headed by the chair of the ethnic and Spanish division to consider better ways of categorizing people. Out of this committee emerged the label "Hispanic" as the preferred category for future use. "Hispanic" offered a way to create political clout. Rather than Puerto Ricans, Cuban Americans and Mexican Americans conceiving of themselves as different groups, the label "Hispanic" highlighted the shared language heritage of these previously separate groups and bound them together as a single ethnic group. It also avoided the confrontational and political edge to the label "Chicano" that was then being used by many Mexican Americans to refer to themselves.

Not everyone, however, was happy with the "Hispanic" label. Giminez,[27] for instance, argued that the label, as is true of any label, led people away from noticing all of the differences among people in the category. A New York Puerto Rican and a new immigrant from Chile were "Hispanic," and yet the two people were pretty different. In addition, the category "Hispanic" reinforces what the author sees as a negative tendency in the United States: seeing everybody in terms of their race and ethnicity rather than, say, in terms of their country of origin or their social class. The label also devalued the Indian heritage that is a significant part of many Mexican Americans' identity: "Hispanic" privileges the colonial Spanish link over the Native American one.[28]

Categories are a way to divide the social world. They are lumping and excluding devices—implicit assertions about which differences among people are of small account and which are big. Put another way, names are rhetorical devices, conveying individuals' commitments and histories. Consider what four of these names do for Dolores Tanno,[29] a communication teacher, often asked by new acquaintances "What are you?"

> *I am Spanish*: Behind this label is the story of my childhood in northern New Mexico. . . . My parents, grandparents, and great-grandparents considered themselves Spanish; rightly or wrongly, they attributed their customs, habits, and language to their Spanish heritage and I followed suit. . . . [B]eing Spanish incorporates into its plot the innocence of youth, before the reality of discrimination became an inherent part of the knowledge of who I am.
>
>   *I am Mexican American*: Behind the name "Mexican American" is the story of classic colonization. . . . The name itself signifies duality; we are, as Richard A. Garcia (1983, p. 88) argues, "Mexican in culture and social activity, American in philosophy and politics."
>
>   *I am Latina*: The name "Latina" is grounded in cultural connectedness. The Spaniards proclaimed vast territories on North and South America as their own. They intermarried in all the regions in which they settled. These marriages yielded offspring who named themselves variously as Cubans, Puerto Ricans, Colombians, Mexicans, etc. but they connect culturally with one another when they name each other Latinas.
>
>   *I am Chicana*: This name suggests a smaller community, a special kind of Mexican American awareness that does not invoke others (Cubans, Puerto Ricans, etc.) . . . the most intense form of ethnic identity because . . . "Chicano/a" is the only term that was selected by us for us.

Other racial and ethnic groups also have multiple names by which to reference selves. Currently the names preferred by African Americans are "black," "Black American," or "African American."[30] Interestingly, it is those people in the most socially powerful group that are the most resistant to having a name to identify their group. As a white student being interviewed about choice of categories to reference self's group noted,

> Labels have negative meanings a lot of the time. Any label—Black, African American, nigger, honkey—any of them so I don't use labels. I'm just me—white.[31]

The irony of the student's statement is that "white" is treated as not a category label. Martin and her colleagues[32] noted how many white college students are reluctant to label themselves. The authors remark that "labeling was somehow different for whites than other ethnic/racial groups."[33] But when white students are pushed to identify names for their group, seven labels emerged: "white," "Caucasian," "white American," "European American" or "Euro-American," "Anglo," and

"WASP" (white Anglo-Saxon Protestant). The most preferred labels were "white," "white American," and "Caucasian," with "European American" and "Anglo" in a second tier, and "WASP" the least favored. Martin argues that the preferred terms are the ones that are the most naturalizing and universalizing ("white is white"), whereas the others highlight the historical and symbolic ties of the category. Put another way, whiteness is invisible; being white is understood as not having ethnicity. But when a white person's ethnic-racial group is named, it is less easy to think of only nonwhites as ethnic or racial. As a respondent in Martin's study noted:

> It was refreshing to see White Americans get defensive about a racial connotation, especially when the class is mostly Anglo. I first heard the term Anglo from friends of mine who are Latino (Chicano) who referred to whites as Anglos back in 1983. When they started the term it was more or less a slang word in the barrio. Since then I've been using it ever since because it catches Whites off their guard.[34]

GENDER-LINKED REFERENCES

Although it is possible in many situations to avoid referring to someone else's race, it is virtually impossible to avoid categorizing people by gender. When we refer to others, we identify them as men or women (rarely as persons), or use first names that are deeply gender-marked (Joshua, Ryan vs. Tricia, Jenny). Moreover, in contrast to Asian languages,[35] English requires identification of an other's sex whenever a third person pronoun is used: *she* smashed the window; *he* ran away. English cannot be spoken without repeatedly marking the gender of the person being mentioned.

When groups seek to bring about societal change, they often focus on language practices, and especially on ways of addressing or referring to people. During the French Revolution that sought to replace hierarchical relationships with equality and brotherhood, there was a movement to replace the more formal second-person pronoun, *vous*, with the informal second-person pronoun *tu*. Similarly, the rise of communism in Eastern Europe and China led to a set of address practices whose goals were to promote more egalitarian relationships.[36] In the last couple of decades, feminists have been arguing for the importance of changing our ordinary person-referencing practices in English in order to bring about fairer, more equitable relations between men and women. In particular, two routine linguistic practices have been identified as unfair and as instances of sexism in language.[37]

A first practice was person referencing that ignored women and made them invisible. Words such as "men" and "mankind," "chairman," and "fireman" or "policeman" were supposed to be terms for both men and women, as was the **generic "he"** (i.e., the use of the pronoun "he" to refer to a person of unknown gender: "If a student wants credit, he can stop by the teacher's office"). The second practice regarded as sexist was the defining of women in terms of their roles to men. The best example of this is the personal address titles that distinguish women in terms of marital status ("Miss" and "Mrs.") but that do not do so for men.

Language reform, then, seeks to replace ordinary talking practices with better, fairer ones. For instance, most language reform proponents argue that fairness would be better served by using pronouns that explicitly recognize women ("he or she" or "they" for the generic "he"), by using address forms that do not describe women in terms of their linkages with men (Ms.), and by replacing male-linked terms with those that do not presume the sex of the referred-to person (chair, firefighter, humanity). The rationale for such language reform flows out of the **Sapir–Whorf hypothesis**.[38] The Sapir–Whorf hypothesis postulated that the language a person has at his or her disposal affects his or her thinking. Although research has pretty clearly demonstrated that people are able to notice distinctions and think ideas for which they have no words, it has also shown that language options (e.g., vocabulary choices, grammatical categories) do shape understanding and meanings. Changing the words we routinely use, not always but sometimes, can make a difference to thought and action. People who routinely think of themselves as "guardians of their pets" very well may treat them better than if they think of themselves as "pet owners."

But there are also arguments for opposing language reform. Three key reasons, quite different in their import, have been offered. A first argument, and perhaps the least persuasive, is that the existing state of affairs between women and men, while not perfect, is reasonable. Since there is no problem, there is no need for language change.

A second reason for opposing language reform is because it is advocating something linguistically suspect: ungrammatical (e.g., "they" and "their" for the generic "he") or awkward ("he or she" for generic "he," "humanity" for "man"). This view tends to treat language as a relatively fixed system that should be preserved whenever possible. Societies should not be in the business of changing language. In fact, terminological changes often do make a language messier with less-clear rules. Thus, if a person sees the keeping of a society's language (e.g., English, French) orderly as a higher priority than the advocated change and what it is expected to accomplish, then he or she is likely to oppose language reform.

A final reason for opposing language reform grants the existence of gender inequality, and admits that such inequality is harmful, but sees language practices as symptoms rather than causes. Treating a symptom, using this line of reasoning, will not cure the problem. Some evidence for this position is seen in the evolution of the title "Ms." The term was initially introduced to allow women to be referred to in a way that did not make their marital status key. Over time, however, this purpose was turned on its head. In the United States in everyday speech "Ms." came to be interpreted as a form single women used to hide the fact that they were unmarried. In Canada, it came to be regarded as the term to refer to a woman who was divorced.[39] Thus, the impetus for introducing the term "Ms."—to make things more equitable—was subverted by the usual way speakers used it. As Erlich and King[40] note, whether a language change takes in its intended way seems to depend very much on whether high-status members of a relevant group support it. In contrast to what happened to "Ms.," the elimination of generic "he" and "man words" in written prose has been highly successful in universities, especially in departments such as communication, sociology, and psychology. By and large, since key players (social science journal editors and professors) were persuaded of the importance of language reform, it happened.[41] Unsurprisingly, attitudes toward language reform are related to a person's gender. In general women are more positive about gender-linked language reform than men.[42]

Referring to others in ways that make salient their ethnicity or gender (and certain attitudes toward it) is one ongoing feature of talk. However, everyday talk is more complicated than this: speakers routinely refer to people in ways that draw upon cultural knowledge and set in motion complex conversational inferencing. Let's next consider how this works.

THE MEMBERSHIP CATEGORIZATION DEVICE

A sociologist named Sacks[43] coined the term **membership categorization device** (MCD) to refer to "collections of categories for referring to persons, with some rules of application."[44] These MCDs include collections like sex (male/female) and race/ethnicity (black, white, Hispanic, Asian), but they also include other groupings of people that we think of as going together. For instance, take a simple comment, "The baby cried. The mommy picked it up." In this case, "baby" and "mommy" are part of what we think of as the *family* category (which includes moms, dads, brothers, sisters, aunts, uncles, etc.). It is also the case, however, that "baby" is part of other membership category systems. Besides the family category, "baby" is a member of the *stage-of-life* category (e.g., baby, toddler, teenager, adult, senior). It is also part of what we might label as an *emotional connection* category. If an 80-year-old woman looked at her 50-year-old son and said, "You're still my baby," we would understand the term "baby" in this way. The sentence about the 50-year-old man being a baby, taken alone, makes sense. Yet if it had preceded the one about the baby crying and the mommy picking it up, it would seem quite bizarre. Although the term is the same, the meaning category that is called up, and thereby what activities reasonably will go with it, are very different.

What Sacks did in his writing was to display the power and significance of a selected membership term and its category. In a nutshell, the membership term a speaker selects does all kinds of work to channel thinking in certain directions, to make actions seem sensible or potentially problematic. Membership categorizations, in Sacks's terms, are inference-rich: they highlight certain features of a situation and downplay others. By using certain membership terms (and avoiding others) a speaker can accomplish having a referred-to person be seen positively or negatively. It is not the case, though, that use of membership terms is necessarily a conscious and highly strategic enterprise. Consider our two-sentence example: "The baby cried. The mommy picked it up."

To see what is being accomplished by membership terms, it is helpful to consider what other terms could have been selected and how they would have led to different inferences. Suppose the speaker had described the baby as *the male,* or even *the boy* or *the child.* Assuming that all of these descriptors technically fit, nonetheless they do not shape thinking in the same way. Each of the membership terms, but especially *male,* makes crying as an activity an action to be disapproved of (i.e., it is not natural or reasonable). This is an example of what it means to say that a membership categorization is inference-rich. It pulls up associations with activities, some of which are taken to be reasonable and others that are implied as not reasonable if a party is that category.

Let's go a bit further with this example. Another inference most listeners will draw is that the mommy that picked up the baby was in fact the baby's mother, not some other woman who was also a mother. Sacks argues that the reason we hear it this way is because if a reference to another person can be heard as a member of the same category (i.e., family in this case), then other references should be heard as members of that category system. This explains, for instance, why we as listeners assume that the mother is the baby's mother, but we would not make the same assumption if the second membership categorization term were changed to *woman* ("The baby cried. The woman picked it up"). One feature of

MCDs is that we expect them to be used together if they can be. Since a second family membership term is not used, listeners will be led to infer that the woman must not be the baby's mother, for otherwise a different membership form would have been used.

Let's now extend the notion of MCD to a more complex situation: an attorney plea bargaining before a judge about a person with regard to her accused crime of shoplifting. One way of describing the woman and her action is as follows:

DESCRIPTION 1

A Mexican woman who is not at all poor went into a department store and tried to sneak a couple of hundred dollars' worth of clothing out under the clothes she was wearing.

This first description can be said to highlight the woman's action as unreasonable and wrong. By categorizing the person as "not at all poor" and "sneaking" we are lead to see this person as someone who is deliberately doing illegal things when she has no good reason (such as poverty) to make her actions excusable. In addition, by using the ethnic reference ("Mexican woman") at this particular juncture (rather than omitting it), the speaker could be seen as drawing on cultural beliefs about the potential link between being a minority and doing illegal actions. This case comes from a study Maynard[45] did investigating how lawyers plea bargained before judges. Consider what the defense attorney actually said:

DESCRIPTION 2

This is a shoplifting case judge. Um on the surface it looks pretty bad. But investigating the case, uh come up with some beautiful defense that I'm anxious to go on trial if the DA is. Situation is this. She's a sixty-five year old lady, Mexic-, speaks uh Castilian Spanish and she's from Spain. Uh, she goes into Davidson's. Oh incidentally by way of background, of 20 years she's worked in the Catholic church of- at San Ramon as the housekeeper for the nuns and fathers and all this stuff, very religious, well known. I've interviewed half of San Ramon concerning her background, wonderful lady no problems 65 years old. But on this particular occasion, she goes into Davidson's, goes into a fitting room, takes two hundred dollars of clothing, pins them up underneath her dress and leaves.

After offering the above description, the attorney noted how the woman was on a medication (an ordinary one but one that in her case, he argued, was causing an extraordinary reaction, leading her to do something completely out of character). Consider how the attorney used membership categorization terms to make plausible that her behavior should be understood as a result of the medication, rather than, as in the first description, creating a view of her as a willful thief.

Of interest is that the woman's age is mentioned twice. Shoplifting, I would suggest, is an activity that goes with certain stages of life more straightforwardly than others. In particular, it is something expected to be common in teens but much less usual in older people, especially seniors. Repeating the woman's age, then, is way to make intentional shoplifting a less plausible meaning. Other details provided about the woman do similar work. Notice how the attorney edits the initial description that she is Mexican and replaces it with a categorization of the dialect she speaks (Castillian Spanish) and mentions her initial origin in Spain (rather than, presumably, her years living in Mexico). Both of these references are class-associated, implying that the woman is not poor, a kind of person for whom shoplifting might be more common. Finally the details about her religiousness, working for nuns and fathers, and the history of her good reputation, all work to mark this instance of shoplifting as something that is truly a bizarre action. That is, through his choice of membership terms that set in motion inferences about what is reasonable for a person of these categories, the attorney implicitly builds a case that the woman's behavior was a reaction to medicine, not really the crime of shoplifting.

SUMMARY

Everyday talk is replete with references to self and other people. The terms we select in ordinary exchanges are an important way we build our own identities as a certain kind of person (e.g., traditional or nontraditional, a feminist or not into feminism). It is also a fundamental part of how we altercast others. Through our use of particular membership categorization devices we frame another and his or her actions as reasonable, stupid, cruel, and so on. In addition, these terms enable us to build relationships with others in which we are distant or close, equal or differing in social rank and status.

The options people have for person referencing are shaped by their language and national community. Since not all speech communities have the same options, the meaning of the same conversational action (giving a child both parents' last names) will differ. Moreover, within any community, some person-reference practices are relatively invisible while others are perceived as a matter of choice. Nonetheless, even for practices that a group at one time perceives as invisible, as was the case in the United States with the use of the generic "he" and ethnic labeling of whites, over time a particular person-reference practice can become visible. That is, a person-reference practice can change from being perceived as the natural way to express self, not a matter of choice, to an identity-implicative option requiring thought and justification.

4

◈ Speech Acts

Early in the 1980s, an Oklahoma horse breeder named Don Tyner was arrested and tried for extortion.[1] The charge against him was brought by Vernon Hyde, a man who had been working for Tyner's organization. Hyde believed that he had purchased a share of a horse; Tyner disagreed. Over a period of time the men had had several angry conversations. Hyde had taped the telephone conversations with Tyner in the hopes of gaining evidence that would lead to Tyner's conviction. The following conversation was introduced at the trial as evidence that Tyner had threatened Hyde. The exchange occurred in the middle of a 30-minute conversation. It had come after a heated exchange between the two men concerning who actually possessed shares of the horse. There was a pause, then the conversation continued:

EXAMPLE 4.1

Tyner: → How's David?

Hyde:　Do what?

Tyner: → How's David?

Hyde:　You mean my son?

Tyner:　Yep.

Hyde:　Don, don't threaten my son. Do a lot of things but don't threaten my son.

Tyner:　I didn't threaten anybody. I just said, "How's David?"

During the trial, the prosecution and the defense claimed radically different speech acts were being performed by the utterance "How's David?" Drawing on an FBI expert witness, the prosecution argued that the utterance was intended as a threat, with a meaning something like "if you don't drop this matter, something could happen to David." The defense stated that this utterance was not intended as a threat. It was meant as a request for information whose purpose was to rebuild a pleasant connection with a coworker who was angry and tense.

One way friends or acquaintances can close down a conflict they are having is to switch to small-talk topics. Was Tyner doing this? Prior to their dispute Tyner had had a friendly relationship with Hyde, as well as with his son, David, whom he had taken to baseball games. At the trial Tyner's attorney argued that this friendly intent was what Tyner's question meant; it was not intended as a threat. Tyner was eventually acquitted. Nonetheless, it is not at all difficult to imagine the circumstances in which an ostensibly benign speech act, such as this question, could have been meant as a threat.

Determining what speech act a communicator means by uttering a phrase is a recurring concern in everyday exchanges. Intimates routinely dispute whether a partner's comment was supporting or criticizing, asking or telling, warning or threatening. Interpretive differences like the one discussed above do not usually end up in court, but they do affect how people feel about each other. In this chapter I (1) provide background on speech acts, (2) examine how speech acts link to a variety of identities, and (3) take a close look at a small set of speech acts that are especially face threatening.

PHILOSOPHICAL BACKGROUND

Some years ago a philosopher named Austin[2] noted that people use words for more than describing and representing the world. Words are used to criticize, praise, request, account, beg, warn, threaten, and so on. The social act that an utterance performs is one aspect of communicative meaning; it is the answer to the question: "What is a person doing in saying X?"

The number of potential speech acts a person could perform is infinite. Austin suggested that there are as many speech acts as there are verbs in a language. In English, for instance, we distinguish between a person ordering, demanding, suggesting, requesting, hinting, pleading, begging, and so on. While these acts are clearly related—each is an attempt to direct the actions of another—they involve a host of subtle differences.

Searle,[3] also a language philosopher, divided speech acts into five categories. Speech acts such as those mentioned above he categorized as

directives, utterances that attempt to get another person to do something. A second category of speech act is **representatives,** utterances that report a state of affairs in the world. Examples of representatives include "It's raining outside" and "Randy was 20 minutes late to the school board meeting." In contrast to other speech acts, representatives can be evaluated as to whether they are true or false statements about the world. A third kind of speech act is **commissives.** Commissives commit a speaker to a future course of action with regard to another. Utterances that threaten, make a promise, or convey an offer to do something are examples of commissives. The fourth category of act is **expressives,** talk whose primary function is to display or reveal a speaker's feelings. If a person apologizes, explodes, or starts shouting at another they are engaged in doing an expressive. Searle's fifth kind of speech act is **declaratives.** Declaratives transform people and situations from one type to another. For instance in an official situation, if a rabbi or priest says, "I now pronounce you husband and wife," a single man and woman are transformed into a married couple. The christening of boats (or babies) and the swearing in of government officials are other instances of declaratives.

By virtue of identifying and distinguishing five important functions of talk, Searle's typology provides a helpful frame. Nonetheless, as is true with any frame, attention is directed toward some features of what people do and away from others. In this chapter, my analysis of speech acts combines Searle's notion of speech act with the notion of speech act/ speech event developed in the ethnography of communication tradition.[4] Drawing on these two traditions, then, a **speech act** will be defined as the social meaning of a short segment of talk. However, rather than assuming that every act falls neatly into one category, I will assume that speech acts are multifunctional. The act of criticizing, for instance, often both expresses a speaker's negative feeling (an expressive) and functions as an attempt to direct the actions of others (a directive). Second, rather than restricting speech acts to single utterances, as Searle would, I include somewhat longer units of talk. Within this broader perspective, *gossiping* or *griping* are also speech acts, socially meaningful speech actions that make sense of a short stretch of connected utterances.[5] Finally, as Hymes[6] shows, and as I will develop later, the meaning of individual speech acts is not universal but is community-flavored. In addition, while most speech acts are defined from the point of view of the doer, speech acts can be defined from other perspectives. Thus, although it would be unusual for a person to set out to *brown-nose*, brown-nosing is a meaningful speech act in institutional situations; American students and workers routinely accuse each other of doing this act and seek to avoid doing it themselves.

LINKS BETWEEN SPEECH ACTS AND IDENTITIES

Speech acts and identities are tied in multiple ways, each both affecting and being affected by the other. The range of relationships that exist between people's identities and speech acts can be stated as four principles. For each of the principles, I provide evidence for its reasonableness.

Principle 1: Preexisting Identities Shape Speech Act Performances

Interactional and master identities will constrain which speech acts will be expected, allowed, or prohibited. Imagine that two people (*X* and *Y*) performed the following sequence of speech acts:

1. *Y asked permission* of *X* to stay at a friend's house for the night.
2. *X denied Y's request.*
3. *Y complained* that *X* was not fair.
4. *X ordered Y* to quit badgering and threatened to withhold TV-watching privileges.
5. *Y began to cry.*
6. *X relented* and *gave permission* for *Y* to stay at the friend's house, bur only after *Y* fed and walked the dog.

Imagine, now, that you are asked to make guesses about *X*'s and *Y*'s identities: What age is each of them? What gender or social class might each be? Are they strangers or acquaintances? If they know each other, what kind of relationship do they have?

We cannot assign *X* and *Y* exact identities, but given the speech acts they performed we can rule some identities as being highly implausible. It is not likely, for instance, that the parties are college roommates. In American culture it would be strange indeed if a college roommate asked for his roommate's permission to spend the night at a friend's house; it would be even stranger if the other took it upon himself to deny such a request, and the person cried in response.

Y's asking permission to spend the night at a friend's, complaining, badgering, crying, and being told to feed and walk the dog make it hard to imagine that *Y* is anything but a child. Probably, too, *Y* is neither very young (under 5 years) nor very old (a teen). A request of this type is unlikely to be made by a toddler, and although it is plausible that a teen would ask permission to spend the night at a friend's, and repeatedly complain if denied such permission, it is unlikely that he or she would burst into tears if reprimanded. Not only is it likely that *Y* is a child and that *X* is older, but these particular speech acts suggest that *X* and *Y* are closely related. Children do not ask just any adult for permission: parents, much older siblings, grandparents, or guardians are the ones likely to be asked about overnights.

For the above sequence of speech acts, it would be a bit more difficult to guess X and Y's gender. In American culture these acts are ones we would regard as typical of caretakers of either gender as well as typical of both male and female children. It may be that in particular speech communities, *crying*, *ordering*, and *relenting* may be gender-tied, but they are at best weak ties. Perhaps less obviously, this set of actions implicates X and Y's social class identities. A dispute over a child spending the night at a friend's house is common in middle-class families but unlikely to occur in a poor family living in a crowded apartment.

Speech acts both go with and become difficult when a person has particular interactional identities. It is far easier to order, praise, criticize, or advise another if one is of higher status than one's conversational partner. Parents with their children, teachers with students, bosses with employees, police officers with citizens, and coaches with players are expected to engage in these kinds of speech acts. In contrast, children, students, and employees are likely to feel constrained in performing these acts, perhaps not avoiding them entirely but putting effort into planning how to do the acts less likely among higher status speakers. In addition, persons with a lower status identity will need to recognize that deciding to perform authority-related acts may make negative interpersonal consequences unavoidable. A player advising a coach how he could coach better may receive a poor response, regardless of the wisdom of the advice.

Similarly, a boss who wants to give an employee a real choice about whether to do something will need to do conversational work to avoid having what she says interpreted as an indirect order. For instance, if the head honcho of a company (Althea) says to the accounts manager (Ann), "Could you complete this report before leaving today?," Ann may feel that she has no choice even though the boss's remark was framed as a question. She may regard the question as a polite way of ordering her to stay. If Althea really wanted Ann to feel free to refuse, she might have said something like: "Don't feel like you have to do this, I want you to feel free to say no, but would you be able to complete the report before you left tonight?" While this extensive conversational prefacing work might do the trick—cueing Ann that it really is a request and not an order—it might not. Ann may still feel as if she has been ordered. At the same time, Althea may be meaning her request as an order, albeit a nice one, and might be angered if Ann were to actually refuse to do it.

Just as certain speech acts seem reasonable (or problematic) with interactional identities of particular statuses, so too do certain speech acts with identities of intimacy/distance. A person cannot tease, flirt, or ask favors of just anybody. Each of the speech acts implies who one is, and thereby can become difficult when a person is not an appropriate identity. This type of linkage also applies to master identities.

Not too many decades ago in U.S. society, being a certain race, religion, or gender completely foreclosed certain interactional identities. Today this is no longer the case, but the historically long association has had communicative repercussions. Men of non-European ethnicity—especially Hispanic, Native, and African Americans—and women of any race may find their performance of authority-related speech acts (criticizing, directing, advising), especially if addressed to white men rather than women, children, or nonwhite men, more difficult than their Anglo male counterparts. Not only may subordinates resist a person's doing of authority-related speech acts that may be accepted in a matter-of-fact manner from a person with the expected master identities (i.e., male, white, middle class), but performing the authority acts may call forth other kinds of negative feelings. Thus, if a speaker's authority is accepted, other master identities may feel challenged, either by the partner or within a speaker herself. A white woman or a Hispanic man may comfortably enact authority identities but experience trouble related to their gender or ethnic identities: Is the female superior being an adequately feminine person? Is the Latino boss selling out and acting white?

At the same time, persons with those master identities that are routinely granted status in a society will find it difficult to perform speech acts that are associated with subordinate status and limited power. Too frequent expression of sad and out-of-control feelings, or easy and frequent acceptance of direction, at least from women, could lead men in many speech communities—Teamsterville, for instance—to question whether they are being men.

Principle 2: Doing Speech Acts Builds Relational and Personal Identities

People's relationships are not fixed but change over time. Strangers become acquaintances, bosses and employees become friends, acquaintances or friends become sexual intimates, intimates become ex's (exgirlfriend, ex-boyfriend, ex-spouse), and so on. In large measure, relational change is accomplished through beginning to do, or refraining from doing, particular speech acts. A request for help can change a pair of acquaintances into people in the beginning stage of a friendship. Invitations and compliments of certain types can transform a friendship into a love relationship. Refraining from polite chitchat or voicing one's criticisms may bring about a new level of relational intimacy, and not inviting someone to go on a vacation may signal a demotion from friend to mere acquaintance.

Identities related to distance/intimacy are especially open to negotiation and renegotiation. But while intimacy-related identities are particularly fluid and constructed through talk, status-linked identities are also modified this way. For instance, it is through different ways of talking that parents and children move from relationships in which parents are authorities to ones in which parents and children are equal or near-equal. Gradually, over time, parents refrain from asking for reports, offering advice, and ordering actions from their children and themselves disclose their feelings and fears to their children, and just as gradually children stop asking for help or for permission from their parents, and themselves provide support and advice to their parents. Thus the parent–child relationship becomes one between equals. Moreover, the speech acts a person selects, as well as his or her characteristic style, is key to how people build personal identities: as tactful or blunt, critical or supportive, trustworthy or unreliable, humorous or serious, and so on. I focus on this topic later in the chapter when I consider the sensitivities in performing face-threatening speech acts.

Principle 3: Speech Acts Are Distinctive to Speech Communities

A speech community evolves ways of talking that are prized within that community and distinctive to it. In Australia, for instance, working-class speakers of both genders, but especially men, have a practice of saying something bad about their conversational partner as a way of sharing fun. This speech act, called **chyacking**, is one of Australians' "favorite national pastimes and forms of entertainment.... Usually the men speak one at a time, making negative remarks about the addressee, while the other men are laughing, so that a group of 'mates' constitutes both a group of participants and an audience." Examples of statements referring to this speech act include "They whooped, they made ribald noises, they chyacked one another" and "I was always civil to the chaps, for all the chyacking they gave me."[7] Chyacking, Wierzbicka suggests, is similar to a speech act common to African American men that has been extensively studied. This act, alternately called *playing the dozens* or **sounding**, involves men and boys making insulting-sounding comments, often about the conversational partner's mother, for the purposes of having fun, displaying self's verbal skill, and jointly enacting a rejection of society's values about proper behavior. While sounding shares chyacking's goal of promoting fun through potentially hostile remarks about the other, sounding differs in its valuing of verbal virtuosity. Sounding is an individual performance and gives weight to verbal skill. In contrast, chyacking involves group-created commenting and allows for minimal verbalizations and grunts or other nonspeech sounds.

There are many examples of community-specific speech acts. Within Israeli society, Katriel[8] has identified a number of distinctive acts, including *dugri*, which I discuss in detail in Chapter 8. *Dugri* is a speech act that involves straightforward direct talk in which a person expresses a negative assessment. Other Israeli speech acts include **kiturim**, a particular ritual of griping. Griping, of course, is a kind of act recognizable in many speech communities, but the Israeli speech act of *kiturim* has features that distinguish it from griping. Within the Israeli speech community, *kiturim* involves talk about problems of public significance: the nation's economy, public morale, a local school district, or teachers' low salaries. *Kiturim* is not about personal problems, nor does it involve all features of public life. A complaint about inflation by a well-off person would be considered *kiturim*, whereas a comment about inflation from a jobless single parent of five kids would not be considered *kiturim*. In addition, if an Israeli complained about U.S. foreign policy, it would also not be considered *kiturim*. *Kiturim*'s purpose is to "relieve pent up tensions and frustrations" and its focus is on problems that Israelis feel that their "society should have been able to deal with through some form of collective or institutional social action."[9]

Speech acts particular to one's own society are much harder to see than those in other societies. One speech act that is quintessentially American is what Katriel and Philipsen[10] have labeled **communicating**. Communicating is the term Americans use to refer to talk about personally important matters where each person experiences a feeling of being deeply understood by the partner. *Communicating*, or *really communicating*, as many Americans refer to this speech act, has an emotional and therapeutic function: its purpose is to make people feel good about themselves and their relationship. In contrast to the Israeli act of griping which also has a therapeutic function, communicating focuses on problems, feelings, and events in one's personal life. Griping and communicating can also be distinguished in terms of the bodily postures that accompany them. As Katriel notes, "one can slouch and gripe, but one can hardly slouch and 'communicate'; one can gripe while doing dishes, but one cannot accomplish the purposeful, concerted activity of communicating under these circumstances."[11]

One consequence of speech acts being local to particular speech communities is that communicators with different backgrounds run into difficulties in dealing with each other. It is all too easy to see communicators who perform unfamiliar speech acts as weird, pompous, obscene, and so on. Similarly, it takes considerable mental effort to realize that speech acts that seem clear and reasonable to self may be local and idio-syncratic, ways of talking that have been acquired through immersion in a community rather than being universal categories of meaning.

Although some speech acts are community-distinctive, many others are common across communities but are performed or interpreted differ-ently. Kreckel, for instance, showed how two families in Britain inter-preted the act of warning differently.[12] In Swahili, much longer greetings are expected among acquaintances than would be typical in Britain or the United States.[13] Additionally, through changing the length of a greet-ing (making it shorter than usual by not inquiring about certain people or events), a Swahili speaker can altercast a conversational partner nega-tively, an option not available for English speakers.

In sum, speech community differences seep into speech acts.[14] Beliefs themselves about what counts as reasonable to include in compliments, greetings, or apologies, and when a particular act type should happen, distinguish one culture from another.

Principle 4: Form and Function Need to Be Distinguished

The utterance *I'm sorry* is a common way people apologize and take re-sponsibility for having done something wrong. An **apology**, according to Goffman,[15] is an attempt to split off the current good self from the bad self. Apologies acknowledge that one's action was bad (i.e., thoughtless, unfair, unreasonable), while suggesting that such action is unusual for self, not normal or ordinary. Yet although the act of apologizing can be accomplished by the phrase "I'm sorry," it may also be accomplished by other words. Even more important, the phrase may not be an apology at all.

To be an apology, then, a speaker must take some responsibility for an action and express regret. Imagine, for instance, that without an ex-planation a man (Jim) ran out and left his friend in the middle of having coffee and conversing at a local shop. The next day, Jim sees his friend and says, "I was a real jerk. ((shaking his head)) I shouldn't have left you like that." Although Jim did not say the words "I'm sorry," his friend probably would hear what Jim was saying as an apology. Apologizing, then, is often done with other words than the phrase "I'm sorry." Ameri-can speakers who were interviewed about how they used and interpreted this phrase, in fact, noted how "I'm sorry" was one of the less suitable things to say when a person was really apologizing.[16] "I'm sorry" more than other words could be taken as conveying a lack of sincerity, being formulaic, and indicating that a speaker did not really feel regret.

Not only are apologies accomplished with a variety of words but the phrase "I'm sorry" has other functions than apologizing. Four other functions have been identified. A first use is as a ritualistic remedy, a token comment or politeness device to be used when, for example, one lets a door slam on another or when one bumps into someone else when a bus lurches to a halt. A second function is to manage and repair minor conversational difficulties. Communicators use this phrase when they have not heard what another said. In this case "I'm sorry" functions as a request for repetition. Speakers also use this phrase when they make minor errors in pronouncing a word or incorrectly retrieving the name of a place or person. The third function of "I'm sorry" is to express sympathy. People use the phrase when something bad or sad happens to another, even though they had nothing to do with it. "I'm sorry" might be said as a response to a coworker who mentions that her bike was stolen. A final function of "I'm sorry" is to express gratitude and indebtedness. Kotani, a communication researcher, identifies this function as especially common among Japanese speakers using English.[17]

It is well documented that Japanese speakers use the phrase "I'm sorry" more often than American speakers. Whether Japanese actually "apologize" more frequently is more difficult to assess.[18] In an interview an American student who had spent a semester in Japan was asked what he thought of Japanese speakers' use of "I'm sorry." He said the following:

EXAMPLE 4.2

It's funny, amusing, I got used to it. First I didn't know what to make of it. "Sorry," "Thank you," "Yes," "Please," "No." I got conditioned to a little polite thing. So when Japanese are straightforward, I'm taken aback.[19]

A Japanese student studying in the United States had this to say about why Japanese speakers say "sorry" even when they are not in the wrong:

EXAMPLE 4.3

It's perhaps a cultural difference. The Japanese have *honne* and *tatemae*. In *tatemae* people try to put a good face on a matter and have a good relationship with others on the surface.

In contrast to what needs to be expressed to create a good relationship on the surface (*tatemae*), *honne* expresses what people think inside. *Tatemae* legitimizes an official and public self that is not necessarily consistent with the private self. Sincerity is not, nor should it be, the main issue affecting what people say. Care about the other person and keeping a smooth relationship should often take priority. To say "I'm sorry," then, may be a way to show recognition of the others' feelings in a situation (e.g., that they feel put out, upset, or offended). It need have nothing to do with whether a speaker feels responsible for that action.

These five functions of the phrase "I'm sorry" are available to both Japanese and American speakers, but which one is intended by speakers or attributed by listeners is likely to differ by speech community. The upshot of this small difference in understanding how a form is likely to link to its potential functions can be quite consequential. Kotani expresses it this way:

> English speakers may interpret Japanese speakers' frequent use of "I'm sorry" as polite, ritualistic or excessively formal depending on situations. They may think that Japanese speakers are "over polite" in their day-to-day encounters but do not admit responsibility when they really need to do so. In contrast, Japanese speakers may interpret English speakers' limited use of "I'm sorry" as the lack of goodwill.[20]

Principle 4 applies to other speech acts as well. Beach and Metzger,[21] for instance, show how the phrase "I don't know," which on its surface is a claim of insufficient knowledge, functions to accomplish other actions than asserting limited knowledge. "I don't know" may be used to indicate a communicator was giving a matter only partial attention or to preface a refusal of an invitation or a request (e.g., "I don't know, I don't think I can make it"). Consider, now, the interactional challenges involved in doing several particularly sensitive acts.

ESPECIALLY FACE-THREATENING SPEECH ACTS

In ordinary family and work situations people view talk and action through a moral lens. They hold themselves and others responsible for *what* is said and done, as well as responsible for *how* something is said or done. Valued personal identities are at stake when speakers perform speech acts, although exactly what will be at stake varies by act. In the pages that follow I examine six speech acts.[22] For each, I give a sense of what the act looks like and how it may threaten valued personal identities for the self or for the conversational partner.

Advising

Giving advice involves presenting information to another for the purpose of helping him or her. When people seek out advice from professionals (e.g., nurses, attorneys, consultants for beauty or computers), the giving of advice is relatively unproblematic.[23] However, advice giving is a staple talk activity among friends, family, and peers who work together. In these relationships, "advice could provide expert opinion on how to solve a problem, another point of view in making a decision, and assistance in laying out options."[24] When advice is taken this way the giver is seen as helpful and caring. At the same time, givers of advice may be perceived as being critical of the other's competence. Giving advice implies that someone would not have done an activity if he or she were not explicitly told. Thus, a wife advising her husband to "make sure to lock up when you leave" can be heard by the husband as implying that he often fails to do this basic safety activity. Advice givers may also be judged to be intruding where they should not.

In a interview study, a small set of Americans were asked about advice episodes that they had experienced. Consider what two women had to say:

EXAMPLE 4.4

When I was in college, I was thinking about moving in with this guy and I asked my parents for their advice. My dad wrote this long pros-and-cons letter that amounted to saying he wasn't happy about the idea. My mom just refused to comment, and I felt like she didn't care at all about me.[25]

EXAMPLE 4.5

I have a friend who drives everybody wild. . . . The other day someone at work was talking about her daughter, she was so upset, and Mona said, "Well what you should do is is . . . " and the person said "Listen, Mona, I don't need you to *butt in*. I just need to kind of talk this through and cry awhile and feel sad."[26]

These women make visible a dilemma involved in the act of advice giving. If one offers advice, a person may be seen as butting in where she should not, but if she refrains from doing so, she may be judged to be uncaring.

Advice giving also involves a second dilemma. In situations where a friend clearly wants advice, so that giving advice won't be perceived as butting in, the advice giver still might need to decide between being supportive or being honest. Sometimes when a person asks for advice what he or she actually wants is for the other to support and comfort him or her (tell the asker what he or she wants to hear). At other times, the advice seeker actually wants an honest opinion, even if it disagrees with what may be the asker's initial inclination. Among close friends, being known as honest and supportive are both valued personal identities. When a friend asks for advice, and a speaker feels that he or she can only be one or the other (honest or supportive), giving advice becomes difficult.

Reproaching

Reproaching is the term used to reference the family of speech acts in which one person raises a question about the goodness or reasonableness of another person's actions. Everyday terms used to refer to reproaching include criticizing, reprimanding, finding fault, accusing, questioning someone's judgment or decision, asking for an account, and confronting. Examples 4.6 and 4.7 give two instances of what reproaches (and responses to them) look like. Example 4.6 offers a segment of a conversation that occurred between a mother and her 18-year-old son. The two are sitting in a parked car together talking about whether the son is going to move back into his mother's house, an action the son is reluctant to do. In the example the son is explaining why he does not want to do so. Example 4.7 offers a conversation between 18- and 21-year-old sisters in their kitchen.

EXAMPLE 4.6

JOEL: Look I mighta broke a window. You didn't have to cuff me up in the head. (pause)

JOEL: Why? (pause)

JOEL: I was a little child and I didn't know what I was doing— maybe I was (pause) vacuuming and "oops I didn't mean to do that."

MOM: Look whenever I hit you it was because you'd lie, you know.[27]

EXAMPLE 4.7

MILLY: People don't like you putting down other people
                                                 [to make
          yourself look good
CLARA: [I did <u>not</u> ((slow
          deliberate voice)) Put   [ANYONE (pause)
          DOWN
MILLY: [<u>yes</u> <u>you</u> <u>did</u>

Cody and McLaughlin[28] found that people reproached each other in four primary ways. A first way was to directly rebuke the other, a second was to request an account, a third was to imply the other's moral/intellectual inferiority, and the fourth was to express surprise or disgust. Table 4.1 illustrates these different kinds of reproaches.

These are not the only ways to perform reproaches. Example 4.6 illustrates a common and especially subtle way to reproach: reproaches can also be done by describing another person's action using words that imply the action's unreasonableness. We see this is Joel's description of his mother hitting him because, as a small child, he had accidentally broken something as he was vacuuming. Joel's description can be heard as a strong reproach of the reasonableness of his mother's actions. All the details of his recalled incident—that he was a small child, that he was helping with a chore, and that his breaking the object was accidental—

TABLE 4.1. Types of Reproaches

Direct rebuke	1. "You shouldn't have borrowed my car without asking." 2. "Well, that's a nice prejudiced statement!"
Request an account	1. "Why did you leave your job?" 2. "What happened to your relationship with Andrea?"
Imply moral or intellectual superiority	1. In response to a person's comment about going to Weight Watchers: "I guess some people just don't know how to shut their mouth without someone else's help." 2. In response to a person's comment about watching TV: "Gosh, since I get out and ski so much, I don't have time to watch sports on TV."
Express surprise or disgust	1. "You're kidding? That's gross!" 2. "What do you mean you haven't graduated yet?"

portray him as reasonable and his mother as unreasonable. But his mother resists this description. Note how she responds. She counters that she hit Joel only when he lied to her, a much more reasonable occasion for cuffs to the head than what Joel had presented.

Reproaching, or criticizing, is invariably relationally sensitive. A reproach altercasts the conversational other as possessing a problematic personal identity—for example, being unusual or immoral, doing questionable things or not doing reasonable things, holding strange or nasty opinions, and so on. While reproaching is a sensitive act, it is also a necessary part of everyday life. People need to let others know when they say or do things that cause them difficulties, and people need to know when their own actions are causing problems for others. Rawlins[29] sees the management of reproaching as one of the basic challenges of friendship, what he labels the dialectic of **judgment and acceptance**. People value their friends because they are accepting of one's self as is—for example, as a balance of charming and irritating qualities. Friends give friends acceptance and support, and expect the same in return. At the same time criticizing can convey caring; criticizing affirms that the criticized person is important enough to a speaker that he is willing to judge her, as well as deal with the consequences.

Reproaching may be done better or worse. In a study that some colleagues and I did we asked college students to describe situations in which another had criticized them in a reasonable way and situations where others did a bad job giving criticism.[30] In these open-ended accounts five features distinguished good and bad criticizing. Criticism regarded as poorly given was more likely to include cursing and strongly negative labels (e.g., "stupid jerk," "idiot") and to be given in a vocal manner that sounded like hollering, screaming, or yelling (i.e., especially loud). In contrast, criticism judged to be effectively given more often provided detail about how the other could improve and included an offer to help. Additionally, good criticism provided reasons that took the criticized person's point of view. For instance, compare an instance of bad criticism ("If you don't stop eating so much sugar you will get fat") with an example of good criticism ("Mr. Big, who is paying money for the project, would treat him better if he would wear a tie and jacket").[31] Finally, criticism perceived as good tended to address smaller problems and have a complimentary flavor that was absent from bad criticism. This last finding is interesting because it suggests that serious reproaches are especially likely to be resisted by a conversational partner and treated as unfair and off-the-mark.

In a study of heated arguments, Dersley and Wootton[32] found that communicators denied they had done the act, as was seen in the exchange between Milly and Clara (Example 4.7), or they justified why doing the act was reasonable, as was seen in the mother's response to

Joel's reproach about hitting him (Example 4.6). This second kind of response to a reproach ties in to a family of speech acts that have been given more attention than just about any others.

Accounts and Accounting

Accounts are speech acts designed to mend social trouble; they are conversational devices used when people's actions are subjected to evaluation.[33] **Accounting** links to the speech act of accounts but references the broader activity of reason giving and explaining. Accounting (reason giving) is a pervasive feature of communicative life. Any time a person explains a choice, he or she can be seen as accounting. If a woman tells a friend why she decided to have rose gowns for her wedding rather than yellow ones, a coworker mentions why he is going to work late rather than leave at 5:00 P.M., a husband tells his wife why they should camp at Rocky Mountain Park rather than the Grand Tetons, accounting is occurring. Accounting, then, includes both explaining problematic events, what is most often meant by the term *accounts*, and the kind of reason giving that occurs whenever a speaker explains why he or she did (or wants to do) something. Figure 4.1 illustrates this relationship.

The distinction between problematic and nonproblematic events is not straightforward; people often do not agree on what counts as inappropriate conduct. Thus, it is not usual for accounting that started off as simple reason giving about a presumably unproblematic event to become *an account* in the narrower sense.

Accounts for problematic events are of two main types.[34] They may try to excuse a problematic action or they may seek to justify it. **Excuses** admit that an act was bad but deny that the speaker had full responsibility for the action. **Justifications**, in contrast, accept full responsibility for

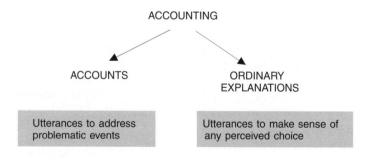

FIGURE 4.1. Links between accounting and accounts.

an action but deny or minimize its presumed badness (e.g., what Mom did with Joel). For instance, if a man (Reid) was late for a meeting, he could excuse himself by mentioning oversleeping, bad traffic, or an earlier meeting running late. Each of these comments would imply that he saw his lateness as problematic but refused to take full responsibility for his action. On the other hand, Reid could justify his lateness. He would be doing this if he said that the real substance of the meeting always begins after folks had their coffee and caught up on small talk.

To take another example, imagine Len and Rudy are roommates. One day when Len comes home from work, he snaps and makes a hostile remark to Rudy. When Rudy reproaches him ("Why are you yelling at me?"), Len might offer an apology and an excuse: "Sorry, I'm exhausted. We had a long, excruciatingly tense meeting at work today." Or he might justify his behavior: "I've asked you multiple times not to call me unless it's urgent" or "What do you expect, given the way you've broken your promises lately." Although excuses and justifications (also apologies) are considered alternative options, it is possible to do them all in a single exchange. In the above situation, for instance, Len might have said: "What do you expect given the way you've broken your promises lately? I'm sorry, though, we had a long excruciating tense meeting at work today, and I'm really feeling out of sorts." Accounts, then, are one of several possible responses to reproaches. Table 4.2 describes the most common types of responses and how they relate to accounts.

The accounting process does not end when a person apologizes, excuses, or justifies. The other person responds, evaluating the speakers' attempt to fix the problem. Response may either fully or partially honor what the speaker has said, reject the account that has been offered, or drop the topic and start talking about other things.[35] As with many communicative actions, the process of honoring is accomplished implicitly. A partner is unlikely to tell a person after she excuses her lateness that "I honor what you told me." Instead, communicators convey their acceptance of an apology and/or an excuse by saying things like "No problem" or "You didn't miss much." In contrast, the rejection of an account is more explicit. In response to an excuse about lateness a conversational partner could say, "That's a new one! Haven't heard that excuse yet" or "You always have a reason, don't you?" At times people refrain from either explicitly honoring or rejecting an account. This is done by changing the topic from the problematic event focus ("Let's get down to business, shall we?").

Some accounts do the work they are officially about—mending troubles—but others do not. Morris and Coursey[36] identified two factors that affected managers' likelihood of accepting an employee's account at work. Employees whose reputations were good (i.e., they had rarely

TABLE 4.2. **Responses to Reproaches**

Features	Apology	Denial	Account Excuse	Justification
1. Speaker acknowledges doing act.	×		×	×
2. Speaker accepts some responsibility and blame for act.	×			
3. Speaker denies doing act.		×		
4. Speaker denies full responsibility for act.			×	
5. Speaker denies or minimizes the act's badness.				×

done inappropriate things) were more likely to have their accounts accepted than those who had a history of error and wrongdoing. In addition, the plausibility of the circumstances affected managers' likelihood of accepting an account. If the manager could envision self in similar circumstances, she would be more likely to accept the account. Thus, an employee who jammed the office copier and excused her act by saying she didn't know that she had to change a copier setting might be more plausible than the same employee attempting to excuse her borrowing from the office's petty cash container by saying she didn't know it was not to be used for personal purchases.

Accounts are highly rhetorical: they are speech acts crafted to accomplish the interactional goal of being seen to be reasonable. The "crafting" aspect of accounts is particularly visible when one has an opportunity to look at the account a person offers over time. Manusov[37] had college students tape-record their talk with five different people about one event in their lives that needed explaining. Such events included canceling a trip, not winning a sorority election, not getting a job, breaking up with a boyfriend, and not wanting a girlfriend to go on a planned trip. As speakers explained the event in their lives a second and then a third time, they often changed their accounts to deal with disagreements that had arisen in earlier tellings. For instance, in explaining why he had canceled out of a trip with a friend, a student initially mentioned his lack of money. The person to whom he offered the initial explanation challenged it, but then went on to ask him how his girlfriend felt about him taking a trip without her. In subsequent accounts, in addition to mentioning his lack of money, the young man excused his pulling out of the trip because of his girlfriend's negative reaction.

Let me conclude by highlighting a nonobvious feature of accounting. Any time a person gives a reason for his thoughts or actions, he marks what has been talked about as a choice. People do not account for what they regard as natural, inevitable, or culturally given. It is quite difficult to respond to questions that ask for accounts of events that a person has never thought of as needing to be explained. In these situations, the most typical response is either to treat the question as a joke or the other as hostile. In American culture, for instance, if a 15-year-old girl were asked why she wore shorts on a hot day, she would probably treat the question as a joke: Who would do otherwise? In other national communities, though, wearing this type of garb would be a highly problematic action that required an account. What actions are routinely accounted for or treated as not needing an account provide a window into what a speech community takes to be normal or questionable. In that sense, accounts expose a cultural group's beliefs about what it means to be a reasonable person.

Disclaimers

Disclaimers are verbal devices to deflect others from assigning negative or inappropriate personal identities to self.[38] They are conversational moves that are done at the time a person says something potentially problematic. Whereas accounts tend to focus on actions, disclaimers are most strongly linked to conversation expressions of opinion. Table 4.3 provides examples of typical disclaimers.

Usually disclaimers come before a problematic utterance (seen in Examples 1–3), but on occasion they may come immediately after (Example 4). Of interest is that disclaimers simultaneously make visible that a speaker regards something as potentially problematic—in the examples in Table 4.3, that she might be regarded as silly, as lacking the skill or expertise to offer advice, or as prejudiced—and are acts to keep others from thinking that the particular problematic identity should apply to the self. In contrast to disclaimers that preface problematic talk, those that come immediately after a comment suggest a different thinking process. Rather than being devices speakers build into their talk to ward off a forthcoming negative assessment, postutterance disclaimers suggest that speakers initially are unaware of an utterance's potential sensitivity, and become cognizant of it as they hear themselves making the comment.[39]

Everyday talk is peppered with disclaimers; after all, almost any comment can be problematic for some audience. Although the use of a disclaimer does not necessarily secure a speaker's desired goal—to have the other see him in a personally positive way, or at least to avoid giving

TABLE 4.3. Examples of Disclaimers

1. "This may sound silly, but I feel as if my great-great grandfather has been trying to communicate with me in my dreams."
2. "I'm not great at directions, but I think we should turn left at the next corner."
3. "I'm not a lawyer, but I think you should sue him."
4. "Ellen Ross is not to be trusted. It's not that I have anything against Jews; some of my closest friends are Jewish."

the other a negative or inappropriate impression—they illustrate the considerable effort communicators give to building desirable personal identities.

Brown-Nosing

In general, performing positive speech acts (e.g., complimenting, expressing interest through a query, making an offer) is considered a nice thing to do. People who routinely do these kinds of actions are seen as helpful and pleasant, someone others like to be around. Yet, when we move these behaviors into institutional settings, such as workplaces or schools, where some people control valued resources, and everyone exists in hierarchical relationships to others, these nice acts may be taken to mean something quite different.

Drawing upon interviews and participant observation in work settings, Hall and Valde[40] explored the cultural meaning of brown-nosing in American work life. **Brown-nosing**, also referred to as *apple-polishing*, *kissing up*, *sucking up*, and, in its most extreme negative form, *ass-kissing*, is a speech act in which a person's niceness is seen to be excessive. Furthermore, in brown-nosing, a person's performance of positive acts is seen as arising from ulterior motives, such as a desire to garner attention, advancement, or rewards merely through these acts. Contrasted to the employee who works hard, and produces real results, the brown-noser is regarded as two-faced and is seen to be either reprehensible or pitiful. Yet it is not just brown-nosers who are negatively evaluated; so too are the recipients of brown-nosing. People who respond well to brown-nosing, who "eat it up," as one interviewee described it, are derogated as narcissistic and insecure.

Brown-nosing differs from other speech acts I have discussed in that it is rarely an act people deliberately set out to do. Most often, the label is applied by fellow workers and is given to persons seen to be performing positive speech acts with an institutional superior from whom they have something to gain. Because people fear having the brown-nosing label attached to self, they may avoid doing actions that contribute to a workplace functioning well. Simply put, to avoid being seen as a brown-noser, an employee may fail to seek out a supervisor to express interest in a project or may withhold ideas about how a problem might be solved.

Consider, now, the sensitivities that surround a last speech act, the giving and receiving of personal information.

Gossiping

From antiquity till the 19th century, gossiping was denounced as evil and as a sign of weak moral character. In today's society, gossip's profile is more complex. On the one hand, gossip is regarded as innocuous, a pleasant and minimally harmful way for neighbors, coworkers, and friends to pass time. On the other hand, gossip continues to carry a moral sting. Much like being known as a brown-noser, being known as a gossiper is not an identity people desire. But what exactly is gossip? What kinds of talk count as gossip? To whom is gossip directed? When, for instance, would talk about an extramarital affair count as gossip? When would it not?

Bergmann[41] supplies an interesting and detailed analysis of this morally controversial speech act. He suggests that for talk to be regarded as gossip, it must be about certain topics and directed to others who stand in certain relationships to the initiator. For instance, a husband talking to a divorce attorney about an affair his wife has had would not be considered to be gossiping. Nor would the husband telling his sister about his wife's affair count as gossip. In addition, the sister telling a close friend about her brother's difficulties is also unlikely to be considered gossip. However, if the sister's friend passed the information on to another friend, it undoubtedly would be judged as gossip. **Gossip** is about absent parties (people who are not participating in the conversation) who are not intimately linked to the speaker (intimates include family members and relational partners). In addition, gossip both presupposes relationships of rough equality and further cements them as such. To gossip with another is to convey a certain amount of trust in the other's judgment, an act unlikely with a stranger. Similarly, to gossip with someone who is not roughly equal to self may be seen as an attempt to curry that person's favor.

Gossip focuses on private matters, giving special attention to the gulf between what people do and say publicly and what they do and say in private. However, because knowledge about people's private affairs is not equally distributed, not all individuals are equally able to gossip. In earlier times, for instance, servants' work gave them access to details about the private lives of those they served. In doing the wash, a servant would come across the physical stains that cued sexual indiscretion. In working for another, assistants get to see what bosses espouse to be proper conduct, as well as how they actually treat others when they are unobserved. Unsurprisingly, those categories of people who have access to the private lives of others (servants, organizational staff who assist others, and women generally) have been regarded as especially susceptible to being gossips. Gossiping, while perhaps more frequent among certain types of people, is a speech act practiced by everybody. Gossiping is an act initiated by one person, but it requires the active participation of a partner. A gossip initiator will test the conversational water to ensure that his or her partner is willing to gossip. Example 4.8 illustrates a typical way a gossip sequence occurs.

EXAMPLE 4.8

Coworker 1: Do you know what's happening with Jim?

Coworker 2: I don't like to say anything bad about people.

Coworker 1: Come on, tell me. What's the dirt? You know you can trust me.

Coworker 2: Well, if you promise . . .

Gossiping, then, is a sequence of talk that implicates both parties. Through one person's act of telling and the partner's active encouragement and elicitation of what is being told gossip gets done.

Gossip serves an important moral function in society by helping to preserve the norms of a community. It is partly because people fear being the object of gossip that they do desirable activities and refrain from doing undesirable ones. At the same time, to talk about others' shortcomings and peculiarities, as gossiping requires, is to be involved in a somewhat sleazy activity. Gossip is both good and bad. This contradictory quality, which is its essence, raises a particular challenge in friendship. On the one hand, being loyal—respecting a friend's confidences (no gossip)—is central to what being a friend is all about; on the other hand, trusting a friend is being willing to share information that officially one is expected to keep private. In the latter case, trusting Friend A is displayed by one's willingness to reveal private information about Friend B (selectively gossiping). Bergmann sees gossip as a form of "discreet indiscretion." For gossip to serve its desirable functions, it must be engaged in selectively. As he notes, "It is only as something bad that gossip can be something good."[42]

Bergmann's view of gossip is a European and American one. Although gossip is a speech act found across communities, it also is an act that takes distinctive shapes within different communities. Goldsmith[43] compared speakers in St. Vincent (West Indies), the Zincanetecos of Mexico, and three other communities and found that all five societies were ambivalent about gossip. They differed, however, as to what kinds of people they saw as most likely to do gossip, what could be talked about, how they divided gossip into subtypes, and the reasons that communities had for evaluating gossip negatively.

SUMMARY

In this chapter I have examined a family of face-sensitive speech acts—gossiping, brown-nosing, disclaimers, accounting, reproaching, and advising—to consider what each act looks like and how it may challenge communicators' personal and relational identities. In addition, I highlighted how performing (and refraining from performing) speech acts is a primary way people enact and change their relational identities. In examining how communicators built closeness (or distance), and the better and worse ways to criticize, I adopted the rhetorical perspective, emphasizing each person's ability to shape close relationships in a direction he or she desires. In highlighting how gossiping or apologizing is done differently when speakers come from different communities, I took a cultural look at speech acts, reminding us that evaluation can never escape being a culturally inflected activity.

◈ The Sound of Talk

One summer morning a 911 call taker in a large city received a sobbing call from a 12-year-old boy who had run across the street to a neighbor's house in his underwear. The boy was calling because his 15-year-old brother was "beating him" up for "little things." The boy wanted the police to come take the brother away. After determining that the older brother was not drinking or on drugs, not using a gun or a knife, and that the two boys fought with each other fairly often, the police call taker tracked down the mother's telephone number and called her at her place of work. The police call taker explained to the mother that there had been trouble at her home and her younger son had called the police. The call taker then connected the telephone lines so that the mother could talk directly with the boy, now at the neighbor's house. The mother ordered her son to go home. Example 5.1 offers part of the conversation that occurred between the mother and her son. Symbols have been added to capture the sound of their talk; these symbols are explained below.

EXAMPLE 5.1. Telephone Exchange between Boy and Mom

1   BOY: I would, NO: I ain't going back home I'm ((sobbing))

2   MOM: I'll be, I (.) am (.) at (.) <u>work</u>.

3   BOY: mum I'm [in my boxer sh-

4   MOM: [I (.) am (.) <u>a:[t</u> (.)work

5   BOY: [I kno:w I'm in my boxer shorts,

6   I ain't goin no= ((less pronounced <u>sobbing</u>))

7   MOM: =you are gonna hafta wait until I can get <u>home</u>.

8 BOY: I ain't <u>goin</u> home till Jackson goes home, you better tell him
9 that he has to go live with his uncle .hh .hh .hh ((sobbing sounds))

10 MOM: I <u>will</u> (.) be <u>home</u>.

11 BOY: <u>when?</u>

12 MOM: Raymond as soon as I kin <u>get</u> there.

13 BOY: well I'm in my <u>boxer</u> sho:[rts ((higher pitched whining quality))

14 MOM: [well I (.) I will hafta <u>get</u> home do (.)
15 you (.) hear (.) me?[1]

One of the most distinctive features of everyday talk is that it has a sound—it is not just a set of words and phrases. How something is said affects what speakers are taken to be meaning. However, to move beyond this commonplace truth (*it's not what was said, but how it was said that's important*), there needs to be a way to represent the sound of speech. Without a written system to represent the subtle ways people use their voice, it is difficult to discuss how meaning making, and identity-work more generally, is accomplished through vocal cues.

In this chapter, I explain the most commonly used symbols for the different sounds of talk. Then I consider how certain communities of people use their voice to portray themselves and their conversational partners as having positively valued personal identities (e.g., *I'm a kind, loving person*) or negatively valued ones (*I see you as a real jerk*). In addition, I examine the assumed identity linkages of more stable features of voice quality. Finally, I explore the meaning of accents and consider how a person's accent both reflects his speech community membership and, on occasion, may be used strategically to present the speaker as a certain kind of person.

TRANSCRIPTION

A number of researchers[2] have developed transcription systems to make written records of the sounds of talk. Each system has advantages, highlighting somewhat different features. The one used most often in communication is the system developed by Gail Jefferson, commonly referred to as the **conversation analysis** (CA) transcription system.[3]

Consider the meaning of the CA symbols used in the conversation between the boy and his mom (Example 5.1). A first feature to note is that words are written as they are pronounced: line 3 "mum"; line 6, "goin." The "NO" in capital letters (line 1) indicates that the word is especially loud. Underlined words (see, for instance, lines 2, 4, 5, and 7) are words that have been stressed, although not as much as the word in capital letters. The series of ".hh" symbols preceded by a period indicate in-breaths; the more h's, the more pronounced is the in-breath. Lowercase "hhh" without the period (there are none in this transcription) indicate out-breaths, like those that occur in small laughing sounds. Double parentheses (( )) describe broader features of talk such as extended sobbing, laughing, or a distinctive voice quality (see lines 1, 6, 9, and 13). In transcribing talk, punctuation is not used as it would be in writing. Instead it captures vocal intonation patterns: a period is a falling intonation, a question mark is a rising one, and a comma signifies continuing intonation.

When a sound in a word is prolonged, colons are used to mark the lengthening. An example of this is seen in line 13 in the word "sho:rts." When short recognizable pauses occur between words, they are marked with parentheses and a period: (.); if the pause were longer the parentheses would include the number of seconds (e.g, (3.5)). Partial words that are cut off are marked with hyphens, as we see in line 3 where the boy starts to mention that he is in his boxer "sh-." Finally, an important part of the sound of talk relates to the timing of what was said. Letting a speaker finish rather than interrupting and overlapping her has different meanings. Where a person starts speaking relative to the person already talking is indicated by square brackets that are aligned in successive lines of the transcription. Multiple overlaps between the mother and the boy occur in lines 3–5. When one person starts to speak at the end of another person's talk with no noticeable pause, this is indicated with equals signs (=; see lines 6 and 7). Table 5.1 summarizes the meaning of these symbols, as well as a few others.

THE IDENTITY-WORK OF PARALINGUISTIC DEVICES

One important part of each person's personal identity is how he or she appears to be feeling at a particular interactional moment. Is he annoyed? Feeling proud? Bored by the conversation? Is she working hard to be patient and not show her anger? Excited? Feeling shame or embarrassment? Amused? Expressions of emotion are done through multiple channels: they are conveyed through voice, through the content of what's said, through the particular words selected, and through the speaker's co-occurring facial expressions and bodily gestures. Arriving at the correct interpretation of other people's feelings about us, the activity being done, and the subject of talk is important but often difficult. Speakers rarely give explicit labels to their in-the-moment feelings. As Parrott and Harré noted, "Words that we use for emotions do not usually figure in displays of emotion. When we hear someone say, 'I'm very angry with you' the chances are that this is a ritual rebuke rather than an expression of genuine anger."[4]

Until recently, most studies of emotion focused on big feelings (e.g.,

TABLE 5.1. Most Commonly Used Transcription Symbols

.	(period) Falling intonation.
?	(question mark) Rising intonation.
,	(comma) Continuing intonation.
-	(hyphen) Marks an abrupt cutoff.
::	(colon(s)) Prolonging of sound.
never	(underlining) Stressed syllable or word.
WORD (all caps)	Loud speech.
°word°	(degree symbols). Quiet speech.
>word<	(more than and less than) Quicker speech.
hh	(series of h's) Aspiration or laughter.
.hh	(h's preceded by dot) Inhalation.
[ ]	(brackets) Simultaneous or overlapping speech.
=	(equals sign) Contiguous utterances.
(2.4)	(number in parentheses) Length of a silence.
(.)	(period in parentheses) micropause, $2/_{10}$ second
( )	(empty parentheses) Nontranscribable segment of talk.
(word)	(word or phrase in parentheses) Transcriptionist doubt.
((gazing toward the ceiling))	(double parentheses) Description of nonspeech activity or sound quality.

anger, sadness, fear, happiness) and were carried out in laboratory settings.[5] Relatively little research had been concerned with analyzing the subtle, often fleeting, feelings that are routine in talk. Yet it is these feelings that are especially important to people in their conversations. One study conducted by Charlotte Bloch,[6] a Danish scholar, is particularly helpful for developing a picture of how the vocal qualities of speech convey information about a speaker's feelings. Bloch asked people to narrate experiences in their lives; the events they chose to narrate could be major or minor. After recording and transcribing their stories, she considered whether systematic relationships could be found between **paralinguistic markers** (audible sounds and the vocal quality of speech) and feelings such as pride, delight, shame, and so on. Bloch concluded that certain paralinguistic markers usually indicate negative feelings about the self (e.g., embarrassment, shame). In particular, she found that a high level of repetition and nonfluent speech (e.g., frequent and long pausing, "uhs" and "ums") and stretches of especially quiet speech expressed negative feelings. She also found that positive self-feelings were evidenced by rapid flowing speech, often melodious in sound, and by laughing and audible inhalations midstream. Finally, she concluded that some paralinguistic markers were ambiguous, with their emotional meaning dependent on what was being said. Table 5.2 shows the likely positive and negative meanings of ambiguous vocal moves.

In arriving at a judgment about a person's in-the-moment feeling state it is important to take account of the person's baseline conversational style. A **baseline** is a person's normal style of speaking. It includes the person's usual loudness level, speaking rate (fast vs. slow), fluency style (smooth vs. lots of repetitions, fillers [uh], pauses), as well as his or her average pitch and the usual amount that he or she varies his or her intonation.

In the exchange between the boy and his mother in the 911 call, the mother's voice cues that she is irritated with her son. This is accomplished not only by her pattern of stressing individual words, seen in line 10 ("I will (.) be home."), but also by her use of **controlled enunciation,** a practice that involves distinct pronunciation of each word followed by a brief pause, seen in lines 14–15 when the mother asks if the boy can hear her: "well I (.) I will hafta get home do (.) you (.) hear (.) me?" Controlled enunciation is a way of presenting self as "working" to be patient but nonetheless feeling irritated. At the same time, the practice altercasts the conversational partner as unreasonable and irritating. As with other paralinguistic practices, this is not the only meaning. Controlled enunciation may also be used in talking to nonnative speakers, the young, the elderly, or the mentally impaired.[8] In these contexts, controlled enunciation altercasts the other as not fully normal, as having a limitation of one kind or another that requires slower, more deliberate speech.

Averill,[9] a psychologist who has studied anger and aggression, found that although the impression that someone is angry draws on facial expressions and speech content, voice was an especially big contributor. Loud, high-pitched speech, what we ordinarily refer to as yelling

TABLE 5.2. Meanings of Ambiguous Paralinguistic Signs[7]

Paralinguistic feature	Potential positive meaning	Potential negative meaning
Laughed word	Joy	Shame
>Quick speech<	Excitement	Discomfort
LOUD or emphatic	Felt significance	Burgeoning anger
°quiet speech°	Relief	Hiding behavior
Inhalation (.hh)	Excitement	Mild shame
Exhalation (hh)	Relief	Feeling burdened

and screaming, cue strong negative feelings. By and large, people attend to the intensity and duration of the person's vocal expression to sort out whether the person is angry or just annoyed.

Voice quality is also a way a speaker altercasts another as an intimate friend or just an acquaintance. A study[10] tape-recorded college women talking with intimate male friends and casual male acquaintances. Women talking with intimates used a relaxed, softer voice with somewhat higher average pitch and more pitch variation than they used in conversations with male acquaintances.

In everyday talk, emotions tend to be treated as if they were genuine expressions of what people are feeling inside. Yet emotions, like other aspects of personhood, are communicatively constructed and strategically chosen. Nowhere is this more common than in workplace settings. Service and professional roles routinely require personnel to express certain positive feelings (e.g., liking, enjoyment, respect) and to repress negative feelings (e.g., impatience, irritation, disgust). To construct self as a good sales clerk, waitperson, telephone operator, and so on requires a significant amount of **emotion labor**—the monitoring of emotional displays to provide the institutionally expected version. As Hochschild remarks,

> Real-time emotions are a large part of what managers manage and emotional labour is no small part of what trainers train and supervisors supervise. It is a big part of white collar "work."[11]

A complexity, though, is that the use of voice cues varies by speech communities. Not all people use voice in the same way as native English speakers do to indicate feeling states. Gumperz and Cook-Gumperz[12] showed how in a public meeting in Britain an exchange between a native English speaker and a West Indian speaker of English went poorly, with members of each community judging each other negatively. To show the consequences of different vocal styles, the authors draw upon a considerably more complicated transcription system than the one I described in this chapter. Their system captured breath groupings (marking exactly where a speaker took a breath and whether or not it was hearable) and prosodic patterns (combined speed, loudness, stress, and pitch changes). Table 5.3 illustrates what members of each community had to say about each speaker when they were interviewed about their impressions. These negative impressions, Gumperz and Cook-Gumperz argue, are strongly affected by the different ways each speech community uses their voice to signal what is important information in what is being said, and whether voice inflection is used to cue feeling states toward the other.

TABLE 5.3. Identity Impressions Based on Speech[13]

	Of British English (BE) speaker	Of West Indian English (WIE) speaker
By BE participants	BE speaker's talk was "calm, factual, and reasoning." He may have had a somewhat "bureaucratic tone" but "points were well made and the argument hangs together."	WIE speaker's talk was "abrupt, impulsive, and perhaps somewhat rude." While some of his metaphors were "quite apt, his statement as a whole lacks clear connections."
By WIE participants	BE speaker exhibited "excessive stiffness and redundancy" and at one key place used a "condescending style." He also "beats around the bush."	WIE speaker was "direct, but not at all impolite." He "says what he means, making clear how he himself feels." His reasoning is "quite clear."

MEANINGS OF STABLE FEATURES OF VOICE

When we first hear someone on the telephone it is pretty easy to tell if a caller is a man or a woman and his or her relative age (child, teen, adult, senior). This is because voices have an average pitch (mean fundamental frequency), with children's pitch generally higher than women's pitch, which in turn is higher than men's pitch. It is also the case that certain particular vocal features are taken to go with certain kinds of people. In general, men use a more restricted pitch range than women.[14] Thus speaking with lots of vocal variation is regarded as a more female talking style. Patches of a quavering voice or a creaky one—technically, a low-pitched staccato sound produced by slow vibration of the vocal folds—are more common in elderly speakers.

A contrasting intonation pattern found commonly among young speakers, especially females, is what has come to be called **uptalk** or *talking in questions*. In uptalk a speaker makes a statement as if it were a question (e.g., "Yesterday? I went to Dillards?"). Uptalk, as Cameron notes, "is held to have originated among young women (typically in the 'Valley Girl' mould, which is to say affluent white girls who are or present themselves as shallow and unintelligent and who do a lot of shopping)." Many listeners see uptalk as "mak[ing] the speaker sound as if s/he does not know what s/he is talking about, or as if s/he cannot express the most straightforward thought without looking to others for approval."[15]

Breathiness—a vocal quality produced by the laryngeal muscles not closing tightly, accompanied by a slightly slower speech—is also more common among women, so much so that it is a voice quality presumed to be feminine. Breathiness is culturally taken as cueing passivity, submissiveness, and a relaxed, sexy style; when it is situation-specific rather than a general style, it is taken to indicate sexual arousal.[16] Although breathiness is biologically linked to sexual arousal, and hence is a quality that will be found in both men and women's voices on certain occasions, this vocal quality has been used strategically to sell sex and sexiness. Hall, a linguist, did a study of sex telephone call-in services where men call in and pay to have a woman talk sexy to them. Hall interviewed the women answering the phones. Consider what Shelia, a European American woman who identified her sexual orientation as butch bisexual had to say about why her talk was so marketable.

EXAMPLE 5.2

I feel like definitely the timbre of my voice has a lot to do with it. I don't know, the ability to sound like, I hate to say it, feminine and kind of that lilting quality, and to sound like you're really enjoying it, like you're turned on and having a good time. I think that has a lot to do with it because they're always telling me, "Oh yes, you have such a great voice! God I love listening to your voice!" I think that's a big part of it, it's just the sound of the person's voice.[17]

To sell the phone service on the fantasy line, callers would get a free taste of the kind of talk they could get if they paid for the service. Example 5.3 offers part of such a sample. Notice how breathy voice is a key talk tactic to entice men to pay money to have these conversations.

EXAMPLE 5.3

Oo::h:: I'm so ((breathy voice)) excited. - I just got a hot new job (0.8) well, ((in slight Southern accent)) I've been bored lately..hh -I live in a small town and my husband travels a lot, (0.5) I have lots of time on my hands. - .hhh of course I've always managed to stay busy. (0.4) lots of girlfriends, you know ((whispered)) I love to shop, I ((laugh)) ^pract^ically live at the mall it seems but still . hhhh (2.0) anyway. - this friend told me about this job I can do at home. - all I need is a phone. - and a lusty imagination. ((laugh))yeah, you've got it - .hh I'm doing h::ot sexy phone calls these days. (0.5) I really get into it too. - .hhh I love that sexy hot fellows from all over the country call me and enjoy my ((whispered)) voice and my fantasies. (0.4) I like to dress the part too. - I went to my favorite lingerie ((in hoarse, breathy voice)) store, - Victoria's Secret? And bought s::atan bikinis . . . when I dress up and look in the mirror ((slower, breathy voice)) I - get - so - crazy .hhhhh I just can't wait for that first ca::ll.[18]

Other aspects of voice also reflect desired (or disdained) personal identities. For instance, a low-pitched voice is regarded as much more commanding and authoritative than a high-pitched one; slow speakers are presumed to be slower thinkers than their faster speaking counterparts; and loud speakers are presumed to be more dominant personalities than quiet ones.[19] As a result of these cultural beliefs, despite the fact that actual evidence for them is thin, members of our culture hold to certain occupational generalizations. Radio announcers and televisions broadcasters, for instance, are likely to have voices that have a lower average pitch than is typical for their gender.[20]

Importantly, judgments that a person is fast or slow speaking, loud or really soft-spoken use a communicator's own speech community to create a baseline and make judgments. The result of communities viewing each other through their baseline is that the negative beliefs one group holds about another get evidenced. Because most Native Americans use a softer, more modulated voice than Anglos, Anglos are likely to judge Native Americans as overly submissive. In contrast Native Americans regard the usual Anglo as shrill and abrasive, a speaker who is always shouting.[21]

DIALECT OR "ACCENT"

A distinctive feature of how talk sounds relates to the dialect a person speaks. A **dialect** is the name for an identifiable and characteristic way of speaking a language. Dialects are associated with communities. The community of speakers may be quite large, as when we distinguish Australian, Jamaican, and American English dialects, or it may be quite small, as when distinctions are made about the dialects in one region of the country (the South) or even a single city (Philadelphia). Generally, if two speakers can understand each other, even if it takes a bit of effort, they are speaking dialects of the same language rather than two distinct languages. The distinction between a dialect and a language, though, is not a hard-and-fast one. Some ways of speaking that are typically treated as two languages (e.g., Spanish and Portuguese) have been argued by language scholars as better described as two dialects of the same language.

A dialect involves three main features: (1) vocabulary, (2) grammar, and (3) pronunciation or accent. Dialect differences in vocabulary refer to differences in everyday word usage; the specialized vocabularies that go with occupations, sports, or hobbies are labeled **jargon**. An example of a dialect difference is seen in how British speakers would describe *lining up* at the post office to *mail* a letter. In contrast to his American counterpart, a British speaker is likely to describe himself as *queuing up* to *post* a letter. Grammatical features that vary across dialects of English include presence or absence of double negatives ("it ain't no good"), usage or omission of "s" in third-person singular ("she go away" or "she goes away"), and many other practices. Typically, the forms of expression that are preferred in written expression of a language are the dialects that will have the most social prestige.

While all three features contribute to what is meant by dialect, pronunciation is the feature of which everyday people are most aware. Although people are described as having an accent or not having one, from a linguistic perspective this characterization is inaccurate. Everyone has a distinct way of pronouncing words, so everyone has an **accent**. What speakers usually mean when they say someone has an accent is that (1) a person talks differently than they do, or (2) the person's pronunciation differs from what is most often heard on U.S. television news (broadcast English) or coming out of the mouths of institutionally high-status speakers.

Dialects can be evaluated linguistically or socially. From the linguistic viewpoint, all dialects are equal. Every dialect is a rule-governed system. Every dialect has pronunciation patterns, grammatical rules, and rules about expected vocabulary. No dialect is better than any other; each reflects coherent rule-governed ways of expressing meaning. Yet while all dialects are equal linguistically, they are not equal socially. Certain dialects will be judged as "better" than others. Social assessments of the goodness of a dialect are tied to the relative value given to different kinds of people in a society. In general, middle-class people are valued more than working-class people; urban residents have more status than rural residents; and whites have more status than blacks. So too are the different dialects valued.[22] The differential valuing of communities' dialects is even reflected in the terms linguists and other language scholars use to refer to kinds of dialects. Those dialects spoken by the elite group(s) in society not only get referred to as **standard dialects**, but also are likely to have become what is expected in good writing; dialects that differ from this small set are grouped together and referred to as **nonstandard**. These labels ("standard," "nonstandard") are not neutral; each strongly implies whether a particular way of speaking is to be desired or avoided. Baldly stated, those groups of people who already possess power and influence will have their ways of speaking assessed as the better ones.

Interestingly, American accents are on their way to becoming the accent of English that speakers worldwide prefer. Until recently, the variety of English that has been spoken by the educated elite in Britain, called *Received Pronunciation* (RP), has been the favored accent worldwide. RP English was the version that most nonnative speakers of English in Europe and Asia would learn. A recent study[23] had college speakers from four English-speaking countries (New Zealand, Australia, England, the United States) read the same message (a letter to parents). Australian and New Zealand college students listened to these different accents and then rated each of the speakers in terms of how friendly and likable they saw the speaker and how competent they thought the person would be. Speakers using an American accent were preferred over the British-accented speakers, sometime even more than speakers with the listeners' own nationality. The explanation for this, Bayard and his colleagues argued, is the widespread use of American media outside the United States. Increasingly, talking like an American, even in places where the United States is strongly criticized, is common. In the BBC's program *The Story of English,* the narrator concluded by saying, "American English seems to be winning hands down" and "American English, not British English, will remain the major global form of English into the indefinite future."[24]

Many group ties shape the dialect a person will use. As already mentioned, nationality and local geographic region shape a person's accent. One of the most important other influences is social class. Social class is a composite way of classifying people that takes account of education, occupation, and income. In the United States class is an uncomfortable way of describing people; to describe someone as *not middle class* to many Americans feels judgmental and intolerant. In surveys, just about everybody—whatever a person's education or occupation—will check that he or she is middle class. How researchers assign a social class category to a person depends on whether the researcher's classification system gives greater weight to education, occupation, or income. In most cases, of course, the three go together, but there are many instances where they do not. When questionnaires give people the option of choosing *working person* (as in *regular working person*) rather than *working class* or *lower class*, a large percentage of people comfortably identify as not middle class.

Speakers from working-class communities speak differently than those from middle-class backgrounds and, in turn, are responded to differently. A middle-class speaking style will be described as "sounding educated." To sound working class will lead many listeners to assume that a speaker is not able to do jobs that primarily involve intellectual labor. In addition to social class, and partly related to it, are the race and ethnic communities of a speaker. Speakers originating from Hispanic, Hawaiian, Asian, and African American communities are likely to have accents distinctive to their groups, especially if the speakers are from working-class communities. By and large, as members of ethnic groups move into the middle class, their speech patterns become increasingly similar to those of other middle-class speakers. That is, middle-class speakers have a more homogeneous style than persons from working-class backgrounds.

De la Zerda and Hopper[25] asked employment interviewers in a variety of large businesses in Austin, Texas, to listen to a tape of several Mexican American speakers using either standard or Spanish-accented English dialects. Employers were asked to rate the suitability of each speaker for three kinds of positions: as an unskilled worker, as a skilled technician, and as a supervisor. Perhaps unsurprisingly, standard-sounding speakers were most favored for the supervisory position; they were also least favored for the unskilled position. At the same time, Spanish-accented speakers were most favored for the unskilled job.

Black English Vernacular (BEV), also called *African American Vernacular English* or *Ebonics*, is undoubtedly the most studied ethnic dialect. Estimates about the number of BEV speakers in the United States range from 60 to 80% of African Americans.[26] Rather than being a single dialect, BEV is best conceived as a family of dialects with a set of grammatical and pronunciation features that can be part of any individual dialect. The roots of BEV can be traced to the Creole language of the first African American speakers. Among the distinctive-sounding features of this dialect are the weakening of final consonants in words, such as saying "coal" for "cold"; pronouncing the "th" sound as a "d" ("dis" and "dat" for "this" and "that"); and stressing the first syllable of a word where other dialects stress the second (e.g., PO-lice, DE-troit).[27] Dialects change over time, as do the frequency and meaning of usage of a specific feature. Pronouncing the word "ask" as "axe," a visible feature of BEV, has become more common in recent years. This change may be a way for African American speakers in predominately white environments to say, "I'm black and I'm proud of it."

This brings us to an important question: Why do dialects that have low prestige and economic disadvantage persist?

The Value of Devalued Dialects

Giles and Coupland[28] offer several reasons as to why speakers keep a low-prestige dialect and do not choose to learn one that has higher prestige. As I noted above, dialects are visible and clear markers of group membership. It is a central way that speakers display who they are. Distinctive dialects, therefore, facilitate in-group cohesion; they are audible signs to mark who is inside or outside the group. An upshot of this is that speakers who want to retain their standing within a group will continue to speak in the way the group values. At the same time, changing one's dialect carries the risk of being judged to be a group traitor. Just about every ethnic group has a derogatory term for members who seek to pass into the dominant group: African Americans use the label *oreo*, Chicanos use *coconut*, Native Americans use *apple*, and Asians use the term *banana*. The latter three terms imply that a person's ethnicity goes no deeper than the skin of the fruit. It accuses a person of changing his/her values and attitudes—made visible through dialect switching—to reflect the white dominant majority.

Another reason that low-prestige dialects persist is because a dialect is an emotionally charged aspect of identity. The dialect a person learns in her home is deeply tied to very basic feelings: of being yourself, of what counts as natural and unpretentious, of feeling warmth and a caring connection with others. Prestige accents, if they are not a person's home dialect, will never have this kind of emotional connection. These, then, are some of the counterforces that encourage people to continue using the dialect they learn in their home communities rather than changing to adopt the dialect valued by prestigious institutions. Although changing dialects is first and foremost an individual issue, it is also a societal issue.

Davies describes the dilemma that a society's leaders face as they craft the public stance to be taken toward dialect diversity:

> In that court, what determines the final decision is an educational philosophy about the kind of society we wish ours to be, with the recognition that for the advantage of pluralism in dialect and language maintenance, there is the price of fragmentation, nonintegration through one standard and lack of proficiency for many in that standard. On the other hand, for the advantage of efficiency, of proficiency in and integration through one standard, there are disadvantages of alienation, overall cultural loss and possible cognitive dissonance.[29]

A final reason that low-prestige dialects persist is that for some speakers they actually carry covert prestige. While prestige of the obvious, unmodified kind goes with the speaking of a standard dialect, nonstandard dialects may have **covert prestige,** a hidden or secondary kind of prestige. Although a nonstandard dialect may signal a lower level of education, it also signals a sense of toughness, strength, and, indirectly, masculinity. That is, by speaking with a nonstandard dialect, a man can portray himself as possessing qualities that are especially valued for men.

In a study of fraternity men that involved tape-recording the men's talk in several sites, Kiesling,[30] in fact, found that the fraternity members increased their use of nonstandard pronunciation when they were in all-male house meetings. Kisling attributed this change to each man's desire to be regarded as a strong, not easy-to-push-around, kind of person. Covert prestige, then, is the tougher image that a nonstandard dialect delivers. Further evidence that nonstandard dialects can furnish men covert prestige is to be found in a study by Trudgill.[31] People were asked to report their usage of nonstandard forms, then each person's self-report was contrasted with his or her actual use. Men were found to overreport their use of nonstandard forms (e.g., "goin" vs. "going"), whereas women underreported their use of nonstandard forms. This pattern ties to broad cultural expectations. In general, working-class people are perceived as tougher and stronger, whereas middle-class speakers are seen as more polite, refined, and correct. Similarly, males are generally perceived as tougher and stronger than females, whereas females are assumed to be more polite and correct. A consequence of the presumed relationship between dialect and these master identities is that middle-class men (and to a certain degree working-class women) will face contradictory injunctions: Should male middle-class speakers talk as is most appropriate for their class or for their gender?

A Rhetorical Perspective on Accent

The dominant perspective researchers have taken toward dialect and identity is a cultural one. Accents and dialects are treated as relatively stable features of talk presumed to be shaped by preexisting identities (e.g., social class, gender, ethnicity, nationality). If, however, we approach accent from a rhetorical perspective, we think about the linkage differently. When and why, we would ask, do speakers choose one accent over another?

One phenomenon that has been well documented is that speakers change their accent as well as their rate of speech and their pausing patterns depending on their conversational partner.[32] In seeking to sell a vacation to a client, a travel agent will shift his pronunciation toward that of the client. A politician may use a regional accent when speaking to her constituency at home, and switch to a more standard accent when addressing public officials at the state capitol. Giles[33] has tried to explain when (and why) in a single encounter people will change their speech. **Communication accommodation theory** (CAT)[34] posits that speakers will talk more like their partners (converge and accommodate) when "they want to be approved of and when they want their communication to be effective." At the same time they are likely to resist accommodating and even accentuate their differences (diverge) when "they want to symbolize and emphasize difference and distance."[35] By and large, similarity is attractive to people; a communicator likes others who talk like she does. Thus when a person wants another to like her, she will shift her accent toward her partner's accent. The shifting is usually unconscious, although it need not be. In situations where people are unequal, such as at a job interview (or the politician or the travel agent), the person with less power (or more to lose) will be the main one to change his or her speech.

Although one or both speakers converging is the most common occurrence, speakers also will talk so that their speech becomes more different from their partner's.[36] Divergence is especially likely in conflict situations between members of different social groups. In a study that had a Welsh person and a British person discuss (in English) whether the Welsh language should be cultivated or left to die out, the Welsh speaker used increasingly Welsh-accented English over the course of the dispute. Besides diverging to indicate dislike or subtle rejection of another, speakers may also diverge to license norm violations. For instance, if a German speaker were speaking English and could do so with no noticeable trace of a foreign accent, nonetheless he might choose to use a more marked foreign accent. When a speaker sounds like a native he is presumed to be a fully functional member of that society. A native speaker will be viewed more negatively for failing to behave in expected ways than a nonnative. Thus, if our English-fluent German was uncertain about whether he knows all the right ways to behave in an American business meeting, he might shift his accent to be more different from the partner's to mark his nonnative status.

SUMMARY

Talk sounds differently when it is spoken by a man, a woman, or a child; a European, a Hispanic, or a Hmong American; a New Yorker, a westerner, or a southerner; a New Zealander or a Scottish speaker. But not only does talk reflect a speaker's geographic, social class, and gender origins, it is also used strategically to display affiliation or hostility. In addition, it may be used as a strategy to claim a particular interactional identity. Consider but one interesting example. Lawyers and judges pronounce the word "defendant" as if they were defending an ant (defend-ant) rather than the more everyday way (defend-ent). Tiersma explains this unusual practice:

> This aberrant pronunciation may well have originated with pedantic law professors who grew weary of students misspelling *defendant* as *defendent,* which is a logical enough way to write it. Perhaps the professors began to articulate the word with added (but unnatural) emphasis on the *a* in the fi-

nal syllable, stressing the final syllable and coloring it to rhyme with *ant*. Students ever eager to begin "talking like a lawyer," quickly mimicked their instructors. Whatever its origin this unusual articulation is now considered a badge of membership in the legal fraternity.[37]

For personal identities related to feelings and attitudes, it is prosodic changes that are most important. Voice gets used to do all kinds of subtle identity-work. It is a big part of what makes talking with people so involving and fun. For sensitive issues, hearing a person's voice seems absolutely necessary. We get much more information about what a friend must mean when we hear her saying the words. And we can count on our own tone of voice to convey things that we may find difficult to put into words. At the same time, and all too often, the sound of talk becomes a site for conflict. Sometimes it is because two people, coming from different communities, attach nonsimilar interactional meanings to a vocal move, and do not realize that this has occurred. Other times— and this is commonplace among intimates—one person accurately interprets the other's intended meaning, whatever he might be saying explicitly, but the meaning is hostile, angry, and blaming. Working through negative feeling that one person has toward another is invariably difficult. For all kinds of reasons, people may not be willing to admit that what the partner inferred (and states) is true. Or it may be only partly accurate. In addition, the vocabulary available to refer to aspects of voice and how vocal features connect to feeling-linked identities is limited, thereby making it a particularly challenging topic. Finally, talking explicitly about feelings (their expression and why they are being felt) may itself be an identity-threatening act. But that is another story.

6

⬖ Language Selection

A mother calls to her children. She repeats the same phrase three times in two languages: "Ven acá. Ven acá. Come here, you."[1] Why did the mother switch from Spanish to English? Would it have made a difference if she had begun with English and ended with Spanish? In this chapter I consider how the language(s) communicators use links to their identities. If a speaker has more than one language at her command, what identity does she construct by choosing one over the other? By mixing them together? This chapter specifically focuses on two issues: (1) the identity implications of language choice and language switching, and (2) the controversy in the United States about English and whether it should be declared the country's official language.

IDENTITY IMPLICATIONS OF LANGUAGE CHOICE AND CODE SWITCHING

Consider the case of Wilson, a teen who had emigrated from the Dominican Republic (a Spanish-speaking country) to the United States when he was small boy. Upon arrival in the United States, Wilson spoke only Spanish. By going to school and playing with English-speaking peers, he gradually became fluent in English. Similar to many immigrant children, Wilson frequently served as a translator for older Spanish-speaking family members when they needed to deal with stores and agencies. As is true for many Dominicans, Wilson is racially black—he has brown skin and the kind of hair and facial features found among persons categorized as African American.

In the United States race tends to be treated as the first and central category to identify a person. For many Dominican Americans their first identification is with their ethnic-language community (Hispanic) rather than with others who share their skin color. This leads to an issue for Dominican Americans in the United States since African American (black) and Hispanic are taken to be either–or categories. Dominican Americans frequently get asked "What are you?" Look at Example 6.1 to see what Wilson said about himself.

EXAMPLE 6.1

A lot of people confuse me for an African American most of the time. They ask me, "Are you Black?" I'm like, "No I'm Hispanic." And they'll be like, "Oh I thought you were Black or something." Most of the time I'll be talking with them, chilling or whatever. They'll be thinking that I'm just African American. Because sometimes the way I talk, my hair, my skin color. It's just that my hair is nappy. I use lots of slang.[2]

Wilson explicitly claims "Hispanic" as his central category, setting it in contrast to "African American." But his use of languages and the dialects within them reveals a more multifaceted sense of self. In speaking, Wilson routinely mixes African American Vernacular English, American English, and Dominican Spanish. Depending on the situation and his conversational partner, Wilson will use one or another language/dialect to highlight a different facet of who he is. Through speaking Spanish and several varieties of English, Wilson resists others' attempts to put him in a single category. As Bailey notes, "language gives Wilson the freedom to highlight diverse facets of his identity."[3] Switching from English to another language (**code switching**), then, is a way for a person to make visible master identities, such as nationality or ethnicity, that may not be inferable from a person's appearance.

Not only does code switching occur as people move from one situation to another, it also occurs within the same situation and, as my opening example showed, even within the same utterance. With regard to the opening example, Spanish–English bilinguals interpreted the meaning of the mother's call to her kids as a mild threat, a way to inform her children that her words were meant seriously. The reverse ordering ("Come here. Come here. Ven acá"), in contrast, was understood as a personal appeal, something along the line of "Won't you please come."[4] In other words, by switching from Spanish to English, the mother signaled a serious relational identity. For most Spanish-speaking Americans, English is the language associated with work, school, and public matters, whereas

Spanish is the language of home, informality, and relaxation. Because of these associations, a bilingual speaker's switching of codes can create a very particular relational meaning. This general kind of association applies to other languages as well.

Consider a conversation in a Hungarian American home. Kristóf (K), an 8½-year-old boy, is talking with his mother (M) about his day at school. As a way to maintain their ethnic heritage, the family typically speaks Hungarian at meal times, and Kristóf usually honors this practice. At one point in the conversation of interest, however, he switches into English to assert that he will make his own salad.

EXAMPLE 6.2. Making a Salad at the Dinner Table[5]

1	M:	Kristóf mi volt az iskolában? Iratok tesztet?
		(Kristóf, how was school? Did you write any tests?)
2	K:	Tessék?
		(Pardon?)
3	M:	Volt teszt? Milyen voltz az AGP?
		(Were there any tests? How was AGP?)
4	K:	Most nem voltam. Nem volt még.
		(I wasn't [in AGP] today. It hasn't started yet.)
5	M:	Kedden van?
		(Is it on Tuesday?)
6	K:	Thursday-n van.
		(It's on Thursday.)
7	M:	Kertek salátát, úgy-e?
		(Would you like some salad, wouldn't you?)
8	K: →	I'll make my own salad.
9	M:	Mi?
		(What?)
10	K: →	I'll make my own salad. (pause)
11	K:	Ilen kicsi tányérokban csinalják a restaurant-okban.
		(They make it in such small plates in the restaurants.)
12	K: →	I need some salad please.

What kind of identity-work is accomplished by Kristóf's speaking mostly Hungarian but switching to English to assert that he will make his own salad? Given the family preference for speaking Hungarian at meals, Kristóf's switch to English can be seen as a small moment of resistance: he is challenging the personal identity of obedient child and the relational identity of being a subordinate party. Refusing to use the preferred language, as Myers-Scotton and Bolonyai state, is "one way Kristóf can fight a battle over power. As he switches to English, he can display that he is about to pull out of a situation that renders him a passive, subordinate recipient of his mother's actions (i.e., being served the salad)."[6] Switching to English allows him to shape interactional meanings toward his own end, showing himself to be "a maturing boy who interacts with peers outside the home."[7] Code switching, then, enables speakers to present themselves in particular desired ways and to resist others altercasting them in negative or unwanted ways. What identities will be made salient depends on what domain and activity each language is associated with.

Language and Immigrant Identity

People immigrating to the United States and other English-speaking countries from non-English-speaking ones usually know only a small amount of English when they first arrive. Many immigrant adults become only partially competent in their new language. Immigrants who arrive as children and teens generally do better, eventually becoming fully competent. However, the process of mastering a second language takes time. Child and teen immigrants spend years in school, struggling with the consequences of not being fully competent in English when such competency is presumed as the mark of a "normal" school child.

Miller[8] studied identity issues for teens immigrating to Australia from non-English-speaking countries, some from European (e.g., Bosnia) and others from Asian ones (Taiwan, China, and Vietnam). The issues confronting the teens as they sought to sound like an Aussie differed based on whether they looked like their Australian peers or were visibly different (blond vs. black-haired). European students generally made the transition from outsider, non-English-speaker to insider, fellow Aussie faster than Asian students. In contrast to a relatively quick mixing of the European immigrants with native Australians, teens from Asian backgrounds tended to group with each other at lunch and on other social occasions and to speak Chinese. In general, Asian students mastered English less quickly.

Sorting out the meaning of the Asian students' segregation and their more limited English language ability, Miller argued, is quite difficult. On the one hand, the students could be viewed as deliberately choosing not to mix with their Anglo-Australian peers, and likewise deliberately choosing not to use English. "This view sits well with the stereotype of Asian students as withdrawn, quiet, and resistant to integration." Such a view of these students sees the problems they face as of their own making, thereby "obviating the need for the institutions to do anything 'extra' for the students."[9] Others would see the situation differently, arguing that schools (and other institutions) value languages and features of communicative expression differently. European-linked languages, and the expressive patterns common to them, quite probably were favored over Asian ones. The Asian students in Miller's study, in fact, experienced their Anglo-Australian peers as not liking them and as actively distancing themselves from them. This second perspective highlights how the Asian master identity, visibly made manifest through the students' appearance, may have led Anglo-Australian students to treat the Asian students as less likely candidates for friends.

Although most Asians were slower learners of English than their European counterparts, not every Asian student was. For instance, one of the girls (Nora) in Miller's study had started working in a family noodle shop soon after her arrival. She quickly became proficient in the English needed to deal with customer orders and problems that arose with disgruntled patrons. Her proficiency with English in this one context led to her feeling comfortable with going shopping. This, in turn, led to her entering additional situations that required her to be able to speak English. Each of these small changes in how she spent her time, and who she spoke with, facilitated her coming to think of herself differently, a self-redefinition in which English language competency became increasingly important to her sense of who she was.

Given increasing globalization, it would seem wise for societies to have citizens who speak a diversity of languages. Speaking Chinese, Vietnamese, Spanish, Hungarian, or whatever should make a child feel special and worthwhile, in possession of a valued skill, rather than make that child feel like a failure or a problem. How schools would accomplish this attitudinal transformation is by no means straightforward: such change would require rethinking the ordinary communicative practices that occur in classrooms that contribute to how children come to see themselves as competent and likable (or the reverse).

Attitudes toward speakers of other languages, however, are not merely a matter for schools. They are stances that are shaped by what is going on in the larger society. Consider what is happening with the social movement to declare English the official language of the United States.

SPEAKING ENGLISH AND AMERICAN IDENTITY

What does it mean to be an American? In what sense is it or should it be linked to speaking English? Should there be laws that declare English as the language of the land? This issue is one that Americans see differently. Consider what four prominent individuals have had to say.

EXAMPLE 6.3.   S. I. Hayakawa, Retired Republican Senator
from California

What is it that has made a society out of the hodge-podge of nationalities and races represented in the immigrant hordes that people our nation? It is language, of course, that has made communication among all these elements possible. It is with common language that we have dissolved distrust and fear. It is with language that we have drawn up the understandings and agreements and social contracts that make a society possible.[10]

EXAMPLE 6.4.   Joseph Leobowicz, Connecticut Lawyer, Author of
an Article in the *Yale Law and Policy Review*

The goal of a unified citizenry committed to democratic ideals is an admirable one, and universal acquisition of the English language by all residents of the United States would no doubt further that goal. But the means by which we promote English should not in themselves run counter to our democratic tradition. Imposing English upon Spanish speakers though a constitutional amendment would likely exclude many from political participation, sacrifice equal justice in the courtroom, narrowly restrict educational alternatives on the basis of political criteria, and mark linguistic minorities as "un-American" in the eyes of the rest of society. Based on undocumented fears of separatism and cultural fragmentation, passage of the E.L.A. [English Language Amendment] would insult and alienate a significant portion of our society in the name of national unity.[11]

EXAMPLE 6.5.   Walter Huddleston, Ex-Senator (Democrat, Kentucky),
Congressional Sponsor of the ELA

National unity does not require that every person think and act like everyone else. However it does require that there be some common threads that run through our society and hold us together. One of these threads is our common belief and support of a democratic form of government, and the right of every person to fully participate in it. Unfortunately, this right to full participation means very little if each individual does not possess the means of exercising it. This participation requires the ability to obtain information and communicate our beliefs and concerns to others. Undoubtedly this process is hindered without the existence of a commonly accepted and used language. In essence what a policy of bilingualism–biculturalism does is to segregate minorities from the mainstream of our politics, economy and society because we are not making it possible for them to freely enter into the mainstream.[12]

EXAMPLE 6.6.   Baltasar Corrada, Ex-Resident Commissioner of Puerto Rico, Nonvoting Delegate to House of Representatives

No one is arguing against the need for all Americans to attain proficiency in English in order to participate in all levels of our society. No one is suggesting that any other language should replace English as the vehicle for interaction in our society. This is the way it is: this is the way it should be. But we do not need the Constitution to mandate this, just as we do not need the Constitution to mandate that we love our mother and our father, or that we have to be patriotic. This is part of the responsibility of citizenship that does not have to be imposed upon us. America is great not because we speak one language or the other but because we are united by the fundamental principles that bind our people together: freedom, justice, equal opportunity for all, fairness, democracy. To say that we make our country stronger because we make it "U.S. English" is like saying we would make it stronger by making it "U.S. white." It is as insidious to base the strength or unity of the United States in one language as it is to base that strength or unity in one race.[13]

The Official English Movement

The **Official English movement** emerged in the United States in the early 1980s. Similar movements have been occurring in Canada, Australia, and New Zealand, although they have been much less successful.[14] Crawford, a scholar who extensively studied the controversy, describes the emergence of the movement as bizarre given that the 1980 census had revealed that all but 2% of speakers over 4 years of age spoke English and only 11% were regular speakers of another language.[15] The movement began in the United States when then-Senator Hayakawaya introduced into Congress a constitutional amendment to declare English the official language of the United States. The proposal failed, but several years later Hayakawa started a lobbying group called U.S. English. The purpose of the group was to lobby states to pass laws declaring English that state's official language. The lobbying group was enormously successful. Five years after its start, the group had over 400,000 members and an organizational budget of six million dollars. By 1990, 17 states had passed Official English statues or approved constitutional amendments; by 2002, the number of states was up to 26.[16] The content of different states' laws varies considerably from single-sentence declarations to complex documents that spell out the contexts in which English is required to be used, and what circumstances would be allowable as exceptions.[17]

Although the movement framed itself as being pro-English, from its start it was very much anti-bilingual.[18] Recruitment of members to the lobbying group (U.S. English) was particularly likely in those geographic areas (e.g., Florida and California) that were feeling the impact of heavy Asian and Hispanic immigration. Scholarly commentators attribute the success of the movement to two main causes. A first cause of the movement's success was the quiet passage in the 1960s and 1970s of legislation that was sympathetic to linguistic minorities.[19] Key pieces of legislation included the Bilingual Education Act of 1968 that made federal funding available for the first time to schools that developed educational programs geared to helping children learn English or to maintain languages other than English. Another especially important event was the class action suit brought in the name of a Chinese student (Lau) in San Francisco in which it was argued that a fair and equal educational opportunity required more than putting a non-English-speaking child into an regular classroom. The Lau case, as it came it be called, made its way to the Supreme Court, where in 1974 the Court ruled that students with limited English proficiency were legally entitled to special help in their schools. A final piece of legislation seen as important was the Voting Rights Act of 1975 that required any voting area in which 5% or more of the citizens spoke a language other than English to have access to ballots in their own language.

Besides these pieces of legislation that gave attention to immigrant speakers' needs, there was a second factor. Contributing to the success of the Official English movement was the sharp increase in immigration in the 1980s, a number exceeded only in the first decade of the 1900s. As a result, some Americans experienced fear that non-English-speakers were taking over the country and beginning to marginalize those Americans who spoke English.

Critics' Views: The English Only Movement

In response to the growing success of the Official English movement, several influential institutions began to speak out. Major newspapers, including the *New York Times*, the *Washington Post, USA Today,* the *Los Angles Times,* and the *Christian Science Monitor* took editorial positions against Official English policies. These newspapers argued that passing laws to recognize English as the official American language was unnecessary. In addition, professional organizations, such as the International Communication Association, the Organization of Teachers of English as a Second Language, and the American Psychological Association, argued that English-only initiatives had had primarily negative impacts. For instance, the American Psychology Association argued that English-only initiatives lessened self-esteem and lowered the academic achievement of linguistic minorities, as well as contributed to creating poorer relationships among ethnic and racial groups in the United States.[20] In labeling the movement "English Only," critics highlighted what they saw as its main effect: promoting an intolerant stance toward racial and ethnic minorities in the guise of patriotism about English. In addition to fostering intolerance, an irony of the English Only movement was that it was occurring "in the face of growing demands for multilingual abilities in the workplace."[21]

How should American identity be linked to speaking English? Does American society need to strengthen the connection? Does the United States need to create a society in which speaking languages other than English becomes sufficiently stigmatized that most Americans will avoid doing so? Or is a weaker link reasonable and desirable? One that regards English as the most usual language spoken by Americans, but not one that is a requirement? As my readers can probably infer from the way I have posed this question, my own position is to favor a weaker link: English speaking, and especially the speaking of certain dialects of English, is a strong cue that a person is a native-born American. However, to make language proficiency a requirement is neither needed nor desirable. English does not need legislation to prop it up, nor is it fair or wise to devalue Americans who speak other languages.

Interestingly, not only is language use linked to identity, but so too is a person's attitude about the issue. Whether a person is for or against Official English laws (as is the case with other politically contested issues) will be taken as an indicator of his likely political tilt. That is, the political identities of liberal and conservative, to identify the most commonly used ones, are attributed to speakers when they express pro- or anti- views toward a single issue. Based on expression of one attitude, a speaker will be assumed to hold a larger set of opinions. This, of course, is highly problematic, but it is a rather common way to make sense of who another person is. For instance, speakers who express negative assessments of Official English would be expected to espouse views that are anti-death penalty, pro-choice, pro-government social services, and so on. Those speakers favoring Official English will be assumed to also favor the death penalty, support minimum government support for services such as health care and welfare, and be pro-life. This knowledge of what attitudes will be taken as clustering together is made visible when people do the rather common action of prefacing an opinion with a disclaimer. In saying "I'm not a bleeding heart, but I don't think we need these Official English laws" or "I don't usually argue the conservative line, but I think we need Official English laws," a communicator makes visible what she is assuming to be the usual attitude package. At the same time these disclaimers instruct the conversational partner not to assume that the speaker holds the other attitudes regarded as going with the focal one.

SUMMARY

In this chapter I have considered an issue that is not a choice for everyone. For some Americans, there is no choice about what language to speak: English (or Spanish or French or Korean) is the only possibility. For other Americans, and for many other nationalities, there is a choice. Speakers can switch back and forth between two or more languages as the occasion, the activity, and the relationship requires. In this chapter I explored some of the reasons why speakers code switch. In addition, I considered what is at stake in proposals to declare English the official language of the United States.

PART III

Complex Discourse Practices

7

◈ Interaction Structures

In the vice presidential debate that occurred as part of the 1992 U.S. presidential election a new interaction format was tried. In response to citizen complaints that political debates were nothing more than displays of canned positions that did not require candidates to think on their feet and deal with the other candidates, the vice presidential debate was redesigned to involve back-and-forth exchanges. Rather than consisting of a panel of reporters who posed a question to a candidate, who then gave a timed answer, the debate format would have a single moderator who posed questions, with multiple opportunities for free-flowing discussion among the candidates. This new format posed significant challenges to the candidates. As communication researcher Beck noted, the candidates now were responsible for "obtaining and maintaining control of the floor during the open discussion while simultaneously appearing to be 'assertive' but not 'rude' or 'indifferent' as behooves a vice presidential contender."[1]

In this context the stakes were high: citizen judgments about each man's interactional and personal identities ("Is this man going to be a good vice president?"; "Is he assertive or is he rude?") mattered, both for the candidates and for the voting public. Although vice presidential debates are events few individuals face, controlling the **conversational floor**—the place and space for talk—in an appropriate manner is a task everybody must manage. In ordinary conversations with friends, as well as in the routine exchanges at work and during public meetings, the way a person handles the structures of interaction affects whether she is seen to be *shy and insecure, overbearing, rude, self-absorbed,* or *poised and competent* (i.e., appropriately assertive and appropriately other-responsive).

What are the structures of interaction? How do they operate? How do they connect with the identities communicators both desire and wish to avoid? I begin this chapter by describing adjacency pairs, a main format in which talk is sequenced. Then I provide an overview of the turn-taking system in which I make visible how people's use of the turn system contributes to positive and negative identity assessments. In the next section I take a close look at talk in two institutional settings and examine the remedial interchange, a much-used sequence to manage relational trouble. I conclude this chapter by identifying several important ways that speech communities do interaction structuring differently.

ADJACENCY PAIRS

Talk involves more than people performing random acts. We, as talkers, have strong expectation that certain kinds of speech acts will be followed by selected others. A greeting (e.g., "Hi," "How ya doing?"), for instance, will usually be followed by a second greeting. That pairs of acts are usually found together is part of the meaning of **adjacency pair**, a concept developed by Schegloff and Sacks[2] to explain the orderliness of conversation. There are many kinds of adjacency pairs. Some pairs involve similar acts, as is the case with greetings or goodbyes, while others involve different acts. Examples of pairs that involve different actions include invitations or offers, followed by acceptances (or refusals), and questions followed by answers. Example 7.1 offers an instance of a common adjacency pair that might occur between coworkers.

EXAMPLE 7.1

TARYN: How bout some lunch?	Invitation
JAY: Sounds good. ((stands up))	Acceptance

In Example 7.1, then, the invitation is the first part of a pair, or first pair part, and the acceptance is the second pair part. Equally possible as a second pair part to an invitation is a refusal, shown in Example 7.2.

EXAMPLE 7.2

TARYN: How bout some lunch?	Invitation
JAY: (pause) Uhh, better not. I've got to get this done by 2:00. Thanks though. How's tomorrow?	Refusal

Adjacency pairs may be expanded in two ways. If a speaker were going to request borrowing a piece of equipment, for instance, a logical prerequisite would be that the requestee actually has the equipment. For a lunch invitation, it is most reasonable to make one if the person being invited has not already eaten. For this reason, communicators often do a **presequence**, an adjacency pair (usually in question–answer format) whose purpose is to determine if the conditions are reasonable for the focal first pair part. Example 7.3 illustrates such a presequence.

EXAMPLE 7.3

TARYN: You eaten yet?	Question
JAY: No.	Answer
TARYN: How bout some lunch?	Invitation

Because presequences are recognizable structures that point to a next act pair, communicators can, if they wish, jump the gun and respond to what they assume is coming next. In response to Taryn saying, "You eaten yet?," Jay may shake his head no, stand up, and say, "Where do you want to go?" Or he might respond, "Sorry, I have to finish this report by 2:00."

A second way adjacency pairs may be expanded is through **insertion sequences**. Similar to presequences, insertion sequences involve an inserted adjacency pair to determine if some condition applies that would make the conversationally preferred option possible. Consider Example 7.4 to see how this applied to our invitation example.

EXAMPLE 7.4

TARYN: How bout some lunch?	Invitation
JAY: You got $5 to lend me?	Request
TARYN: Yeah.	Grant
JAY: Sounds good.	Acceptance

The notion of adjacency pairs in not merely describing the most usual sequences. It is possible for questions not to be followed by answers, greetings by greetings, and so on. However, if an expected second pair part is not forthcoming, it will be **noticeably absent**—and communicators will give social meaning to its absence. The absence of a second greeting or goodbye, for instance, is often taken to mean that the greeted party is feeling irritated or mad unless the greeter decides that the absence is a sign of the greeted party's preoccupation. In other words, one conversational practice used to enact the identity *I'm a person who's mad at you right now!* is to refrain from doing a speech act where it would be expected.

Conversational Preference

A related concept that has the potential to generate powerful inferences is known as **conversational preference**.[3] Conversational preference refers to the structurally preferred second act for adjacency pairs that may take one of two forms. For instance, statements prefer agreement,[4] and following an offer, an invitation, or a request, accepts are conversationally preferred to refusals. To describe an act as "conversationally preferred" is to say that it can be done straightforwardly and simply; in contrast, a nonpreferred act is always longer, more conversationally marked, and elaborated. Consider, for example, the difference between Jay's acceptance of Taryn's invitation to lunch (Example 7.1) and his refusal (Example 7.2). Of note is that Jay did not refuse by simply saying "No" or "No thanks," but instead paused briefly, started his response with an extended "Uhhh" to suggest that he was thinking about the offer, and explained why he was saying no rather than yes.

Jay's response illustrates the conversational clothing of dispreferred acts. They (1) are not immediately adjacent but begin after a pause; (2) they start with "well," "uhm," or other markers; (3) they include an expression of appreciation, apology, or token agreement ("thanks," "yes but"), and (4) they include accounts (explanations for the dispreferred act). To say that acceptance acts are conversationally preferred to refusals is by no means to imply that speakers desire or want to accept. This may be completely untrue. But it is to say that speakers routinely do not, nor are they expected to, do a dispreferred act in the same simple way as a conversationally preferred one can be done. That everyday communicators are aware of the meaning of this conversational structuring principle is cued by the frequency with which pauses before responding to an invitation are often followed immediately by different invitations or requests, as Example 7.5 demonstrates.

EXAMPLE 7.5

| TARYN: How bout some lunch? | Invitation |

JAY: (2.0) Uh[h	Hearable dispreferred second pair part beginning
TARYN: [That's fine. Let's make it later this week?	Reformulated different invitation

One implication of this conversational structuring practice is that one cannot *just say no*. Kitzinger and Frith draw upon this fact of conversation to critique the burgeoning programs designed to teach women how to avoid date rape. Most of the programs, they note, "are deeply problematic in that they ignore and override culturally normative ways of indicating refusal."[5] A direct "No," whether it be to a request for sexual intimacy, an offer of a cigarette, or an invitation to lunch, is quite rare. Just saying no, as most people recognize, says more than "No"; it is frequently perceived as rude and hostile, personal identities most people seek to avoid. Pausing and saying some mildly positive remark before delivering an actual refusal is how refusing is routinely done.

The problem with date rape is not that men misunderstand women's softened refusals; as Kitzinger and Frith argue, men are not cultural dopes. The problem is that men do not want to hear refusals. As evidence they note the following: under a poster with the caption "No means no" in a men's area of a Canadian university, men had scrawled hostile comments like, "No means kick her in the teeth," "No means on your knees bitch," and "No means more beer." One would not need to completely agree with Kitzinger and Frith's feminist analysis of date rape to agree that programs to combat rape between acquaintances, whatever the programs involve, need to consider how conversational acts such as refusal and assent are ordinarily done.

TURN TAKING

In everyday situations outside of school, work, or public settings, there are rarely formal rules about who can talk, when, and about what. Rather, who gets a turn in a conversation, and how frequently, is something that gets negotiated within the local moment. This local negotiation leads to what Sacks[6] identifies as two "grossly apparent facts" about conversation. The facts are that in a small group (three to five people) usually (1) only one person speaks at a time and (2) speaker changes recur. Moreover, how long any person will speak is not predictable; turns may be very short (e.g., single words—"Yes"—or short phrases—"You betcha" or "Around 7:00 tomorrow") or could be quite lengthy (multiple sentences). Put together, these facts create a puzzle.

How is it that conversationalists are generally able to accomplish smooth exchanges in which overlapping speech is infrequent and brief?

Transition Relevance Places

Sacks, Schegloff, and Jefferson[7] argued that the orderliness of conversations could be accounted for by a simple set of sequential procedures. From their participation in speech communities, people develop expectations about places where it is appropriate for speaker change to occur and others where it is not. **Transition relevance places,** or TRPs, are those conversational places where speaker turns could occur. Such places are cued by the use of grammatical forms (ends of questions and statements), the drawing out of a syllable on a final word (so:), rising or falling intonation, hand gestures coming to rest at the body, or engaging someone's gaze.[8] At a TRP, Sacks suggests,

(1) The current speaker may select the next speaker. Speakers may nominate who is to be the next speaker by name (*"I'm not going, how bout you Rich?"*) or cue who the selected other is through gaze or body orientation, or through the mention of a topic that might only be appropriate to one party.

(2) If the current speaker does not select a next speaker, then any of the present persons may self-select and start talking.

(3) If no one self-selects, then the current speaker may continue speaking.[9]

In lively multiperson conversations, people often do considerable work to show that they want to talk next. Cues that a person does want to claim a turn include such actions as leaning forward, opening one's mouth, starting a hand gesture, and looking toward the current speaker. At the same time a speaker may attempt to hold on to the opportunity to talk and keep control of the floor by speeding up speech and rushing through potential TRPs, avoiding the other's gaze, or doing hand gestures that metaphorically push another away.

As mentioned, although most instances of overlapping speech involve no more than a couple of syllables and usually occur at a TRP, there are exceptions. Overlaps may occur in the middle of a turn when one person is interjecting small tokens of attention and listening ("Uhm mm"; "I see") or when a recipient acts to help a speaker who is trying to remember the name of a person or place. Another kind of overlapping speech that may be more than several syllables is what Schegloff[10] calls **choral talk**: segments where several people murmur congratulations, say goodbye, or laugh at the same time. In both of these cases, the overlapping talk is understood as having a cooperative or supportive purpose and is not interactionally troublesome.

The last type of overlapping talk is, perhaps, the most interesting for identity issues. Repeated stretches of simultaneous talking occasionally do occur that are not seen as serving cooperative purposes. At these junctures two people seem to be competing for the floor. Typically the talk of at least one party gets louder, it moves higher in pitch, and its pace becomes either faster or slower. In addition, a person's talk may be suddenly cut off, a sound may be prolonged, or a person may recycle and repeat part of what she is saying.[11] Eventually these segments of overlapping talk conclude with one person dropping out. Sometimes explicit accusations are made that the other *interrupted, always interrupts,* or *is rude,* or that the other *never listens* or *is selfish.* Other times, nothing explicit is said in the moment but one or another party walks away and talks to others about the other's rude, overbearing, or self-preoccupied personality. We all know that people "will get angry at, or feel contrite or guilty about doing such a thing as intruding on X's time, speaking while he is speaking, interrupting him."[12] In other words, built into conversational practice is an emotional motor that helps to keep most people in line most of the time. From how one manages turns, consequential personal judgments will be developed.

Interruption is not the only feature of the turn-taking system that is implicative for identity. The sheer number of turns one takes and the talk content of the turns also shapes identity. By and large, people who take more turns and who take longer ones will be judged as being more expert, influential, or assertive and, in institutional situations, will be assumed to be higher in status than less frequently speaking parties (senior doctor vs. intern or boss vs. secretary).[13] In addition, introducing a new topic for talk is usually regarded as a more assertive act than responding to an ongoing topic; this is especially the case if the new topic is focused on self's interests rather than the other's interests.

Although generalizations abound as to what kinds of moves generally go with what kinds of identities, the picture is quite complex and dependent on how the particular persons and practices come together in a specific situation. For instance, while talk is typically seen as the way a person establishes himself as powerful, under certain conditions silence may be the more powerful tool.[14] Once we move outside of ordinary conversation, though, the rules change.

TURN TAKING IN INSTITUTIONAL ENCOUNTERS

Turn taking in ordinary conversation is locally managed—there are no prespecified rules. In institutional settings, although local management does occur for some activities—for example, a few people chatting about a project—many occasions have formal turn-taking rules that restrict who may speak, when, and on what topic. At one extreme are situations in which the turn system is entirely preallocated. A good example would be the courtroom, where the rights to talk are highly restricted. Not only are parties restricted to speaking in particular slots, their turns are format- and content-restricted. Attorneys, for instance, may not make statements to witnesses but must pose questions, and witnesses must limit what they say to answers to the questions they are asked.

Many institutional encounters have turn-taking systems that are a hybrid between the two extremes of locally managed and preallocated. In business meetings, for instance, there is often an agenda that orders topics of talk and the person who is the meeting chair gets to decide when to close down one topic and start the next topic, as well as decide whether a member's comment is on- or off-topic. However, within the confines of a meeting, discussion may resemble that of ordinary conversation where people do a lot of self-nominating and subtopic introduction. Let's now consider how turn taking links to identities in two important institutional sites.

Turn Taking in Job Interviews

There is no adjacency pair quite so common in institutional settings as that of question–answer pairs. Through long strings of question–answer sequences, participants in a setting enact themselves as one or another party of a discernible pair of interactional identities (e.g., doctor–patient, counselor–client, reporter–interviewee, personnel manager–job candidate). Consider Example 7.6.

EXAMPLE 7.6

1 A: What was your major in college?
2 B: Business administration.
3 A: And did that prepare you for a managerial position?
4a B: Yes, I think my management courses were excellent.[15]

If asked what was going on in Example 7.6, most readers would make an immediate assignment of meaning: it's a job interview. Moreover, it is unlikely that people would have difficulty figuring out who's who. Speaker A appears to be the interviewer and speaker B the interviewee. The self-evidence of these identity attributions flows from the way three particular communicative practices combine in their occurrence. First, A and B perform different speech acts in a recognizable adjacency pair; A asks B for information and B answers A's questions. If in line 2 B had said, "Business administration, and what's yours?," our guess about A's and B's identities would be much less certain. The lack of symmetry in the adjacency pairs that each person initiates cue us that A and B are likely to be in institutional roles where each has different rights and obligations with regard to question asking and question answering. That one person gets to ask most of the questions and the other does most of the answering is a feature of many pairs of institutional identities.

To be sure, our judgment that Example 7.6 comes from a job interview rests on more than this adjacency pair structure. The topical focus and the evaluative stance displayed by B toward the topic of discussion provide further clues. That B is being asked whether her educational training links to preparation for a certain kind of work is just the kind of topical focus to be expected in a job interview, and it is also a subject of talk that is less likely in other situations and relationships. This does not mean that this topic is unimaginable elsewhere: friends and acquaintances in informal conversation do talk about majors and job preparation. If, instead of how B actually responded to being asked as to how her major prepared her, she had responded with the answer in Example 7.7, consider what we would infer.

EXAMPLE 7.7

4b In certain ways it did; in other ways it didn't. I had other things that were more important to me than school at that time. I think if I were doing it now, I would be getting more out of my college classes.

If the content of B's answer were 4b rather than 4a, we would guess that she was talking to a friend rather than to a job interviewer. In 4a it is the sense that the speaker appears to be putting her best foot forward and seeking to show her suitability for the position that further cues us that this is a job interview. In contrast, 4b implicates a more personally reflective and complex evaluation of an experience, a kind of evaluation that might occur between people who have some level of intimacy and trust where one is not performing for the other. Stated a bit differently, the response in 4a suggests that B is operating in a **persuasive frame** rather than simply in an information-giving one. She is responding to each interview question as if its purpose were narrower than the utterance content would suggest. Such a frame, in fact, is the one that job interviewers expect. At recruiting centers on college campuses, the adoption of a persuasive frame was a key practice that distinguished interviewees who received second interviews at the company from those who did not. Interviewees who did not learn about the company in advance and did not do conversational work to display their high level of interest in working for that particular company were much less likely to receive a second interview.[16]

Recently Scheuer[17] taped and studied 12 job interviews where five of the applicants received offers and seven did not. The available jobs were highly desirable professional positions in medium-size corporations. The positions required at least a college degree. The interview was not conducted by a single interviewer but by a three-person committee; two of the interviewers held positions that would make them roughly peers to the position being hired for and one of the interviewers was quite a bit more senior. The 12 people selected for interviews were already among an elite group; they had been chosen from more than 100 applicants. In her study Scheuer wanted to find out if there were conversational differences between successful and unsuccessful candidates in the interviews.

Interesting differences were found between the two groups in how turns were managed. Although in both groups the interviewers talked more than the interviewees, for successful candidates, the amount of talk, as measured by number of words, was closer to equal (46% vs. 34%). This difference was accounted for (1) by successful interviewees giving longer answers to questions, and (2) by turning patches of the interview into conversational episodes in which they took on the role of a storyteller and the interviewers assumed the role of listeners. In the unsuccessful interviews, there were many more question–short answer sequences and fewer conversational kinds of exchanges. What might be the significance of these conversational storytelling moments?

Scheuer suggests that these moments were interpreted by the interviewers as evidence that a candidate had good potential to assume peer relationships with others in the organization and fit in. These conversational moments were treated as "talk evidence" that a person was capable of being someone with whom others would feel comfortable. This fitting-in potential was made visible both through the interviewee's ability to create a relatively equal relational identity in the interview moment, as seen in the close-to-equal amounts of talk, and through enactment of the professionally preferred attitude about work, an important personal identity in job interviews.

Employees in a particular workplace are likely to have similar attitudes about the meaning of work and how it connects to life. Work can be treated "as means" or "as ends."[18] In **the work-as-means** philosophy, work is treated as the means to make money in order to live. Development of self is not done through work but primarily outside of the job.

This view is the dominant one held by people in working-class occupations. Work and personal life are seen as highly distinct categories. A contrasting view, **work-as-ends**, sees work as the primary place for articulating the self. This view, the common one held by people with professional occupations, sees work and the everyday lifeworld as deeply connected. One's work is a crucial part of one's identity. Who a person is is strongly connected to what that person does. Decisions about work and personal life issues are interconnected.

The conversational moments in the successful job interviews often involved the candidate linking some activity in his or her personal life to his or her work interest, as happened, for instance, when an interviewee offered an account of why he went to a business school quite a distance from family and friends. Scheuer found that although the education level and on-paper credentials of unsuccessful and successful candidates were similar, more of the unsuccessful candidates came from working-class families. It is within family communities that teens first observe what are usual and normal ways for adults to talk about (or refrain from discussing) work with friends. These conversational practices are not taught in university but are carried to it, strongly shaped by each person's communities of origin. Successful candidates, then, were more likely to come from middle-class professional families where they had had extensive opportunity to observe and participate in these kinds of conversations. It is mastery of these subtle, not-spoken-about, and class-linked practices that are part of what leads to interview judgments that one person will fit in and make a good colleague and another person will not.

Turn Practices in the 1992 Vice Presidential Debate

Political debates are another type of relatively **preallocated turn system**. How much a debate is preallocated versus **locally managed** is something that varies with the political debate. In the 1992 vice presidential (VP) debate, as I previously noted, there was a moderate amount of local management in which some of the time the parties could speak directly to each other. Consider how the identities of the three contenders (Gore, Quayle, and Stockdale) were shaped by their own and the other candidates' very particular choices and patterns of turn taking.

Let us begin with the media assessments of what the VP debates were taken to show about each candidate. Beck[19] summarized the mainstream public opinion of the three men after the debate as the following:

> *Gore* established himself as more "vice presidential" than the other two candidates; displaying himself as a man of "composed dignity."
> *Quayle* gave an "attack-dog performance." "He didn't look stupid,

merely possessed—by an Urkel-like urge to say 'Liar, liar, pants on fire.' "[20] Quayle displayed himself to be "a fighter" but failed to support that he was a "calm, assertive, and presidential" kind of person.[21]

Stockdale failed to present himself as "presidential." Postdebate polls revealed that voters saw him as "sincere" and "intelligent" but, at the same time, did not regard him to be a "serious" candidate for the office.

Consider, now, how each candidate's management of turns contributed to these widely held impressions. In the 1992 VP debate the format involved a single moderator who raised topics. Each candidate was given 75 seconds to make his response on that topic; then there was a 5-minute open discussion. During the open discussion, there were no rules about length of comments, order for speakers, or how frequently each could speak. In other words, the discussion period was a free-for-all where how much each candidate talked, about what issues, and at what junctures was dependent on the unfolding interaction. Of interest is that in this situation the turn taking itself frequently became a topic of explicit focus. Candidates accused each other of hogging the floor, interrupting, changing the topic at inappropriate spots, and so on. An example of this is seen in Example 7.8, in which we find Gore rebuking Quayle for trying to take the floor. When reading the following examples, remember that brackets indicate overlapping talk and parentheses indicate speech that could be heard but not all the words were understandable. Also note that G = Gore, Q = Quayle, S = Stockdale, and M = moderator.

EXAMPLE 7.8

1G: Yeah I, I, I wanna, I wanna talk about this because the question was not about free trade or education [the question was about, let me finish

2Q: [talk about waffling you're

3G: [now I let you talk

4Q: [the one who brought up the issue of waffling

5G: Da[n let, I let you talk, I- lemme talk now

6Q: [And he's waffled on the abortion issue

7G: It's gonna be a long evening if ya- if you're like this now because[22]

In this instance, Gore's comments altercast Quayle as unfair. In describing Quayle as not letting him finish (1G) and himself as having *let* Quayle have his turn to talk (3G, 5G), Gore strongly implies that Quayle is being unfair by interrupting him. Consider, though, another exchange where Gore is the person who is attempting to claim the floor. In Example 7.9 Quayle is wrapping up an answer to a prior Gore criticism about the Republican position on the family leave act.

EXAMPLE 7.9

1Q: Pass, pass our family leave act and (pause) because it goes to small businesses where the major problem is, your proposal ex-cluded small businesses that's, that's the problem. Now let me talk about health   [care and I'm glad

2G: [did you require it? (pause)

3Q: excuse (pause) my, [my tur- my- my turn

4G: [Did you require it? (pause)

5Q: [( )

6G: [Did you require   [it ( )

7M: [([ )

8Q: [Lighten up Al (pause) my turn

8G: It's a free discussion

10Q: Take a breath Al, inhale ((Audience laughter and applause))

11G: It's a free discussion (pause) did you require it (pause) did you require family leave in that legislation yes or no

12Q: we're we offered incentives to small businesses (pause) yes or no [were small

13G: [yes or no

14Q: Were small businesses exempted under your proposal

15G: yes

16Q: yes and that's where the biggest [problem exists

17G: [did you require it of anyone?

18Q: I'm gonna get back to that topic at hand because

19G: Did you require it of anyone?[23]

At the end of his opening comment (1Q) Quayle is seeking to change the topic from family leave to health care. This juncture is a TRP—it's a place where another could enter to say more on the family leave topic. Gore in fact does so; he pursues information about Quayle's position. This pursuit occurs across the entire exchange and is marked by multiple repetitions of several questions and many spates of overlapping competitive talk. Two possible negative identities are made relevant by this exchange. A first is that Gore could be seen as interrupting, being unfair to Quayle, not letting him finish, and doing more or less what he accused Quayle of doing earlier. On the other hand, Quayle might be seen as trying to evade the question and change the topic, and he could be seen as accusing Gore of not letting him talk just to move attention away from this particular, unpopular Republican position on this issue. Although each interpretation was probably made by at least some viewers, the more frequent one, based on media commentaries, appears to have been the one favoring Gore.

Noteworthy in Example 7.9 is the conversational environment in which Quayle's accusation of unfairness occurred compared to Gore's accusation in Example 7.8: Quayle raised his accusation in response to a question Gore posed to him on the officially sanctioned debate topic; Gore raised his to an off-topic aside ("talk about waffling"). Stated simply, complex and consequential interpersonal assessments are tied to very small differences in use of the turn-taking system.[24]

Thus far I have said nothing about Admiral Stockdale and how his debate performance contributed to a sense that he was not a credible VP candidate. The answer, though, is already implicated in these brief excerpts. Stockdale was invisible in the debate. His comments in the preallocated comment periods rarely took the full 75 seconds, and he had little to say in the open discussion time, mostly standing by and watching Quayle and Gore go after each other. His limited talking, then, became evidence for debate viewers that Stockdale lacked knowledge, political assertiveness, or both—two personal-level identities that made him a nonserious, questionable VP candidate.

THE REMEDIAL INTERCHANGE

In Chapter 4 I examined a set of face-sensitive speech acts (e.g., accounts, reproaches, and apologies). Although these speech acts do not fit into the tight structure of an adjacency pair format, they frequently occur in a more loosely organized structure. In everyday life when an offense occurs, whether it is as small as one person requiring another to move in a crowded airport, or as significant as an accusation that a person's relational partner is self-centered or dishonest, then there is a need for a remedial interchange. The **remedial interchange**[25] is a four-part sequence designed to remedy the feelings of discomfort caused by an offense. The sequence begins with *a remedy*, an act that attempts to solve the trouble. The remedy could be an apology ("Sorry"), a request ("May I get through to get to the plane?"), an account ("Hafta catch my plane"), or some combination of these. The remedy is then followed by an expression of *relief* ("Sure," "Okay"), which in turn is followed by an expression of *appreciation* by the person who had caused the offense ("Thanks"). The interchange concludes with a final move in which the offended party makes a comment that is a *minimization* of the offense ("Yeah, no big deal"). The four-part sequence does not always occur in its elaborated form. For relatively small offenses it may occur in a truncated version that involves only the remedy and the relief. Nonetheless, whether the remedial interchange involves the full or truncated version, it is a powerful, frequently occurring ritual. As Goffman[26] observed, the reason it is so pervasive is that it allows conversational participants to go on their way satisfied that a moment of possible trouble with another person has been managed satisfactorily. Communicators' abilities to participate in remedial interchanges appropriately affect whether they will be seen to possess valued personal identities such as *tactful, sensitive,* and *considerate.* Not initiating a remedial exchange where one is expected or responding inappropriately to another person's initiation is likely to accomplish the reverse: having self written off as *prickly, inconsiderate,* and *not a good person.*

SPEECH COMMUNITY DIFFERENCES

As with other aspects of everyday talk, interaction-structuring processes are culturally inflected. Somewhat different meanings may be attached to a given segment of talk, and, for some occasions, what is taken to be normal will differ. I have already noted how this applies in job interviews. Now let's consider two other differences.

The notion of adjacency pair is cross-culturally relevant. In Chinese, Swahili, and English, speakers are expected to return a first greeting with a second one. However, what counts as an acceptable greeting varies. Spencer-Oatley[27] notes that in Hong Kong "Hello, have you had lunch?" is used by many Chinese speakers as an initiating greeting much like "Hello, a bit colder today?" British English speakers new to Hong Kong routinely hear this greeting as an invitation. In addition, when running into an acquaintance on the street, a usual Chinese way to greet someone is to say "Where are you going?" To British English speakers this greeting seems inappropriate and intrusive—"That's my own personal business, why is this person asking me this?" Yet, from the Chinese point of view, not only is this a legitimate greeting, but it demands no more than a vague response such as "I'm going over there" or "I'm going into town." Thus, for Hong Kong English speakers, the question "Where are you going?" is meant not to solicit information but to build rapport, much as the American English greeting "How you doing?" functions.

A second speech community difference in interaction structuring is to be found in the cues a group uses to request a turn and to signal attention. As illustrated in Chapter 2, the length of a pause that is seen as normal before a new speaker claims the floor varies across Anglo and Native American communities. By and large, Anglo speakers assume shorter pauses at a TRP to be what is normal and as the signal that a speaker is done. Native Americans regard the normal polite pause to be a bit longer. The upshot of this very small difference is consequential, leading to conversations where an Anglo partner keeps self-selecting to continue talking, inferring that her Native American partner has nothing to say since he did not come in after a presumably normal pause.

Another difference between Native Americans and Anglos involves the use of visual cues to give attention. From their earliest years children raised in many Native American communities are taught to make fine visual discriminations. Children will be taught how to identify a person at a distance. On family occasions, infants will be kept in a noisy family gathering room but will have a sheet draped over their cradle to block them from seeing others. In contrast, Anglo families are likely to take a child out of a noisy room to a quiet one. That is, Anglo families train their children to attend to auditory cues whereas Indians put more weight on the visual. In signaling attention, a Native American speaker is likely to use subtle movements around the mouth in the lower region of the face. These movements are much less typically used or attended to among Anglo speakers. Given that Indian children are also likely to avert their gaze as a way of showing respect, it is quite likely that an Anglo partner will not recognize that a Native American is being attentive. Phillips,[28] for instance, documented that Native American children in mainstream American classes are reprimanded for not paying attention far more often than their Anglo peers. Thus, a small, largely out-of-awareness, difference in turn-taking systems, especially when power relations are unequal, may be part of the way well-intentioned members of the dominant speech community (middle-class Americans) produce unfair treatment of ethnic minorities.

SUMMARY

In this chapter I described a set of conversational structures that varied from two utterance sequences (adjacency pairs) to somewhat longer units (the remedial interchange). For each sequence I considered how it did identity-work. In addition, I examined how turn taking works in ordinary conversation when it is locally managed, as well as how it operates in institutional encounters, such as debates and job interviews, in which the situation has prespecified rules about who can talk when and about what. Interaction structures, more than other features of talk, occur across languages and cultures. Nonetheless, we saw that these structures have a cultural dimension: what counts as a greeting, the length of a pause that is judged reasonable, and the function of gaze in giving attention all vary across speech communities.

8

◈ Direct or Indirect Style

To describe someone as having a "conversational style" is to suggest that a person has a distinctive and consistent way of speaking.[1] **Conversational style** is an interaction-rooted version of the psychological concept of personality. But, rather than explaining actions in terms of a fixed set of traits that reside inside a person, explaining conversational style focuses on describing a person's preferences and practices in talk. Style is a broader concept than the particular features of talk I focused on in earlier chapters. In reflecting about style we need to step back from concrete practices to look for patterns across a number of features of talk. Tannen notes that

> *style* does not refer to a special way of speaking, as if one could choose between speaking plainly or speaking with style. Plain is as much a style as fancy. Anything that is said or done must be said and done in some way, and that constitutes style. . . . You can no more talk without style than you can walk or sit or dress without style. Anything you say must be said at a certain rate, at a certain pitch and amplitude, in a certain intonation, and at a certain point in interaction. All these and countless other choices determine the effects of an utterance in interaction and influence judgments that are made both about what is said and about the speaker who says it. All these and countless other necessary choices determine a speaker's style.[2]

Style is an individual's unique signature; at the same time, it is a characteristic way of communicating, partly shared with people with whom one has spent time—family and friends, for example, or national, ethnic, age, and gender groups. There are many different ways to describe style. Norton,[3] for instance, identifies dramatic, open, and attentive as three particularly important aspects of style. This chapter focuses on the aspect of style that is most frequently commented upon in ordinary exchanges: a person's relative directness or indirectness. Of all the ways of describing conversational style, "direct" or "indirect" is one of the most pervasive in people's talk about themselves and others. Yet, as we will soon see, what it means to be direct or indirect is not a straightforward matter. To further complicate this issue, it is virtually impossible to discuss direct and indirect styles without implying that one is better than the other. Each has advantages. Yet, by and large, people react negatively to others whose degree of directness differs markedly from their own. Consider what one Israeli husband said about good communication:

EXAMPLE 8.1

I think that showing consideration for the other means to speak directly and sincerely with people, I think that going round and round shows lack of consideration, I feel hurt and cheated when I feel somebody close is trying to tell me something but does not say it, I think that to talk sincerely, directly is much more civilized, more true. For example I'm always slightly annoyed with Dina [his wife] when as she always does, she asks me if I would mind picking up Yaniv [the baby].[4]

At this point in the interview, the wife, a French woman, intervened to say:

EXAMPLE 8.2

But that's a nice way to ask, I do not force him, I soften the request, I leave him the choice to agree or disagree.[5]

For this husband, and for many other people, being direct is being *sincere, civilized*, and *true*. For this wife, and for many others, being direct about requests involves being *not nice, forcing another*, or *leaving someone no choice*. Style directness, then, becomes a hallmark of especially valued aspects of personal and relational identities—whether one is moral, honest, and fair, treats others as equal, is respectful, and so on.

Style directness is best thought of as an umbrella concept—it includes choices about a set of related but distinct conversational practices. A primary one concerns how a communicator performs speech acts. After examining this primary facet of directness, I identify four other practices that contribute to a speaker's relative directness or indirectness.

SPEECH ACTS

There are many different types of speech acts. With regard to style directness, three kinds of speech acts are especially interesting.

Directives

Directives, as I explained in Chapter 4, are acts in which one person attempts to get another to do something (or to refrain from doing something). We saw one kind of directive in Example 8.1, where the husband complained about the usual way his wife requested that he stop on his way home from work and pick up the baby. Everyday relationships are full of situations in which one person is trying to get another person to do something or is responding to that other person's demand, request, or hint. For instance, a work supervisor could try to get her employee to work an unscheduled shift by demanding "You have to work Saturday night" or by requesting "Would you be able to work Saturday night?" or by just complaining: "Oh no, I don't know what we're going to do. Erin just called in to say she won't be able to work Saturday night." This last strategy, the most indirect, allows the employee to hear the supervisor's comment as a hint asking her to volunteer to work the additional shift.

Directives, according to Kim and Bresnahan, take one of three main forms: (1) direct statement directives, (2) query directives, and (3) hint directives.[6] Table 8.1 gives examples of these three forms for a situation where a person wants to get a friend to repay a loan. The strategies are arranged from most to least direct.

Many factors influence which form a speaker selects. In general, when a person is in a situation where he has the right to direct the actions of another, he is more likely to use direct statement directives. A father, for instance, is more likely to tell a misbehaving child "Go to your room" than he is to use a query such as "How about going to your room?" or a hint such as "I'm not liking the way you're acting right now." In contrast, when the relational situation is not one that gives a party the right to direct the actions of the other, indirect forms are more likely to be selected. For instance, a person who wants a friend to loan her money is more likely to use queries ("Would you be able to loan me $20?") or hints ("Oh gee, I don't have any money with me") than a direct statement ("You have to loan me $20"). When a speech act is indirect it requires listeners to do more inferential work to arrive at a speaker's intended interactional meaning. The literal meaning of the utterance is different than what the speaker is trying to convey. A complexity, though, is that acts always carry both direct and indirect meanings.

TABLE 8.1. Kinds of Directives and Their Relative Directness[7]

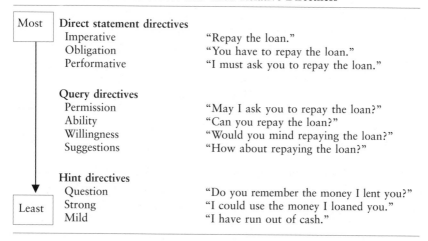

Most	Direct statement directives	
	Imperative	"Repay the loan."
	Obligation	"You have to repay the loan."
	Performative	"I must ask you to repay the loan."
	Query directives	
	Permission	"May I ask you to repay the loan?"
	Ability	"Can you repay the loan?"
	Willingness	"Would you mind repaying the loan?"
	Suggestions	"How about repaying the loan?"
	Hint directives	
	Question	"Do you remember the money I lent you?"
	Strong	"I could use the money I loaned you."
Least	Mild	"I have run out of cash."

A speaker may intend to be direct but this does not rule out the potential that a listener will assign his statement an indirect meaning.

Besides selecting different forms for directives, indirectness may be accomplished through selecting a content than is different than the meaning that is intended. For instance, a criticism of someone's grammar may be heard (or intended) as a criticism of her overall goodness or competence as a person. At the same time it may have been heard (and intended) as no more than its literal meaning—as a small jab about a minor speech choice. An invitation to come up to someone's apartment to hear a new CD may be intended as an invitation to move a relationship to a romantic, sexual level. If the request happens at a culturally significant time (at night, but especially on Friday or Saturday night) between persons regarded as eligibles (of the appropriate gender, age, and sexual orientation), the invitee will be expected to know what the invitation means and not be outraged or surprised when a sexual overture occur. But the invitation to listen to a new CD may be just that, with nothing more intended. Thus an ever-present challenge for communicators is to decide when conversational partners are expressing themselves directly and when their intended meaning is an indirect one.

Misunderstandings are an inescapable part of everyday communication. Because talking is a flexible practice, it enables people to convey subtle and sophisticated meanings. At the same time, talk's chameleon-like potential can make figuring out others' interactional meanings frustrating. In general, the better one knows another or the more routine a talk situation, the more likely that one will infer other people's intentions accurately. But this is not always the case. Tannen describes a pattern typical of many middle-class American women and men in dating relationships. At the beginning of a relationship, couples have relatively few misunderstandings: both see it as necessary to watch out for hints and to give the other party options. As the relationship progresses, however, the men and women begin to change their expectations about how to communicate. With increasing intimacy, women expect more indirectness—"We know each other so well, you should know what I want without me telling you." In contrast, men expect less indirectness, using a logic that assumes, "We know each other so well, you can tell me what you want."[8]

No one expects directness all the time. In a study of seven cultures Blum-Kulka, House, and Kaspar[9] found that every cultural group (e.g., Argentinean Spanish, Australian English, Canadian French) believed that speakers should vary their degree of directness according to the situation. Interestingly, across these cultures there was some agreement about how situations should affect the degree of directness. In particular, the seven communities under study judged it appropriate to use direct statement directives if a police officer was asking a citizen to move her car, but inappropriate if a person were asking a neighbor for a ride. In general, favors were to be performed indirectly and with polite forms, whereas actions involving relational rights could be performed directly. However, while cultural groups saw some situations similarly, they saw others with considerable divergence. For instance, when a college roommate failed to do his or her share of the chores, there were huge differences among the nationalities. The vast majority of Argentineans (76%) used direct statement directives whereas only a tiny percentage (12%) of Australians did.

To give another example, consider a study where Americans and Greeks were asked to interpret the most likely meaning of a husband's response to a question from his wife:

EXAMPLE 8.3

WIFE: John's having a party. Wanna go?
HUSBAND: OK.[10]

Participants in the study were given two possible meanings for the husband's "OK": (1) My wife is asking if I want to go to a party. I feel like going so I'll say yes" (direct meaning); (2) My wife wants to go to this party. Since she asked, I'll go to make her happy" (indirect meaning). Two-thirds of the Americans in the study selected the direct meaning while only one-half of the Greeks did. To generalize, Greeks prefer and use an indirect style somewhat more often than Americans.

Cultural differences in style directness are especially likely in another kind of speech act: talk that seeks to get information from another person.

Information-Seeking Acts

EXAMPLE 8.4

1. "Why don't you have children?"
2. "Were you married before?"
3. "How much money do you earn in your job?"[11]

These three questions are examples of direct acts of information seeking. If asked by an acquaintance in America or Germany, there are likely to be assessed by the speaker's conversational partner as rude and inappropriately direct. In a study of German and Chinese students conversing in Germany, Günther found that both groups of students reacted negatively to each other. Germans found the Chinese to be boring and not interesting conversationalists—they didn't do enough asserting of their own opinions. Chinese regarded the German students as rude, aggressive, and often offensive. Interestingly, while it was the Germans who were generally perceived as more direct, it was the Chinese who saw it as reasonable to seek information directly about the three issues in Example 8.4.

This points to one of the interesting complexities about directness. Although cultural groups are routinely described in terms of their relative directness or indirectness—for example, Chinese and Japanese are more indirect than Germans and Americans—the actual picture is more complex. Cultural groups disagree about what topics are to be regarded as sensitive or private information. So although is may be reasonable to describe Chinese communicators as generally more indirect, there will be particular situations where they will be more direct than Americans or Germans would be. To give another example, Kochman[12] notes that the practice of directly asking someone what he or she does within the first few minutes of meeting, a practice common among middle-class American whites, is sometimes seen as inappropriate for social occasions among African Americans. To ask a new acquaintance straightforwardly about his or her occupation is to treat a person's job as saying something important about who he or she is. In a community where underemployment or unemployment is not uncommon, though, job information becomes a delicate topic and such a question becomes inappropriate intrusiveness.

How, then, do people seek information indirectly? Pomerantz[13] identifies a practice she called **fishing**. Assume that Seth, a friend of Reesa, wants to know where she was last night. He could ask directly: "Where were you last night?" However, to do so might suggest that he sees himself as having the right to know this information, a right usually assumed only in close relationships. Or this comment might be interpreted as evidence that Seth is possessive or jealous, personal identities usually seen as undesirable. One way for Seth to seek the information he wants without asking for it directly would be to report his own actions on the previous night: "Hey, Reesa, I gave you a call last night and you didn't answer" or "I drove by your house last night and your car was gone." Each of these statements is a report of Seth's activities. At the same time, it is quite likely to lead Reesa to spontaneously mention what she was doing the previous night ("Oh, my brother was in town for a meeting and we went out to dinner"). "Fishing for information," then, works by virtue of commenting on something that the speaker has seen or heard that implicates the other. In essence, a "fishing comment" is a piece of talk designed to encourage the partner to disclose information, but it does not have the demand quality that is present in a direct inquiry.

Opinion or News Expression

A third kind of speech act that may be done with different degrees of directness is the giving of news or the expression of opinions. Especially when delivering bad news, it is common for speakers to do so indirectly. Maynard[14] studied a diagnostic clinic where parents brought children who were not developing normally. Clinicians often had bad news to tell parents at the end of the testing period. They had to tell parents that their child was unlikely to ever learn normally—he would always be slow, developmentally delayed, with a lower than normal IQ. Maynard found that rather than delivering the diagnosis straightforwardly, doctors often approached giving out bad news circuitously. A clinician would start the final parent conference by asking the parents to state what they themselves saw as the problem with their child. Then she would confirm and build on the parent's opinion, before finally labeling the trouble in official diagnostic language. The advantage of delivering the news in this indirect fashion rather than directly was that it showed attention to and concern for the parents' perspective on their child. It also conveyed caring in terms of how the bad news was likely to impact the parents. To deliver sad news in a clear, direct way may implicitly convey a message that the speaker does not care whether she hurts the recipient.

However, what exactly directness will convey is culturally variable. Katriel[15] notes that for Israelis direct expression is understood differently than for other nationalities. *Dugri*, a term originating in Arabic and now colloquial in Hebrew, is an important symbol of Zionist socialism. It is the name for an honest person who speaks straight to the point and it also is the name of an act (doing *dugri*) that involves speaking straight to the point. *Dugri* involves speaking plainly and without adornment or softening ("His is not a good plan to follow"; "You shouldn't treat your grandmother that way"). A prototypical act of *dugri* occurs when a subordinate speaks out to someone of higher rank and expresses a negative opinion at some risk to self. To act in this manner is regarded as a courageous and valued kind of expression. To speak *dugri* is to show that a speaker cares about another or is committed to an issue. Other societies, Katriel documents, contrast in interesting ways with this Israeli ideal. Table 8.2 displays these differences.

In Israeli society, expressing opinions directly is valued for both sexes. In American society, speaking directly is used and valued less for women than for men. In Arab society, as in Israeli culture, there is a similar ideal for both sexes. However, Arab women and men are expected to do **musayra**, to work to make relations harmonious. The communicative ideal is to go along, to humor and accommodate others so that an interaction may proceed smoothly. The ideal of *musayra* also goes with a valuing of hierarchy. Among Arab interactants, it is the person of lower rank who is expected to do *musayra*. Finally, in Malagsay, similar to the United States, the valuing of directness is linked to gender. However, the gender linkage is the opposite of that expected in the United States. In Malagasy men are regarded as the subtle communicators, the ones who can handle sensitive situations. In contrast, women are seen as direct in their speech style, lacking subtlety. Women may be able to handle a direct confrontation in the marketplace but they cannot be counted on to manage diplomatically sensitive scenes among people.

There is another kind of indirectness that people frequently use in

TABLE 8.2. Valuing and Use of Directness

	Israeli	American	Malagasy	Arab
Women	+	−	+	−
Men	+	+	−	−

expressing opinions. Rather than saying what they mean, they express the opposite. For example, following a game in which a team lost, one player says to the other, "Great game, wasn't it?" Or at a breakfast when a woman is serving muffins, one rolls off the plate into her friend's lap. The friend looks at the muffin in her lap, then back at the server, and comments, "How elegant." Stated simply, people make ironic comments in which they expect the listener, given the context, to understand what is meant. Irony, then, is a way of being humorous; it fosters a bond between the speaker and the listener. The use of irony can also work to elevate the status of the speaker. If the irony has a critical edge, depending on its exact target and how it is worded, it may either be a way to soften or to intensify a criticism.[16]

In many cultures people use indirectness to be considerate and respectful. It is also used to be funny, to create rapport, or to protect a speaker. Tannen describes the advantages of indirectness this way:

> *Rapport* is the lovely satisfaction of being understood without explaining oneself, of getting what one wants without asking for it. *Defensiveness* is the need to be able to save face by reneging in case one's conversational contribution is not well received—the ability to say, perhaps sincerely, "I never said that," or "That isn't what I meant."[17]

Directness, in contrast, is often seen as being honest and nonmanipulative, sometimes seen as being clearer, and in some cultures (e.g., Israel, Poland) is regarded as the best way to be considerate of others.[18]

People of all cultures perform some acts directly and others indirectly. How frequently communicators select the different options for being indirect (or direct) and the situations in which each device is employed is what gives individuals and their communities their characteristic directness style. But directness involves other conversational practices than those tied to speech act performance.

OTHER FACETS OF STYLE DIRECTNESS

Language Practices

Besides the basic form of a speech act, communicators need to select the act's linguistic clothing: Should the act be carried out in a barebones, minimalist manner? Or should words be added to soften any negative or face-attacking implications? **Mitigation markers** refer to a diverse set of conversational devices that are used to attend to these two purposes. Mitigation markers are forms of indirectness. When they are included in an expression of opinion, an information inquiry, or a directive, the speech act would count as being performed more indirectly or politely than if these bits of talk were absent. In general, the more mitigation markers a speaker uses, the more he or she is using an indirect style.

Brown and Levinson[19] identify a large set of practices speakers can use to accomplish mitigation. One of the most visible devices for mitigating opinions is the use of hedges to minimize the intensity of an assertion ("I sort of disagree"; "I kind of think differently"), apologies ("I hate to say this, but . . . "), words that modify the strength of one's assertion ("probably," "maybe," or "It seems" rather than "It is"), or prefaces that mark one's comment as potentially face-attacking ("Frankly," "to be honest").

Regarding requests for information and directives, people can either highlight their reluctance to impose or seek to minimize the degree of imposition. This is done by including phrases such as "I was wondering if," "Would it be at all possible," "I know this is none of my business, but . . . " "I know this is asking a lot," or "Feel free to ignore this, but . . . " When requesting a person's time or effort, speakers may underscore the smallness of what is wanted ("I *just* need a minute of your time," or "Could I have *a little* help?").

Although the usual result when adding words to a speech act is mitigation and indirection, there are phrases that make a speech act more direct. A clear example of **upgraders**, or directness-increasing devices, is obscenities. To tell someone, "Get the hell in here" is more direct than to merely tell someone to "Get in here." This makes visible a second complexity in deciding whether a cultural group has a direct or an indirect style. In the culture study mentioned earlier in this chapter, Australian students preferred indirect directives (queries or hints to get a roommate to do a chore). At the same time, Australians were the most likely of all the nationalities to use upgraders (e.g., "I was bloody well wondering when you're going to do what you promised?").

Within all societies there are topics that are considered sensitive, at least in certain situations or with particular conversational partners. Sex and mention of sex organs, excrement, illnesses (particularly related to controversial lifestyle choices), judgments about a person's character, certain kinds of religious references, and death are delicate matters in most cultures. Stated more generally, topics that directly or indirectly challenge the goodness and morality of a speaker, a recipient, or a spoken-about person are usually delicate talk activities, requiring speakers to give special thought to the words they select.[20]

Compare the following two comments:

EXAMPLE 8.6

1. *Indirect*: His uncle *passed away* last week. Old Tom probably *liked to have fun in the pubs* with his friends a bit too much.

2. *Direct*: His uncle *died* last week. Old Tom had been an *alcoholic* forever.

In excerpt (1) not only does the speaker use two linguistic devices just noted ("probably" "a bit") but his vocabulary choices for talking about Tom's death and drinking are less harsh. Some of these differences— "passed away" for "died"—are standard **euphemisms**, nicer words for something nasty. Others, such as the phrase "liked to have fun in the pubs," are not euphemisms in the strict sense but share with euphemisms their core impulse of making a reference nicer or more palatable. When speakers refer to something in the world using words that are more positive, cleaned-up, scientific, or vaguer than the lived experience, they are speaking indirectly.

Using indirect language is a way to show self as not a *coarse, crude, vulgar, obnoxious, insensitive,* or *nasty* person. Put positively, referring to sensitive topics indirectly displays self to be *tactful and considerate, a person of good taste.* But as with many communicative choices, the identity dangers don't come only from a single direction. To use indirect references a lot (whatever "a lot" means) can imply that one is *overly sensitive* and *easily offended, prissy,* perhaps *too politically correct, pompous,* or possessing other undesirable personal identities. To use direct references frequently may be taken as evidence that one is *down-to-earth, unpretentious,* or perhaps *comfortable with her sexuality.*

Which set of identity dangers communicators fear more—or which desired identities are more strongly sought—will shape people's usual language choices and contribute to their unique conversation styles. As with other aspects of directness, speech communities differ in their patterns of preferences. Women, for instance, generally use euphemistic and other kinds of indirect references more than men; older people are much more indirect than teens. A common stereotype, although its accuracy is undocumented, is that American and Australian English speakers are more direct than British English speakers.[21]

Amount of Small Talk

It is the beginning of the day in a New Zealand office. Diana, Sally's boss, enters the office to collect her mail. The following conversation occurs:

EXAMPLE 8.7

D: Good morning, Sally, lovely day.

S: Yes, don't know what we're doing here. We should be out in the sun.

D: Mm pity about the work really.

S: How are your kids?

D: Much better, thank goodness. Any mail?[22]

This exchange is a classic example of **small talk,** the friendly chatting that occurs between people about topics such as the weather, sports, food, fashion, and children. Small talk is the everyday term to refer to what the anthropologist Malinowski initially labeled "phatic communion."[23] Coupland describes small talk as "subsuming 'gossip,' 'chat,' and 'time out talk,' " a mode of talk that is "supposedly minor, informal, unimportant and unserious."[24] But as she and other authors show, small talk is anything but unimportant[25]; it is crucial to the smooth functioning of everyday life. Small talk is centrally about building and solidifying relationships; it occurs around the coffeepot and in mailrooms, at the start of meetings, at the beginning of a work lunch, or at the start of a telephone conversation. It differs from business talk (*big* talk?) in that it is about topics not directly relevant to the task at hand. The content of small talk (e.g., weather, sports) could occur in almost any context; it is neither technical nor focused on the task purpose of why one person contacted another.

Small talk is about building bonds with others. A day without small talk would be strange indeed. Yet the amount of small talk that people regard as desirable or necessary is enormously variable. Speakers who do extended "small talking" before getting down to the business at hand are using an indirect style; those who get right down to business with only minimal small talk are being more direct. Similar to other facets of directness, the choice to minimize small talk will be viewed favorable by some people and negatively by others. A direct speaker may be seen as a person who *doesn't waste time* or who *doesn't beat around the bush*, but also as *boorish* or *not understanding how business really works.*

With regard to use of small talk, Americans are more direct than most Latin American or Asian speakers. Americans regard the building of goodwill and a positive relationship as a relatively minor part of business encounters. Most other nationalities give considerably more attention to relational work in business encounters.

This aspect of style directness also plays itself out in informal, outside-of-work contacts. Pavlidou[26] conducted a study that compared telephone conversations among Greeks and among Germans. She found that Greeks engaged in much more small talk than Germans did. In addition, Greek conversationalists would offer a social reason for calling (expressing their desire to know how the other was) before moving on to the explicit purpose of the call. In closing the conversation, Greek speakers spent almost twice as long as Germans in closing rituals (telling the other to keep in touch, saying goodbye). Pavlidou concluded her study this way: the Greek way is "to build the relationship through small talk," whereas the German way is to "refrain from keeping the partner on the phone for too long and letting them know pretty soon the reason for calling."[27] Thus, both Germans and Greeks care about building positive relationships but the way they do so is quite different. The relational concerns of Germans led them to use a relatively direct style whereas Greeks favored a more indirect approach.

Making an Argumentative Point

Another aspect of style directness has to do with how a communicator makes an elaborated point in a discussion. The most indirect way to make an argument is to tell a story. In the next chapter, we will consider how a mother's purpose in telling her teen son a story about their neighbor's arrest for pot smoking might be seen as a strategy to persuade him that pot smoking is bad or, more pointedly, that he shouldn't smoke pot. Telling a story is an indirect way to make an argumentative point. It leaves it up to the listener to figure out the exact point for telling the story. In almost all cases, there are multiple points that could be inferred from a single story. In the situation with the mother and son, the story's point might have been a general one about the dangers of pot, or it might have been that her son was acting badly, making her unhappy, and that he needed to change. Or her story's point may even have been that her son needed to be careful not to smoke in places that would get him arrested. Similar to other kinds of indirection, making a point by telling a story is going to be more ambiguous than stating that point explicitly.

On the plus side, making points by telling stories gives the speaker the ability to deny that she really meant something, and gives the listener more maneuvering room (whatever is implied can more easily be ignored). In addition, telling a story to make a point is likely to make the point more vivid and emotionally compelling. On the other hand, a story has the potential to be less clear than a direct statement. Moreover, telling a story is a long-winded way to make a point. People are often criticized for launching into stories inappropriately ("What a gas bag! I asked a simple question and got a half-hour story!"). In sum, while making a point by telling a story can be memorable and effective, the practice needs to be used judiciously. If a person tells stories too much, it will lead to negative identity inferences. But, as with other conversational practices, what is considered going overboard is likely to vary across communities.

The most common way people make argumentative points, though, is to state an explicit claim and give supporting evidence and reasons. But whether the claim comes first followed by the reasons and evidence, or the reasons and evidence come first followed by the claim, is an organizational choice that the speaker must make. Using either one of these organizational patterns is more direct than telling a story—each makes the point explicit rather than leaving it merely hinted at. However, to make the claim first followed by the evidence is more direct than the reverse order. Compare Examples 8.8 and 8.9 in which the two types of organization are illustrated. In Example 8.8 the speaker is a 14-year-old girl talking with her dad. In Example 8.9 the speaker is a school board member who is arguing to other school board members at a public meeting why it makes sense to add a class in world literature as a graduation requirement in the school district.

EXAMPLE 8.8. Indirect (Inductive)

(R1) GIRL: You know how you've been encouraging me to stick with something and work at it?

     DAD: Yeah?

(R2) GIRL: And you're always saying that I sit around and watch TV too much?

     DAD: Yeah.

(R3) GIRL: And I've saved $200.

     DAD: Okay?

(Claim) GIRL: Well, there's this karate camp in Connecticut for 2 weeks in July. I really need to go if I'm to get any better. Can I go?[28]

EXAMPLE 8.9. Direct (Deductive)

(Claim)   We need to add world literature as a graduation requirement.

(R1)   We are an educated district and we need to be challenging our kids.

(R2)   We need to challenge all of our kids too, not just those in honors classes. For kids not going to college it may be their only opportunity to read literature from other countries.

(R3)   If we're committed to diversity, as we say we are, then we should be exposing our students to authors from diverse cultures.[29]

In making the argument that her dad should both allow her to go to karate camp and pay for it, the girl in Example 8.8 has used an **inductive organization**. Such an organization is especially effective when the point a speaker wants to make is one that the listener may be expected to resist. By gaining her dad's assent for the legitimacy of each reason before identifying what the reason is being used to support, the girl pulls her dad into what she wants. This organization is effective when one is seeking to move the other to action and when the speaker anticipates possible resistance. Organizing an argument inductively is more indirect than organizing it deductively.

In Example 8.9, the school board member uses a **deductive organization**. Unlike the girl with her bid for camp, the school board member has the right to advance his view: his official job is to talk about the issues on the agenda and argue for what he thinks is the best course of action. By beginning with what he favors, the school board member makes it easier for his listeners to make sense of his subsequent information. In essence, a claim as the first part of an argument instructs listeners how to interpret the comments that follow. In that sense, to begin with a general claim and follow it with the particular reasons is an effective strategy when the emphasis is on facilitating the listener's understanding.[30]

Although both patterns are used in all cultures, for the reasons identified above, there are cultural patterns. Asian speakers use the inductive organization more frequently than Americans do.[31] Undoubtedly, Asian speakers' argument organization preference is another piece of evidence that contributes to the widely held belief that Asians are more indirect than Americans.

Emotional Expressiveness

A final facet of style directness concerns how straightforwardly people display their feelings. Consider the following situation. An African American woman named Joan McCartny was watching the play *Lysistrata* at a university theater:

She was laughing heartily enjoying the play's bawdiness and humor, when a white woman turned to her and said, "You are really outrageous!" McCartny, hurt by the remark, asked what was wrong. The white woman

replied, "You are laughing so loud. I mean, come on! It's funny but. . . . "
McCartny said, "Daag, it's a comedy. Ain't you supposed to laugh?" But as
she reflected in her report of the incident, "That was just seen as inappropriate, rude behavior. I guess I was supposed to feel the laughter, but not
express it, at least not in the way I felt it."[32]

Based on observation of college students, faculty, and community
groups in Chicago, Kochman identifies two styles guiding emotional expression that differentiated white and black Americans. In general, African Americans tend to favor forceful expression whereas whites are
likely to prefer a more subdued and restrained style. From a white point
of view, forceful expression is seen as *irresponsible* or *in bad taste*, but
African Americans see whites' low-keyed style as *dead, cold,* or *not for
real*.[33] The different evaluations of the direct and indirect styles of emotional expression can be traced to the ways each speech community
thinks about the rights and responsibilities of communicators. From a
white viewpoint, emotion is a dangerous thing, capable of easily damag-
ing others. Because of the damage potential of emotional expression, it is
the responsibility of speakers to reign their feeling in to protect the sensibilities of listeners. People in their role as listeners have the right to expect others to be tactful and to edit out strong or hurtful feelings. Many
feelings should not be expressed directly.

In contrast, African Americans are likely to regard emotionality and
its expression as an attractive quality in people. We are all emotional be-
ings. Part of making communication lively and interesting is ensuring
that people have the space to express the emotions they feel. People are
strong and quite able to handle intense expressions of feelings from others. It is valuable for each person to be able to express his or her feelings;
in fact, as long as feeling expression does not cross the line to physical
fighting, it is a speaker's right. It is listeners who have the responsibility
of being tolerant of others' expressiveness.

This difference in styles was vividly illustrated in a college-level
communication class that Kochman taught. The class had 14 white and
eight African American students. As their final assignment in the course,
students were asked to talk with the other members of the class about
the communicative style each student had displayed during the class.
The assignment carried a potential that students might be offended; indeed, several students expressed concern about doing it. As a result,
Kochman had the class discuss the assignment. In their discussion white
and black students revealed different attitudes about

whether feelings or sensibilities should receive preemptive consideration.
Specifically the rights of those students who had something to say and
wanted to say it (whether others wanted to hear it or not) versus the rights

of students not to hear what others might want to say about them, irrespective of how much others wanted to tell them. The way the class divided on this issue was culturally revealing. Twelve of the fourteen white students argued for the rights of students *not* to hear what others might want to say to them—thus giving priority to the protection of individual sensibilities, those of others as well as their own, even if this might result in forfeiting their own chance to say what they felt. . . . The eight black students and remaining two white students, on the other hand, argued for the rights of those students to express what they had to say about others even if the protection of all individual sensibilities would be forfeited in the process. On this last point, one black woman said, "I don't know about others, but if someone has something to say to me, I want to hear it."[34]

Similar to African Americans, many Jewish Americans also value a high-keyed, animated emotional style, especially in discussion of issues and ideas. Disagreeing and arguing with people in a direct and lively fashion is often regarded as a good way to connect with people—it is "a method of sociability," in Schiffrin's words.[35] As with the other aspects of directness, when people have different preferences, interaction between persons is likely to be uncomfortable and even contribute to interethnic tension.

In a study of communicative exchanges between African American customers and Korean immigrant store clerks in neighborhood grocery stores in Los Angeles, Bailey[36] showed how the Korean and African American parties assigned radically different interactional meanings to the presence or absence of direct emotion expression. The Korean shop owners saw the African Americans high volume and use of profanity as inappropriate and rude. For them, the African American customers' failure to restrain self's expression was a sign of disrespect. But the African American customers also felt that they were being treated disrespectfully by the Koreans. For them, the lack of personal engagement (small talk) and absence of emotional involvement (signaled by eye contact, smiling, etc.) from the Korean shop owners conveyed contempt and lack of regard.

SUMMARY

In this chapter I have sought to paint a picture of both the complexity and the consequentially of conversational style differences related to directness. Style directness, we saw, arises from each speaker's selection and management of speech acts, several language practices, argument-making style, amount of small talk, and her degree of emotional expressivity. Styles are partly shared within speech communities. At the same time, each person has a style that is uniquely his own, reflecting how he has prioritized desirable but competing beliefs about the right and good ways for people to assert themselves and treat each other in interpersonal life. There is no single "right" style or correct way to prioritize values, even though we often act as if there were. My hope, though, is that a good understanding of how and why style directness and identity judgments are so tightly linked will help readers reflect about conversational options, choose more wisely, and be more tolerant of others whose choices seem irritating.

9

◈ Narratives

Around Christmas in 1996 a young girl named JonBenet Ramsey was found murdered in her locked home. The event had begun as a kidnapping where the parents had called to report their missing child, and to let the police know they had received a ransom note. After many hours of police presence in the home, JonBenet's body was discovered in the basement. The particulars of the case were bizarre and fascinating: JonBenet was a frequent beauty pageant participant, her mother was a former beauty pageant winner, the father was a wealthy businessman. A first version of the ransom note was found in the trash. Upon discovering the child's body, the family hired a PR representative and an attorney, and refused to speak further with the police.

The murder drew international coverage. Reporters from newspapers, magazines, and television flocked to Boulder, Colorado, the site of the murder, to have immediate access to information as events unfolded. News trucks and reporters were everywhere as police investigated. The media criticized the police for not adequately keeping the public informed. The police defended their actions. Then, a couple of weeks into the investigation, Chief of Police Koby agreed to an interview with four local reporters. The interview, broadcast over a local cable channel, was intended for the Boulder community. During the interview one of the reporters asked about the police's poor handling of the media and keeping information from them. Consider Chief Koby's answer, and particularly the story he recounts within it:

EXAMPLE 9.1. Boulder Police Chief's Interview

Well part of the comment about uh the public not having a right to know uh was taken out of context. What has happened in this investigation is this. That it is a, it is something that means a great deal to the Boulder community and that is why we are here tonight. So that we can have this conversation. Uh and that it can be heard in total and uncut by the Boulder community but . . . this situation is a curiosity to the rest of the country and quite frankly it uh, it is a sick curiosity in some ways. Ah to give you an example of that. *A call got through to me a couple of days ago from someone who lives out of state. And it was giggling and laughter and it was Chief, I was late in my office one night, it says, Chief, we're sitting around the table playing Clue and substituting ah th-, the situation for what you have in Boulder. Who was it du dut du dut du dut with the dut in this or that room? That's sick.* And uh so my reference is that there are certain things that everyone is, certain bits of information that every person is entitled to. And we have provided those uh pieces of information. And there are other pieces of information that the public is not entitled to know and doesn't need to know. And so it is simply a desire to have their curiosity satisfied. But it serves no purpose. And that is the information that I'm not going to provide to the public.[1]

Why did Chief Koby tell a story in this public interview? And why did he tell *this* story? What was the story doing for him and the police department? For Boulder citizens? For the reporters? In this chapter I begin by considering what makes a segment of talk a story. I then highlight several distinctive conversational practices employed within stories. Using the police chief's story as an ongoing example, I describe some of the key identity-linked functions of stories. I conclude by considering how the content of stories and storytelling practices differ across speech communities.

EVERYDAY NARRATIVES AND THEIR KEY FEATURES

The more formal name for stories, one used by scholars from a variety of fields, is **narrative**. Narratives include both written and oral forms. Some oral narratives are quite similar to written ones, as, for example, we see in the book-like tales told around a campfire. However, unlike their written counterparts, most oral stories are told to serve personal and relational purposes other than giving information and entertaining. In addition, oral narratives are produced in talk; as such, they must be occasioned and, at least to some degree, jointly produced.

Differences with Written Stories

In contrast to written stories that exist as whole units apart from any specific occasion, everyday stories need to be introduced into conversations; people cannot just launch into telling a story any time they wish.[2] This means that stories are either invited by a conversational partner, as exemplified in Example 9.2, or a speaker who wants to tell one makes a bid to do so (Example 9.3).

EXAMPLE 9.2.   Sample of Story Invitation

A: ((Upon meeting a friend whose face is scraped)) What happened to you?

B: Well, you know the roof I've been trying to patch? I was . . .

EXAMPLE 9.3.   Sample Conversational Bid to Launch a Story

A: You won't believe what happened to me today.

B: What?

A: Well I was walking to the train . . .

In certain kinds of institutional settings, such as the reporters' interview with Chief Koby, the invitation to tell a story is built into the situation format. Interviews by their very nature legitimize people giving extended answers. Typically, interviewees are asked to explain themselves or their actions. In such situations, then, an interviewee may launch a story as a piece of evidence to support a point he is making.

Not only must everyday stories be occasioned, they must also be jointly produced. In institutional settings such as interviews or presentations, these joint markers will be less visible, although even here at least a few will be present.[3] A story's **jointness** can be of two types. The first is the teller–recipient kind of jointness that involves one party telling and the other acknowledging and supporting that telling. At the most minimal level, recipients will produce simple tokens of listening ("hmm," "yeah," head nods). But recipients may also contribute responses that are more enthusiastic such as prolonged "Ohs,"[4] "Really?", small commentaries ("How awful?"; "She's incredible!"), or questions that probe for amplification of particulars in the story.

Though somewhat less frequent in everyday talk, a particularly powerful way to display that one is closely connected to another is for two people to tell a story together, chiming in with different details.[5] An example of a conarrated story is seen in Example 9.4 in which two dating, college-age couples (Shawn and Vickie, Matt and Nina) are having dinner together.[6] The group had just been discussing "going to church," at which point Shawn and Vickie launch a story:

EXAMPLE 9.4

S: I have to start goin' cuz I'm gettin' really tense.

M: Yeah

S: An that really calms you

N: Yeah it does. An it's like medication

S: I was goin' crazy today. On the- on the road

V: Well you know what he did?

S: Went out of my fuckin' mind

V: He made a right. It was in Santa Monica. You know have- the have

S: Oh shit

V: All those bright

S: I made a left- left,

V: They have one-way streets and everything? And then two-way streets? He made a left turn from a one-way street into a two-way street but he THOUGHT it was

S: But in the wrong lane ((laughs))

V: He thought it was a one-way street ((a few lines omitted))

V: He's traveling down

M: Wrong way?

V: The wrong way

S: All of a sudden this guy goes-[AAAAHHH AAAHHH

V: [And how much ( )
     cross the block

S: Very rushed cross the block, an I an I an I

V: AN I'M YELLIN SHAWN at SHAWN ((story continues))

Following Vickie and Shawn's story, Matt and Nina tell another story about a near-accident they experienced together. Everyday stories, then, are not produced alone, whether it be the full collaboration that we see in Shawn and Vickie's storytelling, or the more limited jointness that occurs when one person acts as the story listener. Oral stories are joint accomplishments. In addition, it is particularly common for the telling of one story to serve as the occasion for the telling of another. Stories frequently occur in rounds, where one story occasions another. Telling a second story is a good way for a listener to show she got the point of the partner's story or that she sympathizes and has had a similar experience.[7] It is also a way for a conversational partner to engage in some friendly competition on whatever has become the focus of conversation ("If you think that was bad, you should hear ... ").

What Makes an Everyday Story a "Narrative"?

In a classic article that first appeared in the late 1960s, Labov and Waletsky argued that stories about personal experiences were the simplest and "most fundamental"[8] kind of narrative. Typically everyday stories reconstruct self's and related others' experiences and can be characterized by three features:

1. The talk concerns a particular time when an actor experienced an event; often this event is a problem but it need not be.[9]
2. The event being told about is newsworthy—out of the ordinary and/or interesting in some way.
3. An evaluation of the event is conveyed.[10]

Let us consider what these features look like in Koby's story:

EXAMPLE 9.5. Chief Koby's Story

1. A call got through to me a couple of days ago from someone who lives out of state.
2. And it was giggling and laughter and it was Chief,
3. I was late in my office one night,
4. it says, Chief, we're sitting around the table playing Clue
5. and substituting ah th-, the situation for what you have in Boulder.
6. Who was it du dut du dut du dut with the dut in this or that room?
7. That's sick.

Koby begins by setting the scene, describing a specific time in the past (a couple of days ago), provides a bit more information to orient his listeners (he's working late in his office and gets a telephone call), and then he reports a problem (he received an obnoxious phone call from an "out-of-state" person). Similar to many everyday stories, but quite uncommon in written ones, we hear nothing about how Koby actually dealt with this event. Did he hang up? Holler at the people? Answer the question? To not include information about how a problem was handled keeps a story's point focused on the nature of the problem rather than, say, on the resourcefulness or reasonableness of the person to whom the problem occurred. Thus, Koby's talk manifests the first features of everyday narratives: it tells about a particular time where a person had an experience.

The second criterion, **newsworthiness**, also referred to as "reportability,"[11] is the hardest to assess in stories since what counts as "newsworthy" is very much a matter of judgment and it is not uncommon for people to disagree. At its simplest, though, to tell a story is to implicitly claim that one has something to say that deserves an uninterrupted lengthy turn at talking. Very few people, for instance, would judge Example 9.6 as deserving to be treated as an adequate story even though it includes both of the other features (an agent confronting a problem and an evaluation).

EXAMPLE 9.6

I went into the kitchen, got a bowl out of the cupboard. When I went to get a spoon, they were all dirty so I opened the dishwasher, took one out, and washed it. Then I opened the refrigerator and took out milk. I looked at what cereals we had, picked Cheerios, poured myself a bowl, and ate them. They were good.

Assembling breakfast is so ordinary a "problem" that few of us would think of this event as meriting the label. But if the narrator were only 3 years old and it was the first time he was doing this activity for himself, this story's content becomes imaginable as reasonable. In general, newsworthiness means that an event is at least a little out of the ordinary. The content of Koby's phone call certainly would qualify. Someone comparing a city's murder investigation to the board game Clue, and actually expecting the police officer involved to comment, would count as unusual by just about anyone's standards. In ongoing relationships newsworthiness often becomes tied to events that have led one or another party to have some kind of feelings, whether they be positive (amusement, happiness) or negative (frustration, boredom, anger), strong or mild.

The third criterion, **evaluation** of the event, is seen in Koby's explicit assessment of the out-of-state caller's actions ("that's sick"). Evaluations, however, do not need to be uttered explicitly. Quite often a speaker will leave it up to the listener to infer, by providing guidance through the way he tells the story, as to what the evaluation should be. Consider Example 9.7, and how a husband conveys his evaluation of his wife Connie's actions at a pub one evening and later that same night in their home. The story was told in a marital counseling session that included the husband, the wife, and the therapist.[12]

EXAMPLE 9.7

Connie had a short skirt on I don't know. And I knew this uh, may be I had met him, Yeh I musta met Dave before. But I'd heard that he was a bit of a lad. He didn't care who he chatted up (a few lines omitted) So Connie stood up pulled her skirt right up her side and she was looking straight at Dave like that. And then turned and looked at me. And then she said w-, turned and then back to Dave and said by the way that wasn't for you. (a few lines omitted) Then we went back to the house. Connie and, we all went back to the house at this point. Uh went back there'n I was si- um John and Caroline were together and Dave and Connie were sitting talking. I was sitting on the floor playing records. I sat there for two 'n a half hours. Uh no one come over. Not once did they. ANYthing. Just sat there talking. I was just completely ignored the whole time. (a few lines omitted) Uh I was boiling at this stage and I was real angry with Connie. And uh went up to bed 'n I lay on the bed, got in bed. I could hear giggling and all that downstairs and then the music changed, slow records. And then they changed to slow records. I could hear that Connie was dancing with this bloke downstairs. And Caroline turned around and said something about it. It was wha-, it was oh Connie look out, I'm going to tell Jimmy on you. And next thing I hear is, what he doesn't know doesn't hurt him.

In this story, the husband Jimmy is telling a story about an event that led to him throwing his friends out of his house, yanking his wife up the stairs, and throwing her on the bed. When people narrate events that made them feel angry, an evaluative dimension that becomes relevant is the reasonableness of the person's anger. That is, a judgment people make about their own and each other's anger—certainly in a therapy session but also in everyday exchanges—is whether or not it was reasonable. Because of this, the point of anger stories is often something like "The person [the other] who triggered my anger was bad," or, potentially, albeit less frequently, "I was silly, wrong, and acting unreasonably to get angry." In this story Jimmy does not make his evaluation of his own and Connie's actions explicit. Rather, his assessment is conveyed through the ways he describes particulars in the scene. Through the particular details he chooses to provide and to omit, he is framed as acting reasonably and Connie as acting inappropriately.

Consider how this is accomplished. Jimmy describes how he dealt with the anger he was initially feeling by going up to bed. The details of his story point to Connie as intentionally flirting with a man who did a lot of "chatting up" of women, and as Connie deliberately emphasizing and commenting about her legs and short skirt to Dave. When the group returned to Jimmy and Connie's home, Connie is described as coupled off with Dave and ignoring Jimmy for a long time (2½ hours). By describing himself as going up to bed while guests were still in his home, Jimmy implies that Connie should have known that he was bothered by her actions. Nonetheless, Connie is described as choosing to give no attention to her husband and staying with Dave "giggling and all that." In describing what the two were doing in this way, and especially with the inclusion of the final details—Connie dancing to slow music, her friend Caroline's warning that this action would make Jimmy mad, and the report of Connie's comment ("what he doesn't know doesn't hurt him")—one is left with an image of Connie behaving in overly flirtatious ways with a man who is not her husband. Simply put, through the way Jimmy describes the actions, the story conveys an evaluation that Connie was a bad wife, and Jimmy was reasonable to be jealous and get mad.

That Jimmy's story is his own evaluation of these past events and that others—in this case, Connie—might see things differently is evidenced when we look at what Connie initially said. Consider Example 9.8, in which Connie describes their marital problem to the therapist and her initial version of the same event that precipitated Jimmy's story.

EXAMPLE 9.8

Jimmy is extremely jealous. Extremely jealous person. Has always been from the day we met. You know? And at that point in time there was an episode, with a bloke in a pub, you know? And me having a few drinks and messin. That was it. Right? And this got out of hand. To Jimmy, according to Jimmy I was always doing it and you know always aggravating him. He was a jealous person. I aggravated the situation. And he walked out that time. To me it was totally ridiculous the way he goes on through this problem that he has.

Of note is that Connie describes the episode as involving a "bloke," which is a much more distant impersonal way to describe someone than using his first name. It implies a nonmemorable man with whom she spent an evening in a group. Her actions were "messin. That was it," the usual kind of play and joking that people in bars do. Perhaps she aggravated the situation a bit, she acknowledges, but through her description she strongly implies that her actions were no more than ordinary sociability. These simple sociable acts Jimmy reacted to as Connie's "always doing it" and "always aggravating him." In describing Jimmy as saying that Connie "always" aggravates him and "always" does it, Connie presents us with a person who reacts the same way regardless of the situation. Such a description implicates Jimmy as abnormally and unreasonably jealous, a man with a problem.

Narratives, then, are accounts of past events that convey a teller's point of view. The evaluation of the events may be stated explicitly or it may be built into the story and conveyed through particulars that are included or omitted, as well as by the language used to describe them.

Besides these features, a primary conversational device used to convey evaluation is reported speech. **Reported speech** is stating what self or another person said. It must be kept in mind, however, that it is unlikely to be an accurate replay. People are notoriously bad at remembering exactly what someone else said. Reported speech is a rhetorical device to present what one is uttering *as if* it were the exact words of self or another. In that sense, reported speech might better have been named "reconstructed speech."[13]

Reported speech is of two types: indirect or direct. When it is done indirectly, the gist of what was said is quoted generally. For example, if Jimmy had said at the end of his story, "then Connie told her friend, it didn't matter as long as I didn't find out," he would have been using indirect reported speech. In contrast, direct reported speech enacts what the other actually said. We see an instance of it at the conclusion of Jimmy's story, where he voices Connie's supposed words: "And next thing I hear is, what he doesn't know doesn't hurt him." One indicator of direct reported speech is the pronoun form. References to self in the third person (e.g., "what he doesn't know" said about self) mark a piece of talk as direct reported speech. Usually, too, a storyteller's intonation changes during the quoted other's comment. Another example of direct reported speech is seen in Koby's story (Example 9.1). Immediately before making his evaluation explicit ("That's sick"), Koby reports what the out-of-state caller said ("Chief, we're sitting around the table playing Clue and substituting . . . ").

Direct reported speech is an especially useful way to manage a dilemma frequently faced by storytellers. The dilemma is this: when people recount stories of troubles they have had with others, it is easy for their listeners to discount what they are saying as biased and self-serving, especially when a teller claims to be in the right and portrays the other as in the wrong. A way to manage this presentational dilemma is to recount what was said without offering explicit assessment. Using reported speech allows tellers to position their story as the truth of what happened: they are just "giving the facts" rather than a mere version, an opinionated view.[14] At the same time, through intonation and the emphasis given to certain words, and perhaps also in the choice of words selected to be reported, the speaker makes visible his or her stance toward what is being reported.

A final difference between oral narratives and written ones is that telling a story in everyday life always has a purpose. The answer to the question "Why tell this story to this particular person in this specific situation?" becomes a key part of the meaning of everyday stories. Consider, now, some of the major purposes accomplished by narratives.

FUNCTIONS OF NARRATIVES[15]

A story may often serve more than one purpose: Above its very referential and informative functioning it may entertain, be a piece of moral advice, extend an offer to become more intimate, seek audience alignment for the purpose of joint revenge, and serve as a claim as to "who I really am"—and all that at the same time.[16]

Argument Making

One common purpose for stories is to persuade others to think a certain way or to take a particular action. This, in fact, is the most visible function of Chief Koby's story. A reporter has asked a question that has accused the police of not doing something they have a responsibility to do—keeping the public informed—and also of having denied that they had that responsibility. In this context, Koby's story is a part of an argument that attempts to refute this accusation. His story, along with its surrounding talk, seeks to persuade his listeners (and viewers on cable TV) that the police management of information was reasonable. Stripped to its essence, his argument involves three moves: (1) a statement asserting that he believes the public does have a right to know certain kinds of information, followed by a claim that the Boulder police had released all those kinds of information and will actively work to keep the public informed; (2) a claim that there are certain kinds of information that the public is not entitled to know, a claim that Koby supports by telling the Clue story, which provides a vivid example of people wanting details that they have no right to get; and finally, and clearly the most subtle move, (3) an implication that much of the information that the media is after is of the "Clue story" variety rather than the legitimate kind. Koby concludes his comment by implying that the police will not be bullied into providing the media with this kind of information. In a nutshell, he ends his comment with a counteraccusation—it is the media, not the police, who are behaving inappropriately.

One reason to use stories rather than other kinds of evidence, such as research reports, statistics, or the testimony of experts, is because stories are highly persuasive. Psychologists have described this as the "vividness effect." Stories are memorable and affect emotions more than other kinds of evidence. This feature of stories, in fact, is both the advantage of and the problem with using stories as evidence. Stories say nothing about how typical an event is. If a conversational partner can make salient that a person's story is highly unusual and does not usually happen, one can direct others' thinking away from the conclusion that a story is seeking to argue for.

In Koby's comment, the story functioned as evidence for a claim he had explicitly articulated. However, stories may also be a claim and its evidence all wrapped up together. This practice, in fact, is quite common in families. Imagine a mother talking to her young son. At dinner she tells a story about an older neighbor who was just arrested for smoking pot ("You know what happened to Bill?"). The story recounts how Bill got into trouble with the police, what Bill has to do as punishment, and all the grief Bill is causing his parents. At one level the mom's story is providing newsworthy information about a person both parties know. It is informing. But if we think of the story as an argument, as a claim and its evidence bundled together, we could hear the story as the mom advancing a claim that it's bad to smoke pot and using as her evidence the story of what happened to Bill when he did. If her son is a relatively young child, we are especially likely to hear it as this general type of argument. Should her child be a sometimes-wild teen, the story is likely to be meant (and interpreted as) a more directed speech act.

Performing Speech Acts

If the son is a teen who does things of which the mother disapproves, the story quite possibly was meant (and interpreted) as a warning: something to the effect of "if you continue to do wild things and smoke pot, as I suspect you may be doing, you'll get arrested, hurt lots of people, and face all this grief too." The mother's story, then, is an indirect way to perform the act of warning. Of course, the son could always challenge his mother on the story: "Why are you telling me this story? What has this got to do with me?" And the mother might explicitly acknowledge that her purpose was to warn her son: "Well, I get worried and I don't want that to happen to you." Or, for any number of reasons, she may deny her intent to warn: "I just figured you might want to know what's happening with Bill." In the previous chapter we considered advantages and disadvantages of using an indirect style. In general, telling a story is a relatively common way to perform sensitive speech acts such as advising, criticizing, or reprimanding another. The story enables a speaker to do the sensitive action, but to do so in a manner that is not as straightforwardly taking responsibility for performing it.

Stories may also be used to perform interpersonally positive speech acts—for example, when a friend recounts to a third party a story of another person's accomplishment in front of that person. Or, more complexly, one person can invite another to tell a story about his or her accomplishment in the presence of an influential third party in hopes of eliciting the third party's praise. In middle-class American families, this is an especially common activity for mothers to do with regard to a child in front of Dad.[17] Example 9.9 shows what this kind of exchange looks like.

EXAMPLE 9.9

MOM: BJ, tell Dad what happened in school today.

BJ: Well, you know me and Jade are doing our science project together? Well we were working on making tables on the computer to put some of our results in. And Mrs. Edgar came by. She looked at what we were doing and said, You guys are gonna make our school proud. Biscayne is going to get all the awards.

DAD: Honey, that's wonderful . . .

In Example 9.9 BJ's story narrated her involvement in an activity that led to her teacher, Mrs. Edgar, praising her, which in turn, following the story's telling, led to her father complimenting her. Another function of BJ's story, then, by virtue of its particular content (it is about BJ herself) is that it presents her as a good student in science. In addition, although this single occasion would be insufficient to establish such an identity, the mother's command to tell the story rather than just waiting for BJ to do so altercasts the daughter as *modest*, a girl who needs to be nudged to talk about her successes.

Self-Presentational Devices

Like all talk, stories may be inspected for what they convey about a speaker.[18] But when the story that a speaker tells includes self as a character, a story is twice as informative. Consider what identities the following two narratives build. Each story was told by the same 13-year-old girl who had been away from home and had spent extended time talking on the phone at the hotel where she had stayed. Example 9.10 was told to a female acquaintance in school; Example 9.11 was told to her best friend (another girl) with two boys standing nearby who could over-hear.[19]

EXAMPLE 9.10

We were talking on the phone from the hotel . . . to this kid John . . . for 3 hours and the phone bill came up to $15, for one night, my Mom was like wicked mad at us.

EXAMPLE 9.11

When I was in Connecticut this weekend, my friends, we were staying for competition, right, and they met this boy, right, so they called him out from the hotel, and he was having phone sex with one of my friends, you know how they have phone sex, like, aw, you're wearing this, oh baby, you look so fine, you know, and all, they're having phone sex, I was sitting there, I was cracking up, I was like "no sir."

In Example 9.10 the girl's choice of *we* and *us* versus *my mom* presents her as aligned and in agreement with her friends against her mother who became mad at her for running up the phone bill. In essence, the brief story presents the girl as a typical American teen: a teen who aligns with her peers against adults. In contrast with the first story, in the second one she positions herself as an individual ("I," "my friends" vs. "we") and one who is not fully in agreement with her friends and all their actions ("I was like 'no sir' "). In addition, the content of her talks reveals her to be knowledgeable about sexuality and boys, a valued expertise among 13-year-olds, yet nonetheless a person who does not engage in these activities herself. In other words, the story presents her as *not the type of girl* who does this kind of sexual activity; it presents a view of her stance toward sexual behavior and does so in front of important others (boys and her best friend).

When a speaker tells a story in which she is an actor, she is presenting a picture of what she does (or refrains from doing) under some particular circumstances. Through the details of a person's action, a picture can be built up as to whether she is *trustworthy, fair-minded, a braggart, sexually loose,* and so on. Although tellers do not usually think about themselves as agents making moral claims, nonetheless stories do present speakers in a moral light.[20] This light need not be terribly bright but it is inevitably there.

If we examine Chief Koby's story we can see some of this moral work going on. Consider the significance of one detail that Koby provides in his story ("I was late in my office one night"). As story recipients, we did not need to know when the phone call came to make sense of the story. Yet this detail is important. It makes available to us the information that Koby is a police chief who works late into the night. Working long hours when there is a problem is a routine way to display that one is a serious and committed public official. Koby makes this identity available to listeners by including just this particular detail in the story.

Doing Relational Work

In addition to presenting who a speaker is, the stories people tell, as well as the way they are told, build two kinds of relational identities. First, whenever a person tells another person a story an implication is set in motion of the type "I see you as the kind of person who [would like/ needs to hear/etc.] this particular story" or "We have the kind of relationship in which a story of this type is reasonable to tell." That is, stories altercast their recipients as being particular types of others. For instance, the mother's story about her neighbor's pot smoking and arrest potentially altercast her teen son as someone who needs to hear a warning, and hence, perhaps, as a less-than-ideal child. Koby's Clue story may be taken as altercasting the media as unreasonable, requesting information that is *sick* and that they have no right to expect. It is also the case that Koby's story seeks to altercast the listening Boulder community as generally reasonable. By mentioning that the obnoxious phone call came from *out of state,* Koby implies that inappropriate, prurient interest is common to people outside the community and, by implication, is not a criticism he is directing at his most important audience (i.e., Boulder citizens).

In the 13-year-old girl's story in Example 9.11, the second story recipient is treated as a closer friend than the first one (Example 9.10). This is so because details about one's own sexual experiences, even as a bystander, are seen as a conversational topic that goes with a close relationship, a kind of story that is much less likely or appropriate between mere acquaintances. The selection of a story's topical content, then, can be inspected. Are stories about this kind of event something that one might relate to almost anybody? Or are stories on this subject only likely if the other is a same-sex peer, a family member, a coworker, or so on?

Second, as I noted earlier, joint storytelling, like holding hands in public, is a **tie-sign,** a way to mark that two people are close. Joint story-telling is not possible unless two people have been around each other for extended amounts of time. This sign of closeness may be displayed in a romantic couple, as we saw in Example 9.4 where Shawn and Vickie narrate their near-accident, or it may be manifested between close friends as Cheshire[21] observed among adolescent boys retelling their escapades to an interviewer.

Positioning the Narrator in an Ongoing Conflict

While many stories that people tell involve themselves as a key character, people also recount stories about events they have witnessed. One feature that generally makes an event newsworthy, and hence worthy of telling as a story, is that it relates to a conflict. Thus, if on my way to work I saw a protest occurring outside of a Planned Parenthood clinic, I might tell a coworker about it. I would do this because in American society actions that link to abortion can be assumed to be of widespread interest. In all likelihood my storytelling would allow my coworker to infer whether my sympathies were more with the pro-life protesters or with the pro-choice staff. In social scenes where there are different views of what is going on or what is reasonable, stories invariably position their teller as sympathetic or antagonistic toward one or another player in a conflict. Consider how the story told by a friend of Connie (Example 9.12) about the events recounted in Examples 9.7 and 9.8 might differ if told by a friend of Jimmy (Example 9.13).

EXAMPLE 9.12. Connie's Friend

You won't believe what Connie has been putting up with from Jimmy. The other night when they had some friends in their home, in the middle of the evening Jimmy stormed off and went up to his bedroom without so much as a goodbye. A little later he came down, threw everyone out and yanked Connie upstairs by her hair. He pulled so hard some of her hair came out. As usual the scene occurred out of the blue. Jimmy accused Connie of throwing herself at one of their guests when all she'd done was try to be friendly to a new acquaintance.

EXAMPLE 9.13. Jimmy's Friend

Connie has been at it again. I don't know why Jimmy stays with her. As usual she was dressed to seduce, a skirt that barely covered her ass. Some guy shows interest—surprise, surprise—and Connie, according to her, was quote/unquote, just being friendly. Connie invites this guy back to their home, ignores Jimmy and does one of her exhibitionist cling dances. Jimmy got mad but didn't really do anything. He should have tossed her out the door with her so-called friend and told her it was over.

These two stories position their narrators quite differently in relation to Jimmy and Connie and their marital troubles. The teller in Example 9.12 is sympathetic toward Connie and antagonistic toward Jimmy, whereas the teller in Example 9.13 is just the reverse. Many features of a story may contribute to a narrator's positioning, but two are especially important. A first feature concerns who is presented as the active agent and who is framed as the acted-upon other; the second involves labeling the actions that were taken. Are the actions conveyed by the verbs presented as morally reasonable or morally reprehensible? Contrast how Jimmy is portrayed in the first story compared to the second. Jimmy does things that require Connie to "put up with him," a colloquial expression that implies Jimmy is a troublemaker and unreasonable. Jimmy "storms out," "throws friends out," "yanks hair." In addition, by framing Jimmy's actions as the initiating ones and making Connie's role as an actor invisible, as well as explicitly mentioning how she had "done nothing," Connie is portrayed as the acted-upon victim and Jimmy as the nasty agent.

In contrast, the second story positions the narrator of Connie and Jimmy's conflict as being in Jimmy's camp. Connie is "at it again," dressing to seduce, inviting other men home, ignoring Jimmy, and "doing her exhibitionist cling dances." In addition, the storyteller described Connie's action in a manner that indicates skepticism of Connie's claimed innocence (e.g., with the comment "surprise, surprise" and the preface "according to her"). In this second version, then, Connie is portrayed as the active agent doing nasty things whereas Jimmy is the acted-upon innocent other.

In a rather different arena, Buttny[22] examines how positioning with regard to race relations worked in the stories college students of one ethnic group (black, white, or Latino) told to other members of their same ethnic group following viewing of a video about racism. By and large, white students tended to see minorities as exaggerating the frequency and damage of problematic race incidents on campuses, whereas students of color saw whites as ignoring everyday racism and not taking responsibility to combat it. When telling stories, whites and students of color told them in a manner that displayed which position (and group) they took to be more reasonable. Story positioning drew upon a number of different conversational practices, with the use of reported speech as a particularly prevalent one. Consider, for instance, a conversation among three Latinas. The video, *Racism 101,* had shown an incident is which an African American student had received a nasty racist letter. In a discussion that followed the viewing, C recounted the following story to her two acquaintances.

EXAMPLE 9.14. C's Story

The same exact letter was throw in my building, my dorm, and my friend was the RA and it was the worst experience that I ever had in my life. It was ridiculous the way the white students reacted, was like, *Well I didn't put it out.* And it became an individual thing. And it wasn't a matter of someone of my race offended you and something should be done and the students were taken out of the dorm.[23]

C's story positions herself as in alignment with how other persons of color are likely to assess race relations in the United States. By labeling white students' reactions as "ridiculous," and enacting a white student response ("Well I didn't put it out") that shows insensitivity and on unwillingness to take responsibility, C makes clear which party in this larger society conflict she sees as the more reasonable.

Stories, then, reveal alliances and antagonisms. The telling of a story about multiperson conflict becomes a way people support one person in the situation and criticize some others. It is also true that the way a recipient responds to a story about other people in which she knows both parties conveys whether the recipient agrees with the teller's assessment of events. For this reason, listening to a story where one feels equally connected to the person being portrayed as a bad agent or the helpless victim may be an uncomfortable situation. Such occasions may turn into at least a miniconflict between a teller and his or her listener as to what is a reasonable view of the narrated event.

Expressing Morally Questionable or Devalued Viewpoints

In most Western societies the expression of straightforward bigotry and prejudice against persons of nonwhite ethnic groups is frowned upon. In work or public sites it is unacceptable to use hostile names to reference other people's ethnic groups or to make comments about the stupidity, violence, inferiority, and so on of nonwhite ethnic/racial groups. Nonetheless, many white Americans and Europeans do have at least subtle prejudices toward one or another ethnic/racial group. Based on a two-country study (United States, Holland) of how racism gets communicated in ordinary talk, van Dijk[24] argues that stories are an especially common vehicle for expressing subtle prejudice. Consider the story that a white Dutch woman told when asked in a research interview to talk about experiences in her neighborhood:

EXAMPLE 9.15 (W = Woman, I = Interviewer)

W: But a (pause) long time ago, a Surinamese lady came uhh to the supermarket, which at that time was still on B-square.

I: Oh yes, that was (pause) yes

W: That was in the beginning

I: Yes

W: and what was it, I believe that it was still the Spar [supermarket chain] and that lady bought bread. She leaves the store and comes back and says, "I don't want that bread."

I: Hmm

W: Then the manager very POLITELY (pause) "Madam, we do not exCHANGE bread." No in Holland one doesn't exchange bread, do we? And no meat products either. Well after that the lady took on TERRIBLY, and the manager you know he tried to explain it to her, that bread cannot be exchanged here and in a very polite manner, after which the woman started to SHOUT, like, Don't touch me.

I: (pause) hmmmm

W: She throws the man that bread into his face, walks to the cash register and grabs two packets of Pall Mall.

I: Yes.

W: I still remember that very well.[25]

In this story a (white) Dutch woman tells a story about how a (black) Surinamese woman acted with a (white) Dutch manager in a store. The details of the story—throwing bread, shouting, grabbing—build an image of the woman in the store as dirty, aggressive, and unreasonable. At one level, one could describe the storyteller as merely recounting the kind of unpleasant episode that a person will see or experience with others in the course of living in a city. Anyone who lives in a big city is going to have negative experiences with others, and some of the others are likely to be persons of different races. But, as van Dijk goes on to show in his analysis, this particular kind of story—stories that remember and portray foreigners and nonwhites in negative ways—seem to be especially memorable for whites. Events that reflect negatively on persons of color are particularly likely to be remembered and retold as stories by whites in America and Holland. This, then, is how stories can be, although not necessarily are in any particular case, a subtle way to express racism.

In a rather different vein, narratives of personal experience are an effective way to advance the view that a strange and unusual event should be taken as believable and normal. In a study of tales of the unexpected, Wooffitt shows how stories about unearthly lights, objects moving, or visions of the future are told in ways that present the experiences "as the kind of thing that happens to people, and thereby as existing independently of the speaker's agency, actions and intentions."[26] This "normalizing of the strange" is accomplished by presenting a focal paranormal event surrounded by many highly ordinary particulars (e.g., "I was sitting in my living room watching TV"; "I was e-mailing a friend and having a cup of coffee") that nobody would doubt.

To sum up, stories simultaneously accomplish many different activities: they are useful for making arguments, and, in particular, for advancing questionable claims. They can perform a variety of speech acts, and are particularly potent ways to present the self or enact a relational identity, altercast the conversational partner as well as nonpresent others, and position self in an ongoing conflict. Consider, now, how stories and storytelling practices are likely to differ across speech communities.

CULTURAL DIFFERENCES

As with all facets of talk, storytelling is learned in the national, ethnic, and social class groups in which each person has spent significant amounts of time. As a result, stories reflect their tellers' communities. Cultural membership shapes both the content of stories and communicators' narrating style. As with other communicative differences, differing cultural styles may cause interactional trouble.

Story Content

An American professor was offered a job at a Dutch university. It was a wonderful opportunity to take on new challenges, so she accepted the job. As her stay lengthened, the Dutch students she worked with would ask her how she had come to find herself living away from the United

States. The professor would tell her story. Students would respond with "Oh" and immediately change the topic. The American professor wondered why her story received such a cool reception: Had she said something inappropriate?

The above event happened to Polanyi,[27] who went on to write a book about how the stories Americans tell are distinctive to their community. From a middle-class American point of view, there is nothing more natural than to narrate how one came to be in the line of work one is in, as well as in one's particular job. It is also the case that it is seen as typical and reasonable that people's professions will require them to leave their home communities and go to distant cities. Most middle-class Americans do not go as far as Polanyi did, but leaving family and friends to take a job is a rather routine life event. This is not the case in Holland, or for that matter, in most American working-class communities. To leave family and friends just for work is seen as a negative thing to do. Even if that were a person's main reason, it would be considered inappropriate to admit it. Admitting it would display a person to be callous and ambitious. In fact, the Dutch language has a word for people who act in this inappropriate manner. Polanyi's story was showing her to be a *vakidoot*, a one-sided academic grind who was only interested in her field.

From the Dutch students' point of view, asking a question about how Polanyi became a teacher in Holland was a way to show the American teacher that they had accepted the intimacy and informality that distinguished her classroom from those of many Dutch professors. But when she responded with her career story, her Dutch students felt Polanyi was rejecting them. In their eyes, the story seemed to be a refusal to give an honest answer, for the story she told could not be the real one.

What events can or should be narrated is a deeply cultural matter. Among Americans narrating how one came to meet and commit to the person who ends up being one's significant other is a kind of story people are expected to be able to tell on all kinds of occasions. In cultures in which two people marrying is less a matter of love and more a matter of family and material circumstances, this kind of story is less common.

Moreover, it is not just the general content that is culturally shaped but the stance a storyteller is expected to display self as having. In narratives concerning one's employment and professional choices, Linde[28] showed that middle-class American stories routinely portray selves as spontaneous, open to opportunity and the unanticipated events that happen in one's life—that is, narrators position themselves as not someone who had their career planned from the time they were 5. Portraying the self as a person who is following a life trajectory that is a tightly structured recipe is negatively assessed. At the same time, middle-class American storytellers work to show that they have arrived at where they are through hard work, determination, and focus. This balancing act not only shows that one is ambitious and works hard, but also seizes the moments that come along by chance in life, is not found as commonly in stories among other groups of Americans or other national cultures.

In Colombia a common content for everyday stories, visible but much less frequent in the United States, is the telling of *palanca* narratives.[29] *Palanca* is a Spanish word for a lever. A **palanca narrative** is about how one person used his or her influence to pry open a bureaucratic or institutional exchange to help another. Rather than primarily thinking of themselves as individuals, the more common way Americans think about self, Colombians think of themselves as a set of bonds to others. In Colombia the connections each person has with others are routinely acknowledged and celebrated. People tell stories about what others did for them and what they were able to do for others. Thus, the sheer frequency of *palanca* narratives in Colombian life points to a different view of persons than the view held in the United States.

Narrating Style

In studies of middle-class Americans, an interesting difference has been found between women and men.[30] In women's stories, people have names and do a lot of talking. In men's stories, there are more details about place, time, and objects; people more frequently are nameless and silent. Put another way, direct reported speech is a more common feature of women's than men's stories. This storytelling style difference is evidenced in boys and girls as young as 3–5 years of age.[31] One might conclude that this reflects that men value relationships less than women, but this would be an inaccurate conclusion. Cheshire[32] studied a group of adolescents (11- to 15-year-olds) and asked kids in same-sex groups to recount a real-world event. Cheshire found that the boys were much more likely to tell their stories jointly—chiming in, adding details, revising particulars—than the girls. Girls, in contrast, did more solo storytelling, thereby respecting the autonomy of each storyteller. Thus while there do seem to be differences between boys and girls, and between men and women, they do not support a simple generalization such as boys value autonomy and girls value connection.

Another kind of narrating style difference that has been found among different communities of Americans concerns how parts of a story are to be sequenced and connected. The difference, simply put, is whether a temporal linear organization is preferred over one in which a story is organized around a set of associated topics. The **temporal organization** is the one taught in schools and used more frequently by middle-class Americans. This style orders people and actions within an event along a chronological time line that is signaled explicitly (with words such as "next" or "then"). In contrast, the **topical style** of narrating offers a set of people and events that are linked in the teller's experience (often via emotional connections) and need not be ordered in a strict chronology. It also commonly uses vocal cues (stressing a word to signal a new unit) to create story links rather than using explicit words. The topical style has been found to be more common among working-class speakers of all races and ethnic groups, although particularly African Americans and Latinos.[33] An instance of the topical style is seen in Example 9.16, a story told by a 6-year-old black girl to her teacher during classroom sharing time. The teacher had instructed Deena to share one important thing.

EXAMPLE 9.16

D: In the summer, I mean w- when um I go back to school. I come back to school in September. I'ma have a new coat and I already got it. And it's um got a lot of brown in it. And when um, I got it yesterday. And when I saw it my um my mother was, was going somewhere. When my, when I saw it on the couch and I showed my sister, and I was reading somethin' out on the bag and my big sister said, my big sister said, Deena you have to keep that away from Keesha, cause that's my baby sister. And I said no. And I said the plastic bag because um, when she was with me,

T: wait a minute

D: my cousin and her-

T: Wait a minute, you stick with your coat now. I s-said you could tell one thing. That's fair.

D: This was about my coat

T: OK, alright, go on

D: this was-, and today, and yesterday when I got my coat my cousin ran outside and he, ran to tried to get him, and he, he he start, and when he get in, when he got in my house he layed on the floor. And I told him to get up because he was cryin'

T: mm- what's that have to do with your coat?

D: h- he because he wanted to go outside but we couldn't ((exasperated))

T: why?

D: bec- it um, because, I don't know

T: OK (chuckles) thank you very much Deena[34]

In this storytelling episode Deena was obviously frustrated. When the researchers interviewed her in her home to find out how she felt about her experience in the class, she described her teacher as not interested in what she had to say. Deena said, "She was always stoppin' me sayin' 'that's not important enough' and I hadn't hardly started talkin."[35] Deena's sister also mentioned that she had had the same frustration during sharing time 5 years earlier. For a speaker who assumes a story will have a temporal linear organization, Deena's story may sound incoherent. Deena's teacher apparently thought so. But talking with Deena in her home made it apparent that she had an organized story to convey. She wanted to tell about her new coat and the issue of protection. On the one hand, she needed to protect her baby sister from the plastic bag the coat has come in. On the other hand, she had to protect her new coat from the messy hands of her cousin. However, Deena's organization—associating these two topics—was not a recognizable style to her middle-class white teacher. As a result, the teacher interrupted her multiple times to question where she was going and to ask for details that took her in a different direction than she was thinking.

In schools, storytelling style differences can be highly consequential. For Deena and other children of working-class American parents, it is often the beginning of how they come to see themselves as not very good at what schools are all about. But this narrative style difference is not restricted to children. It plays itself out in differences among adults and what happens to them in important institutions.

In a study of small claims court where citizens stand before a judge to tell their story—their side of a dispute—Conley and O'Barr[36] observed similar differences. In general, working-class Americans, minorities, and women are more likely to tell stories in a topical-linked style, what the authors call a "relationally-based account style," than are middle-class, white, and male speakers. A linear story style in this setting attends to the rules of the courtroom and what is considered relevant in the setting. This storytelling style is more often used by middle-class whites or by male speakers. A topical storytelling style, Conley and O'Barr suggest, is one component that increases the chance of a judge's decision going against a speaker. Thus, how communicators narrate their lives and experiences shape what opportunities they are likely to have.

SUMMARY

Telling stories is a major part of everyday talk. People tell stories to accomplish things: to be seen in a certain ways; to give information; to disagree about an idea; to build, maintain, or sever relationships. Through a story's content, and a large set of stylistic design features, stories do complicated kinds of identity-work. Storytelling, then, is a major part of how everyday talk both builds and reflects identities.

◈ Stance Indicators

"Is Margarita just a friendly person or is she interested in me?"

"Is Roger skeptical of what I've said?"

"Why is she treating me as if I'm ignorant and know nothing about this?"

"Is he antagonistic or open-minded toward gays?"

In ordinary life we give considerable attention to figuring how other people feel about us (Does he like me? Think I'm smart? Believe I'm honest? Think she's better than me?). We also expend considerable energy trying to determine others' attitudes about views we hold dear. Having a reasonably accurate sense of how others regard us is personally desired and practically important.

There's a difficulty, though. For much of what people desire to know, it is problematic to ask straight out. "Do you think I'm smart enough to handle this new assignment?" is not a question people typically ask their boss. To ask such a question may imply either that one doubts one's own competence, doubts the boss's sincerity and goodwill, or both. Asking another for information is itself an informative action. The content and form of a question become fodder for others' inference making about the questioner. In addition, even if we ask and receive an answer, the answer might well prove difficult to interpret. Imagine how a boss might answer the question about being "smart enough":

EXAMPLE 10.1

1. "Of course I think you're smart."

2. "No, I don't" (with a laugh).

3. "Why are you so insecure?"
4. "Would I give you a job if I didn't think you could handle it?"
5. "No, I'm giving you a job that I know you'll fail at."
6. "Don't you trust me?"
7. "We'll find out, won't we?"

Responses could mean what they appear to mean on their surface, they could be ironic and mean the opposite, or they could raise an entirely new issue. Thus, because direct inquiry often is problematic, people will infer a key other's attitude based on a set of clues. Using clues to piece together what kind of person others *really* are, and how they feel about self, has the advantage of sidestepping potentially negative implications set in motion by explicitly asking questions.

Stance indicators[1] is the name we give to the clues used to infer what another person's attitude—his or her stance—is likely to be. Stance indicators may be particular words or phrases, the choice of one speech action over another, hand and facial gestures, tone of voice, the absence of talk, and so on. In essence, just about any aspect of communication can function as a stance indicator in some particular situation. **Stances**, then, are communicative displays of what are presumed to be, and often are, a person's internal state (e.g., being honest/dishonest) and his or her attitudes. We use the concept stance to highlight the communicative display of an individual, actions available for us to process through visual and auditory channels, rather than through focusing on his or her internal psychological state. Stances involve a complex mixture of signs that are given and given off, although particular stances may primarily be of one kind or the other. Another way to describe stance indicators is as the discursive practices that are especially implicative for personal and relational identities. Or, stated more strongly, a person is the stances he or she takes.

People display stances toward social situations (e.g., Is the situation boring or interesting? Formal or casual?), topics (e.g., Is a person involved or disinterested? Skeptical or believing?), the self (e.g., Am I confident or uncertain? Expert or novice?), and the other (e.g., Is one's conversational partner liked or disliked? Seen as equal, higher, or lower in status?). Stance indicators involve a relationship between a focal stance and one or more communicative practices (see Figure 10.1).

In the remainder of this chapter, I consider several issues regarding how stance indicators link to stances. I begin by looking at a family of stances (involvement, liking, disinterest, hostility), their assumed indicators, and the complexities that arise in linking the two. Then I scrutinize one particularly interesting stance indicator—the use of marked and un-

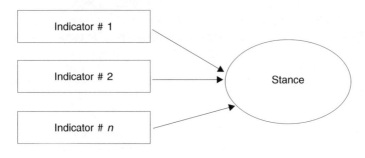

FIGURE 10.1. Relationship between a stance and its indicators.

marked forms—and consider the typical meanings of this indicator in several contexts in which it regularly appears. Finally, I look at a stance that is rarely, in Goffman's words, "given" but can be "given off": being dishonest (deceptive).[2] For stances that are negative and attributed by another person to a speaker—rather than sought by the speaker—the interpretive picture is especially complex.

INTEREST AND INVOLVEMENT (AND THEIR OPPOSITES)

A pervasive concern of most people is whether conversational partners are interested in them and what they are saying or the converse: disinterested or even hostile. Indicators of involvement are reasonably trustworthy; however, there are some complexities in interpreting them that are often not well recognized.

Stance indicators of involvement cut across communicative channels; high levels of involvement differ from lower levels in terms of vocal cues, facial and bodily gestures, and selection of particular discourse forms. Involvement typically goes with increased levels of physiological arousal. Thus the signs of physiological arousal tend to be taken as stance indicators of involvement.

Tannen[3] labels vocal cues of involvement **conversational signals**. When people are involved they (1) talk faster, (2) pause less frequently and for shorter times, (3) use a louder voice, and (4) are more vocally animated (i.e., use more variation in their pitch). Judgments about these vocal features are relative to a communicator's baseline talking style (e.g., how fast and loud does she normally speak?). In addition to vocal cues, involvement is also cued by gestures and facial expressions. Mehrabian[4] named the set of gestures that convey liking and interest **nonverbal immediacy**. Indicators include orienting one's body more directly toward another and leaning forward, gazing more frequently at the other, giving more smiles and nods, and increasing ordinary (non-hostile) touches. For both vocal and gestural indicators of involvement, a relatively low frequency (or low intensity on an indicator) compared to a person's average use is a sign of low interest or involvement (e.g., boredom).

In addition to the nonverbal indicators of involvement, there are also linguistic markers. In group situations, the telling of personal stories, especially lots of them, marks a higher level of involvement than offering abstracted and general statements.[5] Similarly, how turn taking is managed (e.g., How many instances of simultaneous speech or interruption occur?) conveys a group's relative degree of involvement (or lack thereof).

A person's language choices also convey something about how strongly he or she feels about an issue. Jay[6] has done a particularly interesting analysis of the links between anger (high involvement that is hostile) and cursing and obscenity. Table 10.1 offers an overview of some of the most common kinds of cursing and why they are offensive.

The terms noted in Table 10.1 are usually strong cues of hostility. Sometimes, however, if they are used by selected people in particular contexts, they can become terms of endearment or affection. The clearest example of this shift involves racial–ethnic terms. Although terms such as *nigger* and *wop* are insults when used by someone who is not a member of the group, they can become friendly address forms between members of the same ethnic group. Similarly, in certain communities terms such as *bitch*, at least when said with a certain intonation, may be meant as terms of affection.

Complexities in assessing involvement arise from different speech communities and individuals within communities having distinctive usual styles and degrees of expressiveness. In general, Europeans from warmer regions such as Greece and Italy (and American ethnic groups originating from these regions) have more involved conversational styles than communicators from cooler areas (e.g., Germany, Sweden). Thus, to accurately assess a conversational partner's level of involvement, one has to know that other well. The importance of having an accurate baseline for individuals is suggested by comments such as the following:

EXAMPLE 10.2

1. "He may look like he's excited but he's always that way. He just has a hyper personality."
2. "She really liked your idea. I know it didn't look that way, but she has an understated style. For her, she was bubbling over."

TABLE 10.1. Common Kinds of Cursing

Form	Examples	How they work
Cursing and profanity	God damn you, To hell with you	Curses embody attempts to harm a person; profanity conveys disrespect for religion.
References to subnormal thought	Dumhead, numbskull, jerk, moron, shithead, retard	These vary in offensiveness but all convey that the person has not thought carefully about his or her action.
References to sex organ	(To women): cunt	Accuses the other of promiscuous behavior or is used when the offended party hasn't received expected sexual favors.
	(To men): prick, cock, dick	Has done undesirable act.
References to deviant sexual act	Motherfucker, cocksucker, go screw yourself, take a flying fuck	Using generally taboo words to express strong disgust and anger.
References to being sexually violated	I was fucked over, what a ballbreaker, he was jerking us off	Social abuse is conveyed through reference to sexual abuse.
Racial–ethnic references	Spic, nigger, wop, taco, kike	When used by one group about another group conveys derogation.
References to animals	(To men): pig, jackass, turkey (To women): pussy, cow, bitch, dog	Seeks to reduce human; implies that the other is no more than an animal.

In sum, involvement (or its lack) and hostility are cued by a complex set of indicators. When all the indicators line up and one knows the other well, the stance indicators are especially reliable. If the indicators point toward different stances or one does not know the other person well, it is best to treat one's inferences as tentative, as no more than a best guess under problematic circumstances.

MARKED AND UNMARKED FORMS

A linguistic choice that gives information about a person's beliefs is the use of marked or unmarked forms. The idea of conversational marking is a broad one that can be applied to many different talk contexts. The main idea is this: **unmarked forms** reveal what a speaker believes to be typical, usual, or routine; **marked forms** reveal what a speaker regards as atypical, unusual, or uncertain. Unmarked forms are shorter and simpler than marked ones.[7] How marking is done is dependent on the conversational context. Let's consider three examples of how marking works.

Identities Expected to Go Together

Identities are typically understood to co-occur in certain patterns. When identities co-occur in the to-be-expected fashion, speakers referring to others usually leave the co-occurrence unsaid. For instance, if a white male judge came into a courtroom, a speaker recounting her experience is likely to say, "The judge came into the courtroom." But if identities are not what were expected, speakers often note that in their description. For instance, if the judge were a black male, the speaker might say, "The *black* judge came into the courtroom," or if the judge were female, "The *lady* judge came into the courtroom." Other examples include: (1) calling a female nurse "the nurse" and a male nurse "the *male* nurse"; (2) noting a person's sexual orientation only if the person is gay or lesbian ("my *gay* teacher" but not "my heterosexual teacher"); (3) describing a 20-year-old college student as "a college student," but a 35-year-old college student as a "*nontraditional* college student."

In talking about different kinds of Americans, the unmarked form ("American") is typically used when people are of European background. Others are usually referred to as "hyphenated" Americans ("Asian-Americans," "African-Americans") even when, as is becoming the more common practice (illustrated by my normal usages throughout this book), no hyphen is used. While it is possible to use a comparable form for Americans whose ancestors came from Europe (e.g., "Anglo-Americans" or "European-Americans"), it is much less likely to be used.

Of interest is the fact that when a speaker chooses to mark something that is usually unmarked it is taken as evidence that the person is critical of existing social practices. For instance, in a study about women friends, McCullough[8] described a woman as being at that point in the "conventional heterosexual life cycle" where she might be considering having children. This sentence will probably strike most readers as unusual. A feature of the woman's identity (heterosexuality) is marked (i.e., made explicit) that is usually left unmarked. A more expected sentence would have noted that the woman is at a point "in her life cycle" where she might be contemplating having children. In marking heterosexuality, the writer makes visible that differences in sexual orientation and lifestyle are typical differences among people. In essence, by linguistically marking a feature of personhood that is usually left unmarked, the author reveals her commitment to normalizing lesbian and gay lifestyles.

By examining what is marked versus what remains unmarked, we can gain insight into what is believed to be generally true about certain identities. This is nicely illustrated with Lakoff's[9] analysis of "mother" forms. The unmarked form of the word is *mother* but various marking options exist. A person can be a *stepmother,* an *adoptive mother,* a *biological mother, a foster mother,* an *unwed mother,* or a *working mother.* All of these markings point to what is taken to be the prototype mother—the ideal that is presumed. In essence, to use the unmarked form of *mother* suggests that the person is a woman who supplied her half of the child's genes, is married to the child's father, stays home to nurture the child, and is one generation older than the child. That the unmarked form makes assumptions about what is routine and to be expected is further illustrated when we generate utterances that mark one of the implicit features. Consider how unusual it sounds to describe someone as a *wed mother* or a *nonworking mother,* but how normal it sounds to hear another described as an *unwed mother* or a *working mother.*

The phrase *working mother* makes visible an interesting complexity of marking. Although marking is used for what is taken to be atypical, the atypical in an absolute empirical sense may actually be what is usual and commonplace. For instance, at this point in U.S. history, the majority of women who are mothers actually work. Thus, we have a case where an everyday talking practice has not caught up with the societal change in employment patterns.

Being Knowledgeable or Ignorant

A second application of the idea of conversational marking is in question formulations. One identity at stake when a person asks another a question is whether the question asker sees the recipient as knowledgeable. Question formulations cue whether the other is presumed knowledgeable or is seen as not likely to know. For instance, the unmarked form of asking directions would be short and simple: "How do I get to the UMC?" Marked forms would be ones that recognized that the recipient might not know the answer: "*By any chance* could you tell me how to get to the UMC?" or "*I was wondering, do you know how* to get to the UMC?" Of interest here is the fact that either the marked or the unmarked question option could be appropriate. Put another way, selecting a marked form or using an unmarked option may yield smooth communication or cause problems. Whether problems occur will depend on the match between what a recipient knows and whether a marked or unmarked form is used. If a questioner's utterance presumes that the other will or should know something—that is, the unmarked form is used—and the question recipient does not know, she may feel embarrassed. On the other hand, if a question asker uses a marked form—thereby implying the other's possible lack of knowledge—and the question recipient does know she may feel insulted. To be treated as a novice when one is knowledgeable generally offends people.

In a study I did of a discussion group in a university department,[10] I examined how the use of marked and unmarked question forms were consequential to the graduate students and faculty members participating. The departmental discussion, which the group referred to as their "colloquium," was a weekly meeting that brought about 15–20 students and faculty together to talk about research projects. Each week one person would present what he or she was working on for the first half of the meeting; then the group would question the presenter and discuss the research. In this setting, participants wanted others to evaluate them as smart and intellectually creative, and they were concerned that others might not see them this way. One graduate student described his identity concerns during participation in the colloquium in this way:

EXAMPLE 10.3

I was very worried that I might say something and it would show that I didn't grasp everything . . . just worried about general issues, uh how I look and do I seem like a bright individual and have something to say, have original thoughts, any knowledge of well the field or just general classics? Or am I just a person who snuck in here and we're going to have to weed him out because there's really nothing upstairs.[11]

Being knowledgeable is key to most institutional roles; it is something people care deeply about. Salespeople seek to know their product; instructors, what they teach; managers, how their workplace functions; computer programmers, about software; and so on. Part of each individual's sense of whether coworkers regard him or her as good at his or her job or incompetent will depend on how questions are posed.

Belief, Skepticism, and Neutrality

A third application of the notion of conversational marking applies to the stance one takes toward what another has said. Do communicators respond to others as if they believe them or do they seem to be skeptical?

In situations where a person is involved with multiple communicators offering different versions of events, we might be concerned about whether a person is neutral (or not) and how that stance is displayed.

Perhaps the most frequent situation in which people convey skepticism is when they are reporting what another person who is not present said to them. Imagine a conversation between a wife and husband where the wife is reporting that their babysitter called to say he could not make it. Consider the following formulations:

EXAMPLE 10.4

1. Teddy can't make it tonight because he's come down with the flu.
2. *According to Teddy*, he's not going to be able to babysit because he has the flu.
3. *Teddy's story* for why he can't babysit is that he's coming down with the flu.
4. Do you want to hear a good one? *Teddy says* he's getting the flu and that's why he can't babysit.

In (1) the wife gives Teddy's reason for not coming. By not including any markers she conveys the idea that she believes Teddy's story: she has taken what Teddy told her to be true. In the other three cases (2–4), the wife suggests her skepticism by adding certain phrases. The most common markers of skepticism, according to Pomerantz[12] include (1) referencing what another said as "his story" or "his version"; (2) using modifiers like "supposedly" and "allegedly"; (3) highlighting that something is a report rather than a description of the world, for instance, by prefacing a description with the phrase "according to Teddy," "Teddy says," or using the phrase "quote, unquote" to report another person's words; or (4) juxtaposing two pieces of information that are assumed to be incongruous, for instance, if the wife had said, "Teddy called to say he won't be able to babysit because he has the flu. After his call I went to the mall to pick up some things and guess what? I saw him in the food court hanging out with a bunch of friends," she would make visible to the husband her skepticism about Teddy's reason for stating that he could not babysit.

These devices are available for direct use as well. A supervisor could say to a late employee, "What's your story this time?" Such a query not only conveys skepticism regarding what the employee is saying right now, but may also be taken as accusing the employee of a pattern of dishonesty. In other words, being directly skeptical may have relational consequences that a speaker does not wish to incur. It seems likely that there are many other ways to indicate skepticism, some of which are very subtle. Undoubtedly how skepticism is marked will depend on the topic and one's relationship with the other.

One especially interesting twist can be seen for the topic of paranormal experience. Although people are generally expected to believe each other and hence to mark when they do not, there are certain topics where this does not apply. In Western societies where science is highly valued, people are expected to be skeptical of paranormal reports.[13] Thus when people report paranormal experiences, they usually do considerable work to frame their experience as reasonable. In essence, when we move to the context of the paranormal, we see a flip in what gets marked. Whereas for most everyday situations belief is usually unmarked, for reports of the paranormal it is belief that requires elaborate explanation and accounting.

Conveying belief or disbelief becomes more complicated when there are more people and multiple stories involved. People whose job it is to intervene in conflicts and sort out competing stories—for example, marriage counselors, mediators, and judges—need to do significant work to show that they are impartial and neutral, not privileging one person's account over the other's. What the conversational work will be that accomplishes displaying this stance will vary with the interactional identity, and usually will involve more than conversational marking. Of note is that in an institutional context, such as mediation, use of the markers noted above may convey neutrality rather than skepticism. For instance, consider if a mediator in working with a divorcing couple about child custody arrangements said:

EXAMPLE 10.5

According to you [nodding to the husband], you were there and waited an hour to pick up Jessica, and Mary didn't show up and hadn't notified you. And according to you [nodding at wife], you called Bob the night before and let him know you would be an hour later.

In this context, use of the phrase "according to you" marks that the mediator recognizes that what each person is saying is a version of the truth, and thereby indicates neutrality. When multiple stories are part of the situation, such as is the case in a divorce dispute, and the speaker is not one of the disputing parties, then a stance indicator shifts its meaning, cueing a different, albeit related stance: in this case, neutrality.

The use of marking, then, does different things depending on what is being marked. In responding to others' comments, the use of marked forms conveys either skepticism or in certain contexts neutrality. In questioning, the selection of marked forms conveys that the other is seen as not likely to know what is being asked. For identity references, marked forms show that a communicator regards another as not the usual kind of person for the role she is in. In almost any conversational situation, the notion of marking can be applied. Unmarked forms are used for states of the world and attitudes that people take to require no comment. Consider now the complexities that arise when the stance of interest is one people typically seek to *avoid* displaying.

STANCE INDICATOR WITH MULTIPLE MEANINGS: DECEIT?

Virtually no concern is more critical in ordinary relationships than determining if another is being honest with us. Whether a person, as she says, *really* likes a painting, a cake, or a football player may be inconsequential, but for other matters honesty and being believed matter immensely. If Alicia is asked by her roommate whether she borrowed an item belonging to the roommate, if she is asked by a police officer whether she was driving when an accident occurred, if her significant other asks her if she has been seeing other people, honesty is likely to matter. The roommate, officer, and significant other will care if Alicia is telling the truth, and may reflect about how probable it is that she is telling it. Alicia also will care if others believe her and will interrogate their responses for signs of skepticism.

Because of its significance in intimate and institutional life, deception has been extensively studied.[14] Most studies have been done in laboratory settings where a researcher knows in advance if someone is lying or telling the truth. Usually, unlike everyday life, the matter being lied about is not consequential to the participants. There is nothing at stake for lying: in fact, to lie is to be cooperative and do what an experimenter has requested. Neither of these conditions applies in ordinary interaction, which creates problems in interpreting what laboratory results can tell us about everyday interaction. In addition, deception research "often overlooks the role of the interrogator's language in the suspect's response. A question asked with skepticism tends to increase eye-blinks, hand gestures and response length more than probes that convey that the interviewer believes them."[15]

Ekman[16] identifies a large set of contextual features that will affect the ease with which one person will be accurate in assessing whether another is lying. Included, for instance, are factors such as whether the person trying to assess the truth needs to conceal suspiciousness from the other, the consequences of being caught in a lie, and whether the topic one is questioning the other about is inherently emotional. Sorting out when nonverbal cues signal general emotionality rather than deceitfulness is especially complicated. Table 10.2 indicates some of the nonverbal behaviors that have been taken to be indicators of deception and what Ekman has concluded that they actually reveal. The stance linked to these behaviors could be deceit, as deceit is likely to go with these emotions, yet the indicators cue something much broader than deceit.

The issue of honesty and deception is especially salient for law enforcement agencies. Personnel are routinely given training to help them assess whether a suspect is being honest or deceitful. In addition to being sensitized to interpret the kinds of nonverbal behaviors noted in Table 10.2, police and FBI interrogators are trained to look for suspects' usage of certain talk patterns (see Table 10.3).

All the markers in Table 10.3 could be indications that a person is being deceitful, but all of them could have other meanings as well. Hedging, for instance, is a common practice among academics. Besides indicating that a speaker is deceptive, or uncertain, hedges can be used to mark a communicator as careful and precise, as someone not given to overgeneralizations. Shuy, a linguist who is frequently called to testify as an expert witness about tapes and transcripts of people's testimony, had this to say about lists of markers like those in Tables 10.2 and 10.3:

> As much as it is attractive to believe that specific language features associate with deceit, there is simply not enough proof of this to justify using them. I have been asked many times by zealous prosecutors, whether I can

TABLE 10.2. Stance Indicators of Deceit and Most Probable Meaning[17]

Nonverbal behaviors	Information revealed
Raised pitch	Negative emotion, possibly anger, fear, or both
Lowered pitch	Negative emotion, probably sadness, boredom, or both
Frequent swallowing	Emotion, not specific
Increased blinking or pupil dilation	Emotion, not specific
Facial reddening	Embarrassment, shame, anger; maybe guilt
Fewer illustrators (hand gestures that accompany talking)	Boredom, unprepared, weighing each word
Increase in adaptors (gestures of touching self and playing with objects)	Negative emotion

TABLE 10.3. Some Potential Verbal Markers of Deceitfulness[18]

Providing overly detailed statements and referring to self excessively

Repeating and correcting oneself spontaneously

Complicating a story unexpectedly

Giving unusual or marginally relevant details

Admitting memory loss

Hedging

Pausing excessively

Using a more limited vocabulary than expected

tell if a speaker is lying. I answer, quite candidly, that I cannot. But most liars are not good at prevarication, especially during complex and pressure-packed interrogation by law enforcement officers. They tend to slip up somewhere and become inconsistent. When they do, they can get caught in their inconsistent language.[19]

People do not generally seek to be seen as deceitful—it is a personal identity to be avoided. Thus, when people lie—at least where it is inappropriate to do so—they will work to come across as telling the truth. It is also the case that every marker of deceitfulness, whether it be verbal or nonverbal, has at least one plausible alternate meaning. This means that figuring out if another person is being honest is inescapably a difficult judgment. Moreover, in relationships with close others and at work where some degree of trust is taken to be reasonable, to push another person to figure out if he or she is *really* telling the truth may cause more problems than having the information would solve.

SUMMARY

In this chapter I have examined a small set of stances and their indicators; there are many more. Stances are tied to features of personal identity: who a person is, what attitudes she has, how he views others. When viewed rhetorically, the communicative lens of "stance indicators" leads us to consider what conversational practices communicators should select (or avoid) to convey desired character traits and attitudes. When viewed culturally, we are led to remember that personally important stances (e.g., displaying *honesty, respectfulness,* or *interest*) are prioritized differently in different speech communities and may rely on different indicators.

PART IV

The Conclusion

11

◈ Final Thoughts

Endings are communicatively challenging, difficult to get just right. Although they are an ordinary part of every activity, people invest them with extraordinary significance. This is so whether the ending involves an individual encounter, moving away from home, or finishing a book. What the challenges are, of course, varies with what is being ended. For books, authors are expected to end on a thoughtful, interesting note that underscores as well as draws out the implications of the main points they have been making. Toward this end, I offer five final thoughts.

LITTLE STUFF AND BIG EFFECTS

The aspects of discourse that we have been examining in this book could be glossed as "little stuff." We have looked at small thises-and-thats in everyday talk. The words we use to address people, whether phrases such as "sort of," "maybe," or "I don't normally think X, but . . . " are included in our assertions, the content of oral stories and whether stories include interpretations of other individuals' words, a speaker's tone of voice and pronunciation, overlapping speech, whether there are a lot of "uhs" and "ums"—all of these can reasonably be referred to as "little stuff." In the sense that *little stuff* refers to small units within talk, this book has primarily been about little stuff.

There is another meaning of *little stuff*, though. Little stuff is a polite way to name something that a person regards as trivial and unimportant. Little stuff is what can be ignored without harm, as long as attention is given to "big stuff." I hope that the reason this second meaning of little stuff should not be applied is clear. The little stuff we have concerned ourselves with in this book is the bricks and mortar for building selves of one type rather than another. It is the basic ingredients for building and maintaining relationships with those we love and with the people with whom we work and play. This little stuff is the lubricant that keeps public, social, and service encounters moving smoothly. At the same time, it is this little stuff that gums up the works. Little stuff causes hostility, high emotionality, and, at times, conflicts that result in violence.

My aim in this book has been to make the little stuff that so often slips by unnoticed become harder to miss. By providing my readers with a vocabulary to help them notice and analyze ordinary interaction, I have sought to make a more thoughtful kind of reflection possible. Little stuff often has big effects. This book has been about why that is so, and how the inferential connecting process works.

MULTIPLE COMMUNICATIVE GOALS AND DILEMMAS

Talk is both interesting and difficult because communicators have multiple goals that may be challenging to achieve together. When the goals are strongly or completely in tension, a communicator will face a dilemma. Communicative dilemmas arise when different facets of a person's, or group's, belief about how to be a good *fill-in-the-blank* point toward opposite communicative actions. Whatever conversational moves a person chooses, he risks being criticized for not enacting some other valued part of that particular interactional identity. With regard to academic advisors, we saw how their concerns to be both fair gatekeepers and personally helpful pulled their way of talking in opposite directions. In close relationships people constantly juggle being warm and caring but not intruding, building connections but respecting autonomy. We looked at how a dilemma surfaces whenever a person thinks about giving advice to another. Dilemmas are endemic to communicative life.

One dilemma that has been given a lot of attention, and one that I have touched on only indirectly, is the expertise–equality dilemma.[1] The expertise–equality dilemma confronts people in many professional positions. Being a professional is all about having some very particular expertise. Having expertise licenses a person to offer extended information and opinions; it also makes the directing and correcting of others necessary and reasonable. At the same time, many professional work settings define themselves as committed to democracy and equality: doctors and nurses seek to give patients a voice in the system, teachers strive to empower students and encourage them to speak out. Being committed to democratic participation suggests that everyone, not just the experts, is to be treated in a respectful appreciative way (i.e., not discounting any-one's opinions). The dilemma is that the conversational moves that es-tablish expertise are the same ones that may undermine equality. And similarly, moves that affirm equality may undercut one's expertise and right to direct. For teachers, Billig and his colleagues describe the di-lemma this way:

> Within the classroom the teacher is the constituted authority with direct power over the pupils. Yet this authority is not maintained in an authoritar-ian manner. Instead . . . the teachers use democratic semantics: "we" dis-cover things together, rather than "I" the authority, tell "you" the already discovered facts. It is as if the teacher and the pupil have set sail together on a voyage of discovery. Having left the port, the teacher has come down from the ship's bridge and has discarded the old-fashioned uniform with its golden epaulettes of command. Now teacher and crew are gathered on the ship's deck, discussing freely where to head for. Yet authority has not been totally abandoned. For all the discussion, the passage has already been charted. The teacher still possesses the navigational maps, the compass and the power to ring the ship's bell. Even on the deck the teacher must direct the crew, and thereby the ship, but must do so without appearing too direc-tive.[2]

Professionals, then, face a dilemma. Those who are too tentative in directing others may be seen as wishy-washy or judged incompetent; those who are too direct in their style will be judged authoritarian and lacking in "people skills." Steering a communicative course clear of both of these negative identities is invariably difficult. Dilemmas, then, are part-and-parcel of everyday life. Recognizing that this is so is likely to foster an interpretive generosity: making it possible to forgive others, as well as ourselves, for less-than-ideal choices about the handling of a situ-ation.

TALK AND INSTITUTIONAL IDENTITY

Throughout this book I have focused on how talk builds and reflects identities for individuals. But people are not the only entities that have identities; groups and institutions do too! Identity and identity-work could be usefully extended to groups. If we did so we would ask how a group's way of talking contributes to its unique institutional identity. Consider but one example.

Hospice, now a well-established institution, began as a social move-ment to make the process of dying more humane than it usually is in hospitals. Hospice is committed to addressing patients' and families' psychological and spiritual needs as well as their physical ones. As an institution hospice defines itself in contrast to mainstream medical institutions. What does this mean? How do hospice staff use talk to build their group's identity as alternative and caring?

In a study of team meetings in a hospice located in the western United States, Naughton[3] found that the hospice team used a variety of small practices to enact itself as an alternative health care organization. Team meetings, a once-a-week event, brought the staff together for a several-hour meeting. The purpose of weekly meetings was to discuss patients' physical condition, their medications, and their difficulties with caregivers. During the meetings, a common conversational practice that occurred was the making of off-the-agenda, third-party comments (personal remarks about a nonpresent party), most often about a patient but sometimes a patient's family member. Third-party comments were largely positive (e.g., "a lovely couple," "she's a dear soul," "I just love her"). According to the authors,

> These positive comments . . . are one important way hospice professionals display their commitment to an institutional philosophy that commits them to care for the mind and soul of patients in addition to their bodies. . . . It was through making comments such as "he's a charmer," "such a dear" and "so sweet," that hospice staff members enacted themselves as caring professionals, people who saw a patient as a "whole person," as more than a malfunctioning physical organism.[4]

The notions of identity and identity-work that have been central in this book could be applied to institutional groups and families. Moreover, posing questions about identity and identity-work at a group level could be expected to make visible discursive practices that differ from the individual speaker ones that have been my focus here.

SEEING DOUBLE: A GIFT, NOT A DISTORTION

In seeking to understand how talk and identities link, I have drawn on two perspectives. The first perspective has been the rhetorical one. In taking the rhetorical perspective, I recognized that talk is strategic, chosen, and designed to accomplish certain ends and avoid others. Mediators use certain phrases to present themselves as neutral and impartial; speakers in conflict change their accent to emphasize difference from their partner. Storytellers use reported speech to show that they are not being unfair in their description of a conflict with another. Bilingual speakers shift languages to indicate that they mean to be playful rather than serious. The rhetorical perspective is also one that adopts an evaluative stance; it leads us to think about the moral reasonableness and practical effectiveness of different sets of everyday talk choices.

The second perspective I have taken in this book has been a cultural one. In adopting the cultural view, I focused on how everyday talk reflects communicators' identities. Persons of different master and interactional identities will talk and interpret in systematically different ways: Israeli differing from American, men from women, Native Americans from Anglos, teachers from students, older speakers from younger ones, and so on. In adopting a cultural perspective, I treated identities as relatively stable things, existing prior to particular conversational moments, and brought to interaction. I considered how people with different identities were likely to talk and interpret differently.

In adopting a rhetorical perspective, I gave weight to one truth: that each person's choices about how to talk build her unique identity. Each of us can become what we want to be through reflecting about talk and choosing wisely. In adopting a cultural perspective, I gave weight to an alternative truth: that how people talk is stable and not easily changed. People are shaped, one could even say, imprinted, by the communities in which they are born, spend time, and acquire beliefs about how to be a reasonable person. Recognizing these contradictory truths, I suggest, is an essential part of understanding everyday talk.

COMMUNICATIVE EFFECTIVENESS AND PHRONESIS

My focal purpose in writing this book has to foster a better understanding of how everyday talk works. Good understanding, as I have conceived of it, is having a nuanced view of the communicative complexities that inhere in ordinary situations and relationships. With a rich picture of what is likely to be at stake in an everyday talk occasion, it is possible to choose more wisely. There is no algorithm for communicative success; quick fixes that always work do not exist. Yet it is possible for people to become wise situational judges and skilled communicators. Communicating wisely, what Aristotle called **phronesis**,[5] can be cultivated. Through opening up how situations and relationships might be thought about differently, and making the little stuff that achieves the big effects visible, this text has sought to increase your ability to choose wisely, to interpret others' actions generously, and to communicate skillfully.

Notes

CHAPTER 1

1. There is no politically neutral language to write about talk and identities. Choices about how to refer to persons always carry a potential to offend. Many everyday terms imply that something is common (or unusual) about a particular category of people. At the same time, less common forms of reference draw attention to themselves, potentially irritating readers and leading to judgments that an author is going overboard and being "politically correct." Throughout this book I have struggled with this tension. For instance, this opening vignette describing speakers as "sounding American" may be taken as implying that non-native-English speakers are not as fully American as those for whom English is their birth language. I do not believe this (see Chapter 6 and my discussion of the link between English language use and American identity). In this case, however, I have selected the everyday way of describing people since it is just this linkage that I want to highlight.
2. See, for instance, Antaki and Widdicombe (1998), Fitzgerald (1993), Tracy and Naughton (1994), and Ochs (1993).
3. See Grice (1975). This article is also available (Grice, 1999) in an edited reader that brings together classic pieces, such as this reprinted chapter, with more recent studies that illustrate the variety of discourse analytic research (Jaworski & Coupland, 1999).
4. See Grice (1999, p. 79).
5. See Grice (1999, p. 78).
6. The idea that the utterance is the basic unit of speech was first proposed by Mikhail Bakhtin (Morson & Emerson, 1990).
7. Goffman (1959).
8. See Gumperz (1982a, 1982b). In Gumperz (1992) this idea of contextualization cues is developed in more depth. A recent review of some of the key ideas of interactional sociolinguistics, the name of the discourse approach he has developed, is to be found in Gumperz (2001).

9. Gumperz (1982a).

10. How best to distinguish communicative levels is an issue that scholars do not completely agree about. Different writers have used different terms to capture what they regard as most essential. Watzlawick, Beavin, and Jackson (1967) distinguish between the content and relational levels of a message; Searle (1969) separates the locutionary (propositional content) from the illocutionary force or speech act level; Tannen (1986) differentiates the message from the metamessage and the frame; and Bate (1988) distinguishes what's said from what's meant.

11. Whether to assume that meanings are usually shared and it is the exception when they are not, or the reverse, is an issue about which scholars differ. Circourel (1973) has argued that people generally assume they have a reciprocity of perspectives. Although I think Circourel's claim is reasonable—people generally do assume this—I think it is a problematic assumption. Being constantly aware, as Bakhtin (cited in Morson & Emerson, 1990) would advocate, of both the centrifugal and the centripetal forces of language and talk is crucial.

12. Tannen (1993b, 1993c) reviews different approaches to the concept of frame. The notion, initially developed by Bateson (1972), was elaborated by Goffman (1974).

13. Examples 1.4 and 1.5 are taken from Erickson (1999, pp. 116–117). The transcript has been simplified. Pauses and information about breath groupings were eliminated and punctuation was added. The preceptor (P) in the original transcript has been changed to S.

14. Erickson (1999, p. 123).

15. Erickson (1999, pp. 124–125).

16. See Erickson (1999, p. 136).

17. Brubacker and Cooper (2000) provide a nice review of the ways social scientists have used identity. They argue that the term is used in too many different ways to be useful. I disagree. There is some commonality across the multiple meanings. It is the particular pattern of diverse meanings and what unity the term possesses that makes it useful. A view of identity that has some similarities to the one I develop is seen in the anthropologically linked work of Holland, Lachiotte, Skinner, and Cain (1998). Drawing on Bakhtin and Vygotsky, they argue for a view of identity that weaves together the stable structuring forces of culture and a social constructive, agentive role.

18. See Billig (1987).

19. See Billig (1987, pp. 203–204).

20. There is no single way to conceptualize and categorize types of identities. The label "master" is adapted from Harvey Sacks's use in his lectures (1992). The label "interactional identities," my own, collapses a distinction that Zimmerman (1998) makes between situated identities (roles such as teacher and student) and discourse identities, the names for situated activities within a situation (e.g., presenter, discussant, questioner). Based on an analysis of African American communication, Hecht, Collier, and Ribeau (1993) develop a community theory of identity that identifies four layers of

every transaction. Elsewhere their theory is applied to being Jewish (Hecht & Faulkner, 2000).

21. See Goffman (1955). This same article is also published in *Interaction Rituals* (Goffman, 1967).

22. These three distinctions are ones that Lim and Bowers (1991) make. Their three-part distinction builds on the one developed by Brown and Levinson (1987) between positive and negative face. *Positive face* is the desire to be appreciated and approved of, *negative face* is the desire to be free of imposition.

23. *Discourse* is another term that is rich in meaning, potentially referring to units of writing, and even to pictures and graphic layouts. When it is used in the plural (*discourses*), it usually refers to a large and complex set of practices rather than to a specific unit of talk (e.g., the discourses of education). Cameron (2001) does an especially nice job of unpacking the complexities of this term in an accessible manner.

24. In the last several years a number of books have appeared that introduce students to how to do discourse analysis. See, for example, Cameron (2001); Wood and Kroger (2000); Wetherall, Taylor, and Yates (2001a, 2001b); and Gee (1999).

25. I adopt this term from McCall and Simmons (1966). It was initially used by Weinstein and Deutschberger (1963).

CHAPTER 2

1. Rhetoric is by no means a homogeneous perspective, as is evidenced in the recent *Encyclopedia of Rhetoric* (Sloane, 2001). My characterization is most consistent with Aristotle's view as developed by Kenneth Burke (1969).

2. See Hauser (1986, p. 28).

3. See Hauser (1986, p. 3).

4. See Sanders (1995) and Duck (1994). My own studies of institutions, such as academic colloquia (e.g., Tracy & Baratz, 1993), calls to the police and 911 (e.g., Tracy & Agne, in press), and school board deliberations (e.g., Tracy & Ashcraft, 2001; Tracy & Muller, 2001) are one kind of rhetorically informed discourse analysis. Recently I have begun to develop what exactly that means (Tracy, 2001, 2002, in press).

5. See Billig (1987, p. 143).

6. Kellermann (1992) makes the argument that communication is inherently strategic and primarily automatic.

7. Erickson and Shultz (1982).

8. Conley and O'Barr (1998) review discourse research on mediation. They argue that mediation has some unintended negative consequences. In particular, the cooperative structure of mediation ends up disadvantaging women such that wives, in general, do less well financially than they do when they go to court.

9. The first tape from the Academy of Family Mediators was called *Initial Mediation* (1989a) and focused on the opening session. The second tape, called *Yours, Mine and Ours: Property Division Mediation* (1989b), focused on issues surrounding property division.

10. Tracy and Spradlin (1994, p. 117).

11. See Jacobs, Jackson, Stearns, and Hall (1991).

12. See Smith and Eisenberg (1987) for an explication of the idea of root metaphor.

13. Tracy and Spradlin (1994, p. 125).

14. In developing these two perspectives I have assigned the structuring and constraining forces to the cultural view and the agentive force to the rhetorical view. This is a simplification. Ways of conceiving of culture are enormously diverse. My version of culture is most similar to that developed by ethnographers of communication (e.g., Hymes, 1974; Philipsen, 1975) and interactional sociolinguists (Gumperz, 1982b; Tannen, 1984).

15. Fitch (1998).

16. Hymes (1972).

17. See Swales (1998).

18. See Eckert and McConnell-Ginet (1992, 1995).

19. This term is used in the works of Fitch (1994) and of Carbaugh (1996).

20. See Scollon and Scollon (1981, pp. 12–13).

21. Scollon and Scollon (1981) suggest that American English speakers are the extreme case of regarding spectatorship and dominance as linked. British and Canadian English speakers are less extreme, and hence somewhat less different from Athabaskan in this component of interpersonal ideology.

22. Scollon and Scollon (1981, p. 17).

23. Scollon and Scollon (1981, p. 17).

24. Philipsen (1975, 1992).

25. *Nacirema* was a term originally coined by Horace Miner (1956). It is "American" spelled backward.

26. Why, one might ask, do authors select different names if they are referring to the same set of people? Wouldn't it be better to use the same name? A primary reason authors use different names is because the choice of a name suggests those characteristics that are shared by people with the same name, as well as implies a dimension of contrast for people who differ. Thus, for instance, while the group Scollon and Scollon labeled "Athabaskans" shared historical ties to the Native American language of Athabaskan, no singular language background tied Teamsterville residents. Teamsterville members came from language backgrounds that included Italian, Polish, and many others. Instead of a common language heritage, what distinguished this speech community was its place in American society as a white working-class community.

27. Philipsen (1992, p. 21).

28. Philipsen (1992, p. 29).

29. Philipsen (1992, p. 16).

30. See Rubin's (1976) *Worlds of Pain* and Komarovsky's (1962) *Blue-Collar Marriage*.

31. Scollon and Scollon (1995, p. 125).
32. These are paraphrases from *Webster's New World Dictionary* (1970).
33. Middle-class American culture is my starting point. However, I assume that there will be many similarities with other societies, particularly European or European-based ones, and especially those in which English is the dominant language (Australia, Canada, New Zealand, United Kingdom).

CHAPTER 3

1. Carbaugh (1996, p. 94).
2. Arliss (1991, p. 35).
3. Maggio (1988, p. 171).
4. Carbaugh (1996).
5. The percentage of women in the United States keeping their birth name upon marriage ranges from 14% for women under 40, to 10% for women 41–50, to 5% for women above 50. Less than 5% of women with a high school education, 15% with a BA, and 20% with postgraduate education keep their birth name ("Why Wives," 1994).
6. Carbaugh (1996, p. 95).
7. Carbaugh (1996, p. 97). Note, the original had "MN" (maiden name) in brackets rather than birth name.
8. Carbaugh (1996, p. 100).
9. Stafford and Kline (1996) labeled women who kept their birth name as a middle name or who hyphenated their last name as "combiners." Carbaugh (1996) identifies these women as adopting the integrative option. Of note is the more positive flavor of Carbaugh's name for this position.
10. Carbaugh (1996, p. 101).
11. See Fitch (1998) for a more elaborated discussion of Colombian address practices.
12. Fitch (1998, p. 38)
13. Fitch (1998).
14. Kondo (1990).
15. See Sequiera (1993) for a review of issues of personal address and how they are applied in an American church community.
16. This description uses Fitch's (1998) general typology. She developed it to describe Colombian culture; I use it to describe English speakers.
17. Thanks to Alena Sanusi for this example.
18. See Fitch (1998, p. 41).
19. See Hopper, Knapp, and Scott (1981, p. 25) for American examples and Langford (1997) for British examples.
20. Winchatz (2001) discusses this for uses of the German *Sie*. Fitch (1998) examines this issue in Spanish.
21. Carbaugh (1996) argues that FN–FN usage no longer is a strong sign of intimacy in the American scene. Under certain circumstances reciprocal title + LN may be more intimate (e.g., husband to wife: H: "Mrs. Smith, are you going to join me?"; W: "Mr. Smith (big smile), I believe I will.").

22. Scollon and Scollon (1981).
23. The above example is the way requests were formulated in a Western city where the main groups in the city were Hispanic, white, and black (see Tracy, 1997b). What choice citizens are provided will vary with the ethnic groups in an area.
24. See Wander, Martin, and Nakayama (1999).
25. Martin, Krizek, Nakayama, and Bradford (1999).
26. Gomez (1992).
27. Giminez (1992).
28. See Oboler (1992).
29. See Tanno (1997, pp. 29–30).
30. See Hecht et al. (1993).
31. See Nakayama and Krizck (1999, p. 101).
32. Martin et al. (1999).
33. Martin et al. (1999, p. 28).
34. See Martin et al. (1999, p. 46).
35. Malay does not require gender identification for third-person singular.
36. See Prentice (1994) for an overview of language reform movements and effects.
37. Weatherall (1998) reviews this research.
38. See Whorf (1956).
39. See Erlich and King (1992, 1994).
40. Erlich and King (1992).
41. See Prentice (1994).
42. See Prentice (1994).
43. See lectures 1 and 2, Spring 1966, in Sacks (1992).
44. Sacks (1992, p. 238).
45. Maynard (1984, p. 215).

CHAPTER 4

1. Shuy (1993) analyzes a series of trials in which the crime a person is accused of focuses on language, that is, one person saying something to another. See Chapter 5 and especially pages 108–109 for this case.
2. Austin (1962).
3. Searle (1979).
4. The notion of speech act developed here merges the speaker-focused intentional stance developed by Austin (1962) and Searle (1979) with the anthropological and community-rooted notion seen in the work of Hymes (1974) and other ethnographers of communication (e.g., Katriel, 1986).
5. Many authors (e.g., Hymes, 1974) distinguish smaller units that get labeled as *speech acts* from bigger units that get labeled as *speech events*. However, as Wierzbicka (1991) argues, other than size of unit, the key features are highly similar. For this reason, I do not make a distinction.
6. Hymes (1974).

7. See Wierzbicka (1991, pp. 166–168).
8. See Katriel (1986, 1991).
9. See Katriel (1991, p. 40).
10. Katriel and Philipsen (1981).
11. See Katriel (1991, p. 45).
12. See Kreckel (1981).
13. See Yahya-Othman (1995).
14. Gass and Neu (1995) have edited a volume that examines speech act differences across cultures with a focus on acts performed in a second language.
15. See Goffman (1971).
16. See Sugimoto (1999b) and Kotani (2002).
17. The summary of functions as well as the explication of the gratitude function of "I'm sorry" is taken from Kotani (2002). Interesting analyses of Japanese apology are to found in an edited volume by Sugimoto (1999a) with comparisons to Americans highlighted in chapters by Sugimoto (1999b, 1999c) and Kotani (1999). Blum-Kulka, House, and Kasper (1989) explore cultural differences in apologies and requests, focusing primarily on Europeans.
18. See Sugimoto (1999a, 1999b) and Barnlund and Yoshioko (1990).
19. See Kotani (2002, p. 53).
20. See Kotani (2002, p. 61).
21. Beach and Metzger (1997).
22. These six are not the only face-sensitive acts that have been studied. Others include, for example, *complaining* (Alberts, 1988a, 1988b; Boxer, 1996; Murphy & Neu, 1996) and *asking for or responding to favors* (Craig, Tracy, & Spisak, 1986; Goldschmidt, 1996; Tracy, Craig, Smith, & Spisak, 1984).
23. Professionals sometimes are called upon to provide advice even though it was not asked for. Such scenes are also delicate (Heritage & Sefi, 1992).
24. Goldsmith and Fitch (1997, p. 461).
25. Goldsmith and Fitch (1997, p. 462).
26. Goldsmith and Fitch (1997, p. 463; italics in the original).
27. This is a simplified transcript from Dersley and Wootton (2000, p. 382).
28. Cody and McLaughlin (1985).
29. See Rawlins (1992).
30. See Tracy, van Dusen, and Robinson (1987).
31. Tracy et al. (1987, p. 54).
32. Dersley and Wootton (2000).
33. The literature on accounts is extensive. Reviews that tackle the issues in distinctive ways are available in Antaki (1994), Benoit (1995), and Buttny (1993). I draw most heavily on Buttny and Morris's (2001) recent review where they highlight this distinction between accounts as reason giving and accounts as seeking to mend social trouble.
34. Some authors (Schönbach, 1990) have extended Scott and Lyman's (1968) notion of accounts to include apologies and denials that one committed the problematic action. Because this broader definition is contrary to our everyday usage of accounts, I stick with the narrower meaning.

35. See Cody and McLaughlin (1985).
36. Morris and Coursey (1989).
37. Manusov (1996).
38. Hewitt and Stokes (1975).
39. Naughton (1996) finds postutterance disclaimers common in hospice staff meetings where staff discuss the problems they are having with the families with whom they work.
40. Hall and Valde (1995).
41. Bergmann (1993).
42. See Bergmann (1993, p. 153).
43. See Goldsmith (1989–1990). Blum-Kulka (2000) also disagrees with Bergmann (1993), suggesting that gossip may occur among family members. Her chapter provides a nice review of some of the more recent research on gossip.

CHAPTER 5

1. This exchange is one taken from a telephone call set of more than 650 calls that were made to 911 and police dispatch that I have been working with for the last 5 years. With colleagues I have written papers that analyze different interactional problems in these calls. See Tracy (1997b), K. Tracy and S. Tracy (1998), S. Tracy and K. Tracy (1998), Tracy and Anderson (1999), and Tracy and Agne (in press).
2. Edwards and Lampert (1993) provide an overview of many of the transcription systems that linguists have used to analyze talk. Their edited book, however, gives little attention to the conversation analytic system, the one most used in communication research.
3. Detailed descriptions of the CA transcription conventions can be found in a number of places, including Atkinson and Heritage (1984, 1999), Ochs, Schegloff, and Thompson (1996), and Psathas (1995). Two particularly nice introductions to the logic and findings of conversation analysis are Hutchby and Wooffitt (1998) and ten Have (1999).
4. See Parrott and Harré (1996, p. 42).
5. Planalp (1999) provides a review of research investigating emotion and how it is communicated. The majority of the work she reviews, as is true of the research itself, has been carried out in laboratories. Exceptions to this generalization are to be found in the growing research area of emotions in organizational life (see Fineman, 1993, 1996, for a review).
6. Bloch (1996).
7. See also Pittam (1994) for a discussion of vocal features related to feelings.
8. See K. Tracy and S. Tracy (1998) for a discussion of controlled enunciation and its use by police call takers in talking to angry callers.
9. Averill (1982).
10. Pittam (1994) reviews this research.
11. Hochschild (1993, p. xii).

12. Gumperz and Cook-Gumperz (1982).

13. See Gumperz and Cook-Gumperz (1982, p. 155).

14. See Pittam (1994).

15. See Cameron (2001, p. 112).

16. See Pittam (1994).

17. See Hall (1995, p. 200).

18. See Hall (1995, p. 192). To make the transcript easier to read, lower case i's were changed to uppercase.

19. See Tusing and Dillard (2000) and Pittam (1994).

20. See Pittam (1994).

21. See Basso (1979).

22. Linguist Walt Wofram offers this generalization in the video *American Tongues*.

23. Bayard, Weatherall, Gallois, and Pittam (2001).

24. The quotations from the BBC, *The Story of English* TV series, programme 1, were quoted in Bayard et al. (2001, p. 44).

25. See de ka Zerda and Hopper (1979) and Bradac (1990).

26. Dillard (1972) estimated 80%, whereas Spears (1992) estimated 60%.

27. Johnson (2000) overviews the phonological and syntactic features of BE.

28. Giles and Coupland (1991).

29. See Davies (1984, p. 231).

30. Kiesling (1998).

31. Trudgill (1974).

32. Bradac (1990) reviews this research.

33. Giles (1973).

34. In earlier versions of the theory, the name of the theory was "speech accommodation"; for instance, contrast Giles (1973) with Giles, Malac, Bradac, and Johnson (1987). The reason for changing names was to extend the process to a broader array of communicative features than the more focused ones of dialect and speech rate that were the initial focus of the theory. I use the current name but emphasize accent, the focus of the earlier work.

35. Ylänne-McEwen and Coupland (2000, p. 191) identify the core of accommodation theory this way. Their chapter provides a nice review and critique; see also Shepard, Giles, and Le Poire (2001) for an elaboration of the theory's development across time. Communication accommodation theory has also been applied to conversations with the elderly, although here the focus has been on features such as vocabulary and sentence and topic structure rather than primarily accent (e.g., Ryan, Giles, Bartolucci, & Henwood, 1986; Ryan, Hummert, & Boich, 1995). Fox (1999) reviews much of this research, with an emphasis given to communicating in families with aging parents.

36. See Giles and Coupland (1991) for a review of communication accommodation research. A more recent review essay, although it has a broader focus, is Cargile and Bradac (2001).

37. See Tiersma (2000, p. 52).

CHAPTER 6

1. This example is taken from Gumperz (1982a, p. 92).
2. See Bailey (2000b, p. 565).
3. See Bailey (2000b, p. 557).
4. See Gumperz (1982a, p. 92).
5. This is a slightly modified version of a transcript appearing in Myers-Scotton and Bolonyai (2001, p. 7).
6. See Myers-Scotton and Bolonyai (2001, p. 14).
7. See Myers-Scotton and Bolonyai (2001, p. 14).
8. Miller (2000).
9. See Miller (2000, p. 97).
10. See Hayakawa (1992, p. 94).
11. See Leibowicz (1992, p. 111).
12. See Huddleston (1992, p. 117).
13. See Corrada (1992, pp. 120–121).
14. See Barker et al. (2001).
15. See Crawford (1992b, p. 1).
16. See U.S. English, Inc. (2002).
17. Crawford's (1992b) edited volume is a source book documenting the controversy.
18. See Crawford (1992a) and Barker et al. (2001).
19. Draper and Jiminez (1992).
20. See Barker et al. (2001).
21. Draper and Jiminez (1992, p. 89).

CHAPTER 7

1. See Beck (1996, p. 168).
2. Schegloff and Sacks (1973).
3. See Heritage (1984) and Nofsigner (1991) for fuller discussions of this notion.
4. Whether there is a general conversational preference for agreement has been vigorously debated. The interactional picture appears to be quite complex. Pomerantz (1978) has shown that compliments often are not straightforwardly agreed with. Bilmes (1991) suggests that once an argument gets going the conversationally preferred response is disagreement. Hutchby (1996) illustrates the preference for disagreement in an analysis of call-in radio shows.
5. Kitzinger and Frith (1999, p. 293).
6. Sacks (1992, Vol. 2, pp. 32–43).
7. Sacks, Schegloff, and Jefferson (1974).
8. See Duncan (1972; Duncan & Fiske, 1977). In this discussion I have combined the conversation analytic sequential model of turn taking (Sacks et al., 1974) with the signaling model described by Duncan and his colleagues.

Wilson, Wiemann, and Zimmerman (1984) describe the advantage of such a combination.

9. Sacks (1992, Vol. 2, pp. 32–43).
10. Schegloff (2000).
11. See Schegloff (2000) for a discussion of overlapping talk and turn taking. James and Clark (1993) review research on interruption and gender differences.
12. Sacks (1992, Vol. 2, p. 50).
13. Tracy (1997a) claims that in graduate student–faculty colloquia in university departments, faculty members routinely talk more than graduate students. Ng, Brooke, and Dunne (1995) show that the number of turns a student took in a group discussion influenced how influential he or she was perceived to be. Tannen (1993a) reviews some of the complexities going with use of language strategies and judgments of dominance.
14. See Sattel (1983) for a discussion of how silence is used by men to exercise power over women.
15. Ragan (1983, p. 157).
16. See Goodall and Goodall (1982).
17. Scheuer's (2001) study was conducted among Danish businesses. An earlier study by Einhorn (1981) in the United States with different industries found similar patterns related to turns for successful and unsuccessful job interviews.
18. See Scheuer (2001, p. 201).
19. Beck's (1996) analysis of the turn taking in the VP debates draws upon newspaper and magazine articles published in *USA Today* and *Newsweek*.
20. Beck (1996, p. 177).
21. See Beck (1996, p. 177).
22. This is a simplified version of the transcript published in Bilmes (1999, p. 216).
23. This transcript excerpt is pieced together from Bilmes (1999, p. 221) and Beck (1996, p. 175). Both authors analyze this exchange. Each transcript has small differences. The one here is simplified from both of theirs.
24. Bilmes (1999, 2001) and Beck (1996) provide in-depth analyses of various features of this debate.
25. See Goffman (1971, pp. 138–148).
26. Goffman (1971).
27. Spencer-Oatley (2000a, 2000b).
28. Phillips (1983).

CHAPTER 8

1. The concept of *style* has been important in both communication (Norton, 1983) and linguistics (Tannen, 1984, 1986). Norton identifies the dimensions of style as, to name but a few, dominance, dramatic, contentious, animated, relaxed, open, and friendly. Tannen focuses on direct/indirect and in-

volvement. This chapter is informed by both notions but aligns more closely with Tannen's.

2. See Tannen (1984, p. 8; italics in original).
3. Norton (1983).
4. Blum-Kulka (1989, p. 66).
5. Blum-Kulka (1989, p. 66).
6. This analysis uses Kim and Bresnahan's (1994) three-category typology because it is relatively clear and straightforward. The earliest and a particularly influential typology is Ervin-Tripp's (1976) study of children's requests.
7. This is a much simplified version of a table in Kim and Bresnanhan (1994, pp. 326–328).
8. Gumperz (1982a) overviews this work by Tannen; it is also referred to in her bestseller (Tannen, 1990).
9. Blum-Kulka et al. (1989).
10. See Tannen (1982, p. 224).
11. See Gunther (2000).
12. Kochman (1981).
13. Pomerantz (1980).
14. See Maynard (1992).
15. Katriel (1986).
16. See Dews, Kaplan, and Winner (1995).
17. See Tannen (1982, p. 218).
18. See Wierzbicka (1991) for a discussion of Polish and English speaker differences in directness.
19. This list of mitigation strategies is based on Brown and Levinson's (1987) negative politeness strategies.
20. Bergmann (1998) provides an interesting analysis of how morality plays out in ordinary talk situations.
21. I am unaware of any research that would document whether this cultural generalization has an empirical base.
22. This transcript excerpt comes from Holmes (2000). Punctuation was added to aid reading.
23. See Malinowski (1923).
24. See Coupland (2000, p. 1).
25. See, for instance, Coupland and Ylanne-McEwen (2000), Ragan (2000), Cheepen (2000), and Tracy and Naughton (2000).
26. Pavlidou (2000).
27. Pavlidou (2000, p. 138).
28. This is a constructed example but it is based on conversations that I have heard or that have been reported to me.
29. This is a gist version of several points made in a discussion that occurred at a meeting of the Boulder Valley School Board in Boulder, Colorado, in 1996.
30. Deductive and inductive organization style is developed by Scollon and Scollon (1995). The advantages identified for each also are taken from their analysis.

31. See Yamada (1992) and Scollon and Scollon (1995).
32. See Kochman (1981, pp. 107–108); this discussion is also available in Kochman (1990).
33. Kochman (1981, p. 107)
34. Kochman (1981, pp. 122–123; italics in original).
35. See Blum-Kulka (1997), Schiffrin (1984), and Tannen (1984). Directness in emotional expression is sometimes treated as a matter of involvement style rather than of style directness (e.g., Tannen, 1984).
36. Bailey (2000a).

CHAPTER 9

1. An analysis and more excerpts of this interview may be found in Agne and Tracy (1998).
2. Schegloff (1997) makes this point.
3. The exception is talk that is designed for overhearing audiences, as is the case in news interviews on radio or television. On such occasions it is rare to hear these conversational tokens that acknowledge listening (Hutchby, 1996).
4. "Ohs" are common ways people show that what the other has said is newsworthy (e.g., Heritage, 1984; Schiffrin, 1987).
5. Mulholland (1996) distinguishes between conarration that is centrally cooperative, what she labels *duetting*, and that in which participants are competing over a version of events.
6. This story is a simplified version of what appeared in Mandelbaum (1987).
7. Hamilton (1998) examines how stories and reported speech accomplish this is a family support group for bone marrow transplants,
8. Labov and Waletsky (1997, p. 3).
9. These features are my attempt to cull a workable definition for everyday stories from the different literatures, but especially the linguistic structural approaches (Labov & Waletsky, 1997) and discourse processing (e.g., Shapiro, van de Broeck, & Fletcher, 1995). I draw in these two, but recast them with a more conversation analytic orientation. Two features that have often been identified as defining stories—(1) temporal structure and orientation and (2) a resolution or outcome to a confronted problem—I do not include. Temporal structure is excluded since this is a key features that has been argued to be culturally variable, an issue I discuss later in the chapter. Resolution/outcome is excluded since van Dijk (1987) finds this feature to frequently be absent when people are telling stories that are criticizing or complaining about people.
10. Different theorists have offered proposed different versions of what the main parts of a narrative are. Within linguistic traditions the most common is Labov and Waletsky's (1997) six-part structure that includes (1) abstract, (2) orientation, (3) complication, (4) evaluation, (5) resolution, and (6) coda. In studies of story comprehension the structure is described a bit differently. For instance, Trabasso, van de Broeck, and Suh (1989) identify five

features: the setting (S), the goals of the protagonist (G), attempts to achieve the goals (A), outcomes of the attempt (O), and reactions (R). For another version, see Resier, Black, and Lehnert (1985).

11. See Labov (1997).
12. The excerpts are simplified from the way they originally appeared in Edwards (1995). The analysis of the exchange draws heavily from the Edwards article, although extending it in ways to focus on story features.
13. See Holt (2000) and Buttny (1997) for overviews of the kinds and functions of reported speech.
14. Potter (1996) offers a descriptively rich account of how people work to construct their views as just the facts.
15. Sunwolf and Frey (2001) offer an overview of the functions of narrative, present different definitions of narrative, and discuss narrative as a methodology.
16. Bamberg (1997, p. 341).
17. Ochs and Taylor (1995) analyzed how family stories position mothers and fathers differently. Other articles examining family narratives include Ochs and Taylor (1992) and Taylor (1995).
18. Shaw (1997) examines some of the ways stories reveal self and reflect other.
19. The two excerpts are taken from a master's thesis (Crawford, 1996), with the first excerpt from page 45 and the second one from pages 59–60. The excerpts are included and analyzed in Bamberg (1997).
20. Bergmann (1998) notes this; he examines how ordinary talk, including stories, do moral work.
21. See Chesire (2000).
22. See Buttny (1997) for a discussion of the role of reported speech in talking about race on campus. Other articles that look at this same focus group's conversations about the racism video tackle different issues (Buttny, 1998, 1999; Buttny & Williams, 2000).
23. This story has been simplified from its original transcript format. Punctuation has been added to make it more readable. See Buttny (1997, p. 485).
24. van Dijk (1987).
25. van Dijk (1987, p. 66).
26. Wooffitt (1992, p. 103).
27. Polanyi (1985).
28. Linde (1993).
29. Fitch (1998).
30. See Johnstone (1995).
31. See Ely, Gleason, Narasimhan, and McCabe (1995).
32. See Cheshire (2000).
33. See Michaels and Collins (1984), Riessman (1997), and Conley and O'Barr (1990).
34. This is a simplified version of the story that appears in Michaels and Collins (1984, p. 227).
35. Michaels and Collins (1984, p. 230).
36. Conley and O'Barr (1990).

CHAPTER 10

1. My notion of stance and stance indicators draws on the work of Ochs (1993).
2. Goffman (1959, p. 4).
3. Tannen (1984, 1986).
4. Mehrabian (1972).
5. See Tracy (1997a), Tannen (1989), and Gamson (1992).
6. Jay (1992).
7. The notion of marking has some similarity to the conversation analytic notion of preference (see Chapter 6 and Nofsinger [1991]). However, marking focuses on the language choices within an utterance rather than the interactional devices (longer pause, giving of an account) that occur when a structurally dispreferred second act follows a first speech act (e.g., an offer being followed by a rejection rather than an acceptance).
8. McCullough (1992).
9. Lakoff (1987).
10. Tracy (1997a).
11. See Tracy (1997a, p. 88).
12. See Pomerantz (1989–1990). Clayman (1988, 1992) provides an analysis of how neutrality, a cousin of skepticism, is achieved in news interviews.
13. Wooffitt (1992).
14. For reviews, see Tornquist, Anderson, and De Paulo (2001), Galasinski (2000), Robinson (1996), and Miller and Stiff (1993).
15. See Miller and Stiff (1993, p. 91).
16. Ekman (1992).
17. Adapted from Robinson's (1996) book examining deception. This table is draws especially on the work of Ekman (1992).
18. See Shuy (1998, pp. 76–77).
19. See Shuy (1998, p. 78).

CHAPTER 11

1. See Billig et al. (1988).
2. See Billig et al. (1988, p. 65).
3. Naughton (1996). See also Tracy and Naughton (2000).
4. See Tracy and Naugton (2000, p. 77).
5. Jasinski (2001, pp. 462–470) sourcebook on key rhetorical terms provides an overview of the history and meaning of phronesis.

References

Academy of Family Mediators. (1989a). *Initial mediation* [A training videotape]. (Available from Academy of Family Mediators, P.O. Box 10501, Eugene, OR 97440)

Academy of Family Mediators. (1989b). *Yours, mine and ours: Property division mediation* [A training videotape]. (Available from Academy of Family Mediators, P. O. Box 10501, Eugene, OR 97440)

Agne, R., & Tracy, K. (1998). Not answering questions: A police chief's strategies in a sensationalized murder. In J. F. Klumpp (Ed.), *Argument in a time of change* (pp. 238–242). Annandale, VA: National Communication Association.

Alberts, J. K. (1988a). A descriptive taxonomy of couples' complaints. *Southern Communication Journal, 54,* 125–143.

Alberts, J. K. (1988b). An analysis of couple's conversational complaint interactions. *Communication Monographs, 55,* 184–197.

Antaki, C. (1994). *Explaining and arguing: The social organization of accounts.* Thousand Oaks, CA: Sage.

Antaki, C., & Widdicombe, S. (Eds.). (1998). *Identities in talk.* London: Sage.

Arliss, L. P. (1991). *Gender communication.* Englewood Cliffs, NJ: Prentice-Hall.

Atkinson, J. M., & Heritage, J. (Eds.). (1984). *Structure of social action: Studies in conversation analysis.* Cambridge, UK: Cambridge University Press.

Atkinson, J. M., & Heritage, J. (1999). Jefferson's transcript notation. In A. Jaworski & N. Coupland (Eds.), *The discourse reader* (pp. 158–166). London: Routledge.

Austin, J. L. (1962). *How to do things with words.* Oxford, UK: Oxford University Press.

Averill, J. R. (1982). *Anger and aggression: An essay on emotion.* New York: Springer-Verlag.

Bailey, B. (2000a). Communicative behavior and conflict between African-American customers and Korean immigrants in Los Angeles. *Discourse and Society, 11,* 86–108.

Bailey, B. (2000b). Language and negotiation of ethnic/racial identity among Dominican Americans. *Language in Society, 29,* 555–582.

Bamberg, M. G. W. (1997). Positioning between structure and performance. *Journal of Narrative and Life History, 7,* 335–342.

Barker, V., Giles, H., Noels, K., Duck, J., Hecht, M., & Clement, R. (2001). The English-only movement: A communication analysis of changing perceptions of language vitality. *Journal of Communication, 51,* 3–37.

Barnlund, D., & Yoshioka, M. (1990). Apologies: Japanese and American styles. *International Journal of Intercultural Relations, 14,* 193–206.

Basso, K. (1979). *Portraits of the whiteman.* Cambridge, UK: Cambridge University Press.

Bate, B. (1988). *Communication and the sexes.* Prospect Heights, IL: Waveland Press.

Bateson, G. (1972). *Steps to an ecology of mind.* New York: Ballantine Books.

Bayard, D., Weatherall, A., Gallois, C., & Pittam, J. (2001). Pax Americana?: Accent attitudinal evaluations in New Zealand, Australia, and America. *Journal of Sociolinguistics, 5,* 22–49.

Beach, W. A., & Metzger, T. R. (1997). Claiming insufficient knowledge. *Human Communication Research, 23,* 562–588.

Beck, C. S. (1996). "I've got some points I'd like to make here": The achievement of social face through turn management during the 1992 vice presidential debate. *Political Communication, 13,* 165–180.

Benoit, W. L. (1995). *Accounts, excuses, and apologies: A theory of image restoration strategies.* Albany: State University of New York Press.

Bergmann, J. R. (1993). *Discreet indiscretions: The social organization of gossip.* New York: Aldine de Gruyter.

Bergmann, J. R. (1998). Introduction: Morality in discourse. *Research on Language and Social Interaction, 31,* 279–294.

Billig, M. (1987). *Arguing and thinking: A rhetorical approach to social psychology.* Cambridge, UK: Cambridge University Press.

Billig, M., Condor, S., Edwards, D., Gane, M., Middleton, D., & Radley, A. (1988). *Ideological dilemmas.* London: Sage.

Bilmes, J. (1991). Toward a theory of argument in conversation: The preference for disagreement. In F. A. van Eemeren, R. Grootendorsts, J. A. Blair, & C. A. Willard (Eds.), *Proceedings of the Second International Conference on Argumentation* (pp. 4622–469). Amsterdam: International Centre for the Study of Argumentation.

Bilmes, J. (1999). Questions, answers and the organization of talk in the 1992 vice-presidential debate: Fundamental considerations. *Research on Language and Social Interaction, 32,* 213–242.

Bilmes, J. (2001). Tactics and style in the 1992 vice presidential debate: Question placement. *Research on Language and Social Interaction, 34,* 151–182.

Bloch, C. (1996). Emotions and discourse. *Text, 16,* 323–341.

Blum-Kulka, S. (1989). Playing it safe: The role of conventionality in indirectness. In S. Blum-Kulka, J. House, & G. Kasper (Eds.), *Cross-cultural pragmatics: Requests and apologies* (pp. 37–70). Norwood, NJ: Ablex.

Blum-Kulka, S. (1997). *Dinner talk: Cultural patterns of sociability and social-ization in family discourse*. Mahwah, NJ: Erlbaum.

Blum-Kulka, S. (2000). Gossipy events at family dinner: Negotiating sociability, presence and the moral order. In J. Coupland (Ed.), *Small talk* (pp. 213–240). Harlow, UK: Pearson.

Blum-Kulka, S., House, J., & Kasper, G. (Eds.). (1989). *Cross-cultural prag-matics: Requests and apologies*. Norwood, NJ: Ablex.

Boxer, D. (1996). Ethnographic interviewing as a research tool in speech at anal-ysis: The case of complaints. In S. M. Gass & J. Neu (Eds.), *Speech acts across cultures: Challenges to communication in a second language* (pp. 217–239). Berlin: Mouton de Gruyter.

Bradac, J. J. (1990). Language attitudes and impression formation. In H. Giles & P. Robinson (Eds.), *Handbook of language and social psychology* (pp. 387–412). Chichester, UK: Wiley.

Brown, P., & Levinson, S. C. (1987). *Universals in language usage: Politeness phenomena*. Cambridge, UK: Cambridge University Press.

Brubaker, R., & Cooper, F. (2000). Beyond "identity." *Theory and Society, 29*, 1–47.

Burke, K. (1969). *A rhetoric of motives*. Berkeley and Los Angeles: University of California Press.

Buttny, R. (1993). *Social accountability in communication*. London: Sage.

Buttny, R. (1997). Reported speech in talking race on campus. *Human Commu-nication Research, 23*, 477–506.

Buttny, R. (1998). Putting prior talk into context: Reported speech and the re-porting context. *Research on Language and Social Interaction, 31*, 45–58.

Buttny, R. (1999). Discursive constructions of racial boundaries and self-segrega-tion on campus. *Journal of Language and Social Psychology, 18*, 247–268.

Buttny, R., & Morris, G. H. (2001). Accounting. In W. P. Robinson & H. Giles (Eds.), *The new handbook of language and social psychology* (pp. 285–301). Chichester, UK: Wiley.

Buttny, R., & Williams, P. L. (2000). Demanding respect: The uses of reported speech in discourse constructions of interracial contact. *Discourse and Soci-ety, 11*, 109–133.

Cameron, D. (1995). *Verbal hygiene*. London: Routledge.

Cameron, D. (2001). *Working with spoken discourse*. London: Sage.

Carbaugh, D. (1996). *Situating selves: The communication of social identities in American scenes*. Albany: State University of New York Press.

Cargile, A. C., & Bradac, J. J. (2001). Attitudes toward language: A review of speaker-evaluation research and a general process model. In W. B. Gudy-kunst (Ed.), *Communication yearbook 25* (pp. 347–382). Mahwah, NJ: Erlbaum.

Cheepen, C. (2000). Small talk in service dialogues: The conversational aspects of transnational telephone talk. In J. Coupland (Ed.), *Small talk* (pp. 288–311). Harlow, UK: Pearson.

Cheshire, J. (2000). The telling of the tale?: Narratives and gender in adolescent friendship networks. *Journal of Sociolinguistics, 4*, 234–262.

Cicourel, A. V. (1973). *Cognitive sociology: Language and meaning in social interaction*. New York: Free Press.

Cicourel, A. V. (1999). Interpretive procedures. In A. Jaworski & N. Coupland (Eds.), *The discourse reader* (pp. 89–97). London: Routledge.

Clayman, S. E. (1988). Displaying neutrality in television news interviews. *Social Problems, 35*, 474–492.

Clayman, S. E. (1992). Footing in the achievement of neutrality: The case of news interview discourse. In P. Drew & J. Heritage (Eds.), *Talk at work: Interaction in institutional settings* (pp. 163–198). Cambridge, UK: Cambridge University Press.

Cody, M. J., & McLaughlin, M. L. (1985). Models for the sequential construction of accounting episodes: Situational and interactional constraints on message selection and evaluation. In R. L. Street & J. N. Cappella (Eds.), *Sequence and pattern in communicative behaviour* (pp. 50–69). London: Arnold.

Conley, J. M., & O'Barr, W. M. (1990). *Rules versus relationships*. Chicago: University of Chicago Press.

Conley, J. M., & O'Barr, W. M. (1998). *Just words: Law, language, and power*. Chicago: University of Chicago Press.

Corrada, B. (1992). Viva la roja, blanca y azul. In J. Crawford (Ed.), *Language loyalties: A source book on the official English controversy* (pp. 118–120). Chicago: University of Chicago Press.

Coupland, J. (Ed.). (2000). *Small talk*. Harlow, UK: Pearson.

Coupland, N., & Ylanne-McEwen, V. (2000). Talk about the weather: Small talk, leisure talk and the travel industry. In J. Coupland (Ed.), *Small talk* (pp. 163–182). Harlow, UK: Pearson.

Craig, R. T., Tracy, K., & Spisak, F. (1986). The discourse of requests: Assessment of a politeness approach. *Human Communication Research, 12*, 437–468.

Crawford, J. (1992a). Editor's introduction. In J. Crawford (Ed.), *Language loyalties: A source book on the official English controversy* (pp. 1–8). Chicago: University of Chicago Press.

Crawford, J. (Ed.). (1992b). *Language loyalties: A source book on the official English controversy*. Chicago: University of Chicago Press.

Crawford, V. (1996). *Identity construction in conversational narratives*. Unpublished master's thesis, Department of Psychology, Clark University, Worcester, MA.

Davies, A. (1984). Idealization in sociolinguistics: The choice of the standard dialect. In D. Schiffrin (Ed.), *Meaning, form and use in context: Linguistic applications* (pp. 229–239). Washington, DC: Georgetown University Press.

Dersley, I., & Wootton, A. (2000). Complaint sequences within antagonistic argument. *Research on Language and Social Interaction, 33*, 375–406.

Dews, S., Kaplan, J., & Winner, E. (1995). Why not say it directly? The social functions of irony. *Discourse Processes, 19*, 347–367.

Dillard, J. E. (1972). *Black English*. New York: Vintage Books.

Draper, J. B., & Jimenez, M. (1992). A chronology of the official English movement (1990).In J. Crawford (Ed.), *Language loyalties: A source book on the official English controversy* (pp. 89–93). Chicago: University of Chicago Press.

Duck, S. (1994). *Meaningful relationships: Talking sense and relating.* Thousand Oaks, CA: Sage.

Duncan, S. D. (1972). Some signals and rules for taking turns in conversations. *Journal of Personality and Social Psychology, 23*, 283–292.

Duncan, S. D., & Fiske, D. W. (1977). *Face-to-face interaction.* Hillsdale, NJ: Erlbaum.

Eckert, P., & McConnell-Ginet, S. (1992). Think practically and look locally: Language and gender as community-based practice. *Annual Review of Anthropology, 21*, 461–490.

Eckert, P., & McConnell-Ginet, S. (1995). Constructing meaning, constructing selves: Snapshots of language, gender and class from Belten High. In K. Hall & M. Bucholtz (Eds.), *Gender articulated: Language and the socially constructed self* (pp. 469–507). London: Routledge.

Edwards, D. (1995). Two to tango: Script formulations, dispositions, and rhetorical symmetry in relationship troubles talk. *Research on Language and Social Interaction, 28*, 319–350.

Edwards, J. A., & Lampert, M. D. (Eds.). (1993). *Talking data: Transcription and coding in discourse research.* Hillsdale, NJ: Erlbaum.

Einhorn, L. J. (1981). An inner view of the job interview: An investigation of successful communicative behaviors. *Communication Education, 30*, 217–228.

Ekman, P. (1992). *Telling lies.* New York: Norton.

Ely, R., Gleason, J. B., Narasimhan, B., & McCabe, A. (1995). Family talk about talk: Mothers lead the way. *Discourse Processes, 19*, 201–218.

Erickson, F. (1999). Appropriation of voice and presentation of self as a fellow physician: Aspects of a discourse of apprenticeship in medicine. In C. Sarangi & C. Roberts (Eds.), *Talk, work and institutional order: Discourse in medical, mediation and management settings* (pp. 109–143). Berlin: Mouton de Gruyter.

Erickson, F., & Shultz, J. (1982). *The counselor as gatekeeper: Social interaction in interviews.* New York: Academic Press.

Erlich, S., & King, R. (1992). Gender-based language reforms and the social construction of meaning. *Discourse and Society, 3*, 151–166.

Erlich, S., & King, R. (1994). Feminist meaning and the (de)politicization of the lexicon. *Language in Society, 23*, 59–76.

Ervin-Tripp, S. (1976). Is Sybil there?: The structure of some American English directives. *Language in Society, 5*, 25–66.

Fineman, S. (Ed.). (1993). *Emotion in organizations.* London: Sage.

Fineman, S. (1996). Emotions and organizing. In S. Clegg, C. Hardy, & W. Nord (Eds.), *Handbook of organizational studies* (pp. 543–564). London: Sage.

Fitch, K. L. (1994). Culture, ideology, and communication research. In S. Deetz (Ed.), *Communication yearbook 17* (pp. 115–135). Newbury Park, CA: Sage.

Fitch, K. L. (1998). *Speaking relationally: Culture, communication, and interpersonal connection.* New York: Guilford Press.

Fitch, K. L. (2001). The ethnography of speaking: Sapir/Whorf, Hymes and Moerman. In M. Wetherell, S. Taylor, & S. J. Yates (Eds.), *Discourse theory and practice* (pp. 57–63). London: Sage.

Fitzgerald, T. K. (1993). *Metaphors of identity: A culture communication dialogue.* Albany: State University of New York Press.

Fox, S. A. (1999). Communication in families with an aging parent: A review of the literature and agenda for future research. In M. E. Roloff (Ed.), *Communication yearbook 22* (pp. 377–429). Thousand Oaks, CA: Sage.

Galasinski, D. (2000). *The language of deception: A discourse analytical study.* Thousand Oaks, CA: Sage.

Gamson, W. A. (1992). *Talking politics.* Cambridge, UK: Cambridge University Press.

Gass, S. M., & Neu, J. (Eds.). (1996). *Speech acts across cultures: Challenges to communication in a second language.* Berlin: Mouton de Gruyter.

Gee, J. P. (1999). *An introduction to discourse analysis: Theory and method.* London: Routledge.

Giles, H. (1973). Accent mobility: A model and some data. *Anthropological Linguistics, 15,* 87–105.

Giles, H., & Coupland, N. (1991). *Language: Contexts and consequences.* Pacific Grove, CA: Brooks/Cole.

Giles, H., Mulac, A., Bradac, J. J., & Johnson, P. (1987). Speech accommodation theory: The first decade and beyond. In M. McLaughlin (Ed.), *Communication yearbook 10* (pp. 13–48). Newbury Park, CA: Sage.

Gimenez, M. F. (1992). US ethnic politics: Implications for Latin Americans. *Latin American Perspectives, 19*(4), 7–17.

Goffman, E. (1955). On facework: An analysis of ritual elements in social interaction. *Psychiatry, 18,* 213–231.

Goffman, E. (1959). *The presentation of self in everyday life.* New York: Anchor Books.

Goffman, E. (1967). *Interaction ritual.* Garden City, NY: Anchor Books.

Goffman, E. (1971). *Relations in public: Microstudies of the public order.* New York: Bantam Books.

Goffman, E. (1974). *Frame analysis.* New York: Harper & Row.

Goldschmidt, M. (1996). From the addressee's perspective: Imposition in favorasking. In S. M. Gass & J. Neu (Eds.), *Speech acts across cultures: Challenges to communication in a second language* (pp. 241–256). Berlin: Mouton de Gruyter.

Goldsmith, D. J. (1989–1990). Gossip from the native's point of view. *Research on Language and Social Interaction, 23,* 163–193.

Goldsmith, D. J., & Fitch, K. (1997). The normative context of advice as social support. *Human Communication Research, 23,* 454–476.

Gomez, L. E. (1992). The birth of the "Hispanic" generation: Attitudes of Mexican-American political elites toward the Hispanic label. *Latin American Perspectives, 19*(4), 45–58.

Goodall, D. B., & Goodall, H. L., Jr. (1982). The employment interview: A selective review of the literature with implications for communication research. *Communication Quarterly, 30*, 116–123.

Grice, H. P. (1975). Logic in conversation. In P. Cole & J. Morgan (Eds.), *Syntax and semantics: Vol. 3. Speech acts* (pp. 41–58). New York: Academic Press.

Grice, H. P. (1999). Logic and conversation. In A. Jaworski & N. Coupland (Eds.), *The discourse reader* (pp. 76–88). London: Routledge.

Gumperz, J. J. (1982a). *Discourse strategies.* Cambridge, UK: Cambridge University Press.

Gumperz, J. J. (Ed.). (1982b). *Language and social identity.* Cambridge, UK: Cambridge University Press.

Gumperz, J. J. (1992). Contextualization and understanding. In A. Duranti & C. Goodwin (Eds.), *Rethinking context: Language as an interactive phenomenon* (pp. 229–252). Cambridge, UK: Cambridge University Press.

Gumperz, J. J. (2001). Interactional sociolinguistics: A personal perspective. In D. Schiffrin, D. Tannen, & H. Hamilton (Eds.), *The handbook of discourse analysis* (pp. 215–228). Oxford, UK: Blackwell.

Gumperz, J. J., & Cook-Gumperz, J. (1982). Interethnic communication in committee negotiations. In J. J. Gumperz (Ed.), *Language and social identity* (pp. 145–162). Cambridge, UK: Cambridge University Press.

Gunther, S. (2000). Argumentation and resulting problems in the negotiation of rapport in a German–Chinese conversation. In H. Spencer-Oatley (Ed.), *Culturally speaking: Managing rapport through talk across cultures* (pp. 217–239). London: Continuum.

Hall, B. J., & Valde, K. (1995). "Brown-nosing" as a cultural category in American organizational life. *Research on Language and Social Interaction, 28,* 391–419.

Hall, K. (1995). Lip service on the fantasy lines. In K. Hall & M. Bucholtz (Eds.), *Gender articulated: Language and the social constructed self* (pp. 183–216). London: Routledge.

Hamilton, H. E. (1998). Reported speech and the survivor identity in on-line bone marrow transplantation narratives. *Journal of Sociolinguistics, 2,* 53–67.

Hauser, G. A. (1986). *Introduction to rhetorical theory.* New York: Harper & Row.

Hayakawa, S. I. (1992). The case for official English. In J. Crawford (Ed.), *Language loyalties: A source book on the official English controversy* (pp. 94–100). Chicago: University of Chicago Press.

Hecht, M. L., Collier, M. J., & Ribeau, S. A. (1993). *African American communication: Ethnic identity and cultural interpretation.* Newbury Park, CA: Sage.

Hecht, M. L., & Faulkner, S. L. (2000). Sometimes Jewish, sometimes not: The closeting of Jewish American identity. *Communication Studies, 51,* 372–287.

Heritage, J. (1984). A change-of-state token and aspects of its sequential placement. In J. M. Atkinson & J. Heritage (Eds.), *Structure of social action:*

Studies in conversational analysis (pp. 299–345). Cambridge, UK: Cambridge University Press.

Heritage, J., & Sefi, S. (1992). Dilemmas of advice: Aspects of the delivery and reception of advice in interactions between health visitors and first-time mothers. In P. Drew & J. Heritage (Eds.), *Talk at work: Interaction in institutional settings* (pp. 359–417). Cambridge, UK: Cambridge University Press.

Hewitt, J. P., & Stokes, R. (1975). Disclaimers. *American Sociological Review, 40*, 1–11.

Hochschild, A. (1993). Preface. In S. Fineman (Ed.), *Emotion in organizations* (pp, ix–xiii). London: Sage.

Holland, D., Lachiotte, W., Jr., Skinner, D., & Cain, C. (1998). *Identity and agency in cultural words.* Cambridge, MA: Harvard University Press.

Holmes, J. (2000). Doing collegiality and keeping control at work: Small talk in government departments. In J. Coupland (Ed.), *Small talk* (pp. 32–61). Harlow, UK: Pearson.

Holt, E. (2000). Reporting and reacting: Concurrent responses to reported speech. *Research on Language and Social Interaction, 33*, 425–454.

Hopper, R., Knapp, M. L., & Scott, L. (1981). Couples' personal idioms: Exploring intimate talk. *Journal of Communication, 31*, 23–40.

Huddleston, W. (1992). The misdirected policy of bilingualism. In J. Crawford (Ed.), *Language loyalties: A source book on the official English controversy* (pp. 114–117). Chicago: University of Chicago Press.

Hutchby, I. (1996). *Confrontation talk: Arguments, asymmetries, and power on talk radio.* Mahwah, NJ: Erlbaum.

Hutchby, I., & Wooffitt, R. (1998). *Conversation analysis.* Cambridge, UK: Polity Press.

Hymes, D. (1972). Models of the interaction of language and social life. In J. J. Gumperz & D. Hymes (Eds.), *Directions in sociolinguistics: The ethnography of communication* (pp. 35–71). New York: Holt, Rinehart & Winston.

Hymes, D. (1974). *Foundations in sociolinguistics: An ethnographic approach.* Philadelphia: University of Pennsylvania Press.

Jacobs, S., Jackson, S., Stearns, S., & Hall, B. (1991). Digressions in argumentative discourse: Multiple goals, standing concerns and implicatures. In K. Tracy (Ed.), *Understanding face-to-face interaction: Issues linking goals and discourse* (pp. 43–61). Hillsdale, NJ: Erlbaum.

James, D., & Clarke, S. (1993). Women, men and interruptions: A critical review. In D. Tannen (Ed.), *Gender and conversational interaction* (pp. 231–280). New York: Oxford University Press.

Jasinski, J. (2001). *Sourcebook on rhetoric.* Thousand Oaks, CA: Sage.

Jaworski, A., & Coupland, N. (Eds.). (1999). *The discourse reader.* London: Routledge.

Jay, T. (1992). *Cursing in America.* Philadelphia: John Benjamins.

Johnson, F. (2000). *Speaking culturally: Language diversity in the United States.* Thousand Oaks, CA: Sage.

Johnstone, B. (1993). Community and contest: Midwestern men and women creating their worlds in conversational storytelling. In D. Tannen (Ed.),

Gender and conversational interaction (pp. 62–80). New York: Oxford University Press.

Katriel, T. (1986). *Talking straight: Dugri speech in Israeli Sabra culture.* Cambridge, UK: Cambridge University Press.

Katriel, T. (1991). *Communal webs: Communication and culture in contemporary Israel.* Albany: State University of New York Press.

Katriel, T., & Philipsen, G. (1981). What we need is communication: "Communication" as a cultural category in some American speech. *Communication Monographs, 48,* 301–317.

Kellermann, K. (1992). Communication: Inherently strategic and primarily automatic. *Communication Monographs, 59,* 288–300.

Kiesling, S. F. (1998). Men's identities and sociolinguistic variation: The case of fraternity men. *Journal of Sociolinguistics, 2,* 69–99.

Kim, M.-S., & Bresnahan, M. (1994). A process model of request tactic evaluation. *Discourse Processes, 18,* 317–344.

Kitzinger, C., & Frith, H. (1999). Just say no?: The use of conversation analysis in developing a feminist perspective on sexual refusal. *Discourse and Society, 10,* 293–316

Kochman, T. (1981). *Black and white styles in conflict.* Chicago: University of Chicago Press.

Kochman, T. (1990). Force fields in black and white communication. In D. Carbaugh (Ed.), *Cultural communication and intercultural contact* (pp. 193–918). Hillsdale, NJ: Erlbaum.

Komarovsky, M. (1962). *Blue-collar marriage.* New York: Vintage Books.

Kondo, D. K. (1990). *Crafting selves: Power, gender, and discourses of identity in a Japanese workplace.* Chicago: University of Chicago Press.

Kotani, M. (1999). A discourse-analytic approach to the study of Japanese apology: The "feel-good" apology as a cultural category. In N. Sugimoto (Ed.), *Japanese apology across disciplines* (pp. 125–154). Commack, NY: Nova.

Kotani, M. (2002). Expressing gratitude and indebtedness: Japanese speakers' use of "I'm sorry" in English conversation. *Research on Language and Social Interaction, 32,* 39–72.

Kreckel, M. (1981). *Communicative acts and shared knowledge in natural discourse.* London: Academic Press.

Labov, W. (1997). Some further steps in narrative analysis. *Journal of Narrative and Life History, 7,* 395–415.

Labov, W., & Waletsky, J. (1997). Narrative analysis: Oral experiences of personal experience. *Journal of Narrative and Life History, 7,* 3–38.

Lakoff, G. (1987). *Women, fire, and dangerous things: What categories reveal about the mind.* Chicago: University of Chicago Press.

Langford, W. (1997). "Bunnikins, I love you snuggly in your warren": Voices from subterranean cultures of love. In K. Harvey & C. Shalom (Eds.), *Language and desire* (pp. 170–185). London: Routledge.

Leibowicz, J. (1992). Official English: Another Americanization campaign. In J. Crawford (Ed.), *Language loyalties: A source book on the official English controversy* (pp. 101–111). Chicago: University of Chicago Press.

Levinson, S. C. (1983). *Pragmatics*. Cambridge, UK: Cambridge University Press.

Lim, T., & Bowers, J. W. (1991). Facework, solidarity, approbation, and tact. *Human Communication Research, 17*, 415–450.

Linde, C. (1993). *Life stories: The creation of coherence*. New York: Oxford University Press.

Maggio, R. (1988). *The nonsexist word finder: A dictionary of gender-free usage*. Boston: Beacon Press.

Malinowski, B. (1923). The problem of meaning in primitive languages. In C. K. Ogden & I. A. Richards (Eds.), *The meaning of meaning*. New York: Harcourt, Brace & World.

Mandelbaum, J. (1987). Couples sharing stories. *Communication Quarterly, 35*, 144–170.

Manusov, V. (1996). Changing explanations: The process of account-making over time. *Research on Language and Social Interaction, 29*, 155–179.

Martin, J. N., Krisek, R. L., Nakayama, T. L., & Bradford, L. (1999). What do white people want to be called? In T. K. Nakayama & J. N. Martin (Eds.), *Whiteness: The communication of social identity* (pp. 27–50). Thousand Oaks, CA: Sage.

Maynard. D. W. (1984). *Inside plea bargaining: The language of negotiation*. New York: Plenum Press.

Maynard, D. W. (1992). On clinicians co-implicating recipients' perspective in the delivery of diagnostic news. In P Drew & J. Heritage (Eds.), *Talk at work : Interaction in institutional settings* (pp. 331–358). Cambridge, UK: Cambridge University Press.

McCall, J. G., & Simmons, J. L. (1966). *Identities and interaction: An examination of human associations in everyday life*. New York: Free Press.

McCullough, M. (1992). *Black and white women's friendships: Claiming the margins*. Annor Arbor, MI: UMI Dissertation Services.

Mehrabian, A. (1972) *Nonverbal communication*. Chicago: Aldine-Atherton.

Michaels, S., & Collins, J. (1984). Oral discourse styles: Classroom interaction and the acquisition of literacy. In D. Tannen (Ed.), *Coherence in spoken and written discourse* (pp. 219–244). Norwood, NJ: Ablex.

Miller, J. M. (2000). Language use, identity, and social interaction. *Research on Language and Social Interaction, 33*, 69–100.

Miller, J. R., & Stiff, J. B. (1993). *Deceptive communication*. Newbury Park, CA: Sage.

Miller, L. (2000). Negative assessments in a Japanese-American workplace encounter. In H. Spencer-Oatley (Ed.), *Culturally speaking: Managing rapport through talk across cultures* (pp. 240–254). London: Continuum.

Miner, H. (1956). Body ritual among the Nacirema. *American Anthropologist, 58*, 503–507.

Morris, G. H., & Coursey, M. (1989). Negotiating the meaning of employees' conduct. *Southern Communication Journal, 54*, 185–205.

Morson, G. S., & Emerson, C. (1990). *Mikhail Bakhtin: Creation of a prosaics*. Palo Alto, CA: Stanford University Press.

Mulholland, J. (1996). A series of story turns: Intertexuality and collegiality. *Text, 16,* 535–556.

Murphy, B., & Neu, J. (1996). My grade's too low: The speech act set of complaining. In S. M. Gass & J. Neu (Eds.), *Speech acts across cultures: Challenges to communication in a second language* (pp. 191–216). Berlin: Mouton de Gruyter.

Myers-Scotton, C., & Bolonyai, A. (2001). Calculating speakers: Codeswitching in a rational choice model. *Language in Society, 30,* 1–28.

Nakayama, T. K., & Krizck, R. L. (1999). Whiteness as a strategic resource. In T. K. Nakayama & J. N. Martin (Eds.), *Whiteness: The communication of social identity* (pp. 87–106). Thousand Oaks, CA: Sage.

Naughton, J. M. (1996). *Discursively managing evaluation and acceptance in a hospice team meeting: A dilemma.* Ann Arbor, MI: UMI Dissertation Services.

Ng, S. H., Brooke, M., & Dunne, M. (1995). Interruption and influence in discussion groups. *Journal of Language and Social Psychology, 15,* 369–381.

Nofsinger, R. E. (1991). *Everyday conversation.* Newbury Park, CA: Sage.

Norton, R. (1983). *Communicator style: Theory, applications and measures.* Beverly Hills, CA: Sage.

Oboler, S. (1992). The politics of labeling Latino/a: Cultural identities of self and others. *Latin American Perspectives, 19,* 45–58.

Ochs, E. (1993). Constructing social identity: A language socialization perspective. *Research on Language and Social Interaction, 26,* 287–306.

Ochs, E., Schegloff, E. A., & Thompson, S. A. (Eds.). (1996). *Interaction and grammar.* Cambridge, UK: Cambridge University Press.

Ochs, E., & Taylor, C. (1992). Family narrative as political activity. *Discourse and Society, 3,* 301–340.

Ochs, E., & Taylor, C. (1995). The "father knows best" dynamic in dinnertime narrative. In K. Hall & M. Bucholtz (Eds.), *Gender articulated: Language and the socially constructed self* (pp. 67–96). New York: Routledge.

Parrott, W. G., & Harré, R. (1996). Embarrassment and the threat to character. In R. Harré & W. G. Parrott (Eds.), *The emotions: Social, cultural and biological dimensions* (pp 39–56). London: Sage.

Pavlidou, T.-S. (2000). Telephone conversations in Greek and German: Attending to the relationship aspects of communication. In H. Spencer-Oatley (Ed.), *Culturally speaking: Managing rapport through talk across cultures* (pp. 121–140). London: Continuum.

Philipsen, G. (1975). Speaking "like a man" in Teamsterville: Cultural patterns of role enactment in an urban neighborhood. *Quarterly Journal of Speech, 61,* 13–22.

Philipsen, G. (1992). *Speaking culturally: Exploration in social communication.* Albany: State University of New York Press.

Phillips, S. (1983). *The invisible culture: Communication in classroom and community on the Warm Springs Indian reservation.* New York: Longman.

Pittam, J. (1994). *Voice in social interaction.* Thousand Oaks, CA: Sage.

Planalp, J. (1999). *Communicating emotion: Social, moral and cultural processes*. Cambridge, UK: Cambridge University Press.

Polanyi, L. (1985). *Telling the American story: A structural analysis of conversational storytelling*. Norwood, NJ: Ablex.

Pomerantz, A. (1978). Compliment responses: Notes on the co-operation of multiple constraints. In J. Schenkein (Ed.), *Studies in the organization of conversational interaction* (pp. 57–101). Cambridge, UK: Cambridge University Press.

Pomerantz, A. (1980). Telling "my side": Limited access as a "fishing device." *Sociological Inquiry, 50*, 186–198.

Pomerantz, A. (1984). Agreeing and disagreeing with assessments: Some features of preferred/dispreferred turn shapes. In J. M. Atkinson & J. Heritage (Eds.), *Structures of social action: Studies in conversation analysis* (pp. 57–101). Cambridge, UK: Cambridge University Press.

Pomerantz, A. (1989/90). Constructing skepticism: Four devices used to engender the audience's skepticism. *Research on Language and Social Interaction, 22*, 293–313.

Potter, J. (1996). *Representing reality: Discourse, rhetoric and social construction*. London: Sage.

Prentice, D. A. (1994). Do language reforms change our way of thinking? *Journal of Language and Social Psychology, 13*, 3–19.

Psathas, G. (1995). *Conversation analysis: The study of talk-in-interaction*. Thousand Oaks, CA: Sage.

Ragan, S. L. (1983). Alignment and conversational coherence. In R. T. Craig & K. Tracy (Eds.), *Conversational coherence: Form, structure and strategy* (pp. 157–173). Beverly Hills, CA: Sage.

Ragan, S. L. (2000). Sociable talk in women's health care contexts: Two forms of nonmedical talk. In J. Coupland (Ed.), *Small talk* (pp. 269–287). Harlow, UK: Pearson.

Rawlins, W. K. (1992). *Friendship matters: Communication, dialectics and the life course*. New York: Aldine de Gruyter.

Resler, B. J., Black, J. B., & Lehnert, W. G. (1985). Thematic knowledge structures in the understanding and generation of knowledge. *Discourse Processes, 8*, 357–389.

Riessman, C. K. (1997). A short story about long stories. *Journal of Narrative and Life History, 7*, 155–158.

Robinson, W. P. (1996). *Deceit, delusion, and detection*. Thousand Oaks, CA: Sage.

Rubin, L. B. (1976). *Worlds of pain: Life in the working-class family*. New York: Basic Books.

Ryan, E. B., Giles, H., Bartolucci, G., & Henwood, K. (1986). Psycholinguistic and social psychological components of communication by and with the elderly. *Language and Communication, 6*, 1–24.

Ryan, E. B., Hummert, M. L., & Boich, L. L. (1995). Communication predicaments of aging: Patronizing behavior toward older adults. *Journal of Language and Social Psychology, 14*, 144–166.

Sacks, H. (1992). *Lectures on conversation* (2 vols.; G. Jefferson, Ed.). Cambridge, MA: Blackwell.

Sacks, H., Schegloff, E. A., & Jefferson, G. (1974). A simplest systematics for the organization of turn taking for conversation. *Language, 50,* 696–735.

Sanders, R. (1995). The sequential inferential theories of Sanders and Gottman. In D. P. Cushman & B. Kovacic (Eds.), *Watershed research traditions in human communication* (pp. 101–136). Albany: State University of New York Press.

Sattel, J. (1983). Men, inexpressiveness and power. In B. Thorne, C. Kramarae, & N. Henley (Eds.), *Language, gender and society* (pp. 119–124). Cambridge, MA: Newbury House.

Schegloff, E. A. (1997). "Narrative analysis": Thirty years later. *Journal of Narrative and Life History, 7,* 97–106.

Schegloff, E. A. (2000). Overlapping talk and the organization of turn-taking for conversation. *Language in Society, 29,* 1–63.

Schegloff, E. A., & Sacks, H. (1973). Opening up closings. *Semiotica, 8,* 289–327.

Scheuer, J. (2001). Recontextualization and communicative styles in job interviews. *Discourse Studies, 3,* 223–248.

Schiffrin, D. (1984). Jewish argument as sociability. *Language in Society, 13,* 311–335.

Schiffrin, D. (1987). *Discourse markers.* Cambridge, UK: Cambridge University Press.

Schiffrin, D. (1994). *Approaches to discourse.* Oxford, UK: Blackwell.

Schonbach, P. (1990). *Account episodes.* New York: Cambridge University Press.

Scollon, R., & Scollon, S. B. K. (1981). *Narrative, literacy and face in interethnic communication.* Norwood, NJ: Ablex.

Scollon, R., & Scollon, S. W. (1995). *Intercultural communication.* Cambridge, MA: Blackwell.

Scott, M. B., & Lyman, S. (1968). Accounts. *American Sociological Review, 33,* 46–62.

Searle, J. R. (1969). *Speech acts.* Cambridge, UK: Cambridge University Press.

Searle, J. R. (1979). *Expression and meaning.* Cambridge, UK: Cambridge University Press.

Semin, G. R., & Manstead, A. S. R. (1983). *The accountability of conduct.* New York: Academic Press.

Sequiera, D. L. (1993). Personal address as negotiated meaning in an American church community. *Research on Language and Social Interaction, 26,* 259–285.

Shapiro, B. P., van de Broeck, P., & Fletcher, C. R. (1995). Using story-based causal diagrams to analyze disagreements about complex events. *Discourse Processes, 20,* 51–77.

Shaw, C. L. M. (1997). Personal narrative: Revealing self and reflecting other. *Human Communication Research, 24,* 302–219.

Shepard, C. A., Giles, H., & Le Poire, B. (2001). Communication accommodation theory. In W. P. Robinson & H. Giles (Eds.), *The new handbook of language and social psychology* (pp. 33–56). Chichester, UK: Wiley.

Shuy, R. W. (1993). *Language crimes: The use and abuse of language evidence in the courtroom*. Malden, MA: Blackwell.

Shuy, R. W. (1998). *The language of confession, interrogation, and deception*. Thousand Oaks, CA: Sage.

Sloane, T. O. (Ed.). (2001). *Encyclopedia of rhetoric*. Oxford, UK: Oxford University Press.

Smith, R. C., & Eisenberg, E. M. (1987). Conflict at Disneyland: A root metaphor analysis. *Communication Monographs, 54*, 367–380.

Spears, A. K. (1992). Reassessing the status of black English. *Language in Society, 21*, 675–682.

Spencer-Oatley, H. (2000a). Introduction: Language, culture and rapport management. In H. Spencer-Oatley (Ed.), *Culturally speaking: Managing rapport through talk across cultures* (pp. 1–9). London: Continuum.

Spencer-Oatley, H. (2000b). Rapport management: A framework for analysis. In H. Spencer-Oatley (Ed.), *Culturally speaking: Managing rapport through talk across cultures* (pp. 11–46). London: Continuum.

Stafford, L., & Kline, S. (1996). Married women's names: Choices and sense of self. *Communication Reports, 9*, 85–92.

Sugimoto, N. (1999a). A Japan–US comparison of apology styles. In N. Sugimoto (Ed.), *Japanese apology across disciplines* (pp. 79–104). Commack, NY: Nova.

Sugimoto, N. (1999b). Norms of apologies depicted in American and Japanese literatures on manners and etiquette. In N. Sugimoto (Ed.), *Japanese apology across disciplines* (pp. 47–78). Commack, NY: Nova.

Sugimoto, N. (Ed.). (1999c). *Japanese apology across disciplines*. Commack, NY: Nova.

Sunwolf, & Frey, L. R. (2001). Storytelling: The power of narrative communication and interpretation. In W. P. Robinson & H. Giles (Eds.), *The new handbook of language and social psychology* (pp. 119–135). Chicester, UK: Wiley.

Swales, J. (1998). *Other floors, other voices: A textography of a small university building*. Mahwah, NJ: Erlbaum.

Tannen, D. (1981). Indirectness in discourse: Ethnicity in conversational style. *Discourse Processes, 4*, 221–228.

Tannen, D. (1982). Ethnic style in male–female conversation. In J. J. Gumperz (Ed.), *Language and social identity* (pp. 217–231). Cambridge, UK: Cambridge University Press.

Tannen, D. (1984). *Conversational style: Analyzing talk among friends*. Norwood, NJ: Ablex.

Tannen, D. (1986). *That's not what I meant!: How conversational style makes or breaks relationships*. New York: Ballantine Books.

Tannen, D. (1989). *Talking voices: Repetition, dialogue, and imagery in conversational discourse*. New York: Cambridge University Press.

Tannen, D. (1990). *You just don't understand: Women and men in conversation*. New York: Ballantine Books.

Tannen, D. (1993a). The relativity of linguistic strategies: Rethinking power and solidarity in gender and dominance. In D. Tannen (Ed.), *Gender and conversational interaction* (pp. 165–188). New York: Oxford University Press.

Tannen, D. (1993b). What's in a frame?: Surface evidence for underlying expectations. In D. Tannen (Ed.), *Framing in discourse* (pp. 14–56). New York: Oxford University Press.

Tannen, D. (Ed.). (1993c). *Framing in discourse*. New York: Oxford University Press.

Tanno, D. (1997). Names, narratives, and the evolution of ethnic identity. In A. Gonzalez, M. Houston, & V. Chen (Eds.), *Our voices: Essays in culture, ethnicity, and communication* (2nd ed., pp. 28–32). Los Angeles, CA: Roxbury.

Taylor, C. E. (1995). "You think it was a fight?": Co-constructing (the struggle for) meaning, face, and family in everyday narrative activity. *Research on Language and Social Interaction, 28,* 283–317.

ten Have, P. (1999). *Doing conversation analysis.* London: Sage.

Tiersma, P. M. (1999). *Legal language.* Chicago: University of Chicago Press.

Tornqvist, J. S., Anderson, D. E., & De Paulo, B. M. (2001). Deceiving. In W. P. Robinson & H. Giles (Eds.), *The new handbook of language and social psychology* (pp. 271–284). Chicester, UK: Wiley.

Trabasso, T., van de Broek, & Suh, S. Y. (1989). Logical necessity and transitivity of causal relations in stories. *Discourse Processes, 12,* 1–26.

Tracy, K. (1997a). *Colloquium: Dilemmas of academic discourse.* Norwood, NJ: Ablex.

Tracy, K. (1997b). Interactional trouble in emergency service requests: A problem of frames. *Research on Language and Social Interaction, 30,* 315–343.

Tracy, K. (2001). Discourse analysis in communication. In D. Schiffrin, D. Tannen, & H. Hamilton (Eds.), *Handbook of discourse analysis* (pp. 725–749). Oxford, UK: Blackwell.

Tracy, K. (2002). Rhetorically-informed discourse analysis: Methodological reflections. In T. Goodnight (Ed.), *Arguing communication and culture* (Vol. I, pp. 243–250). Annandale, VA: National Communication Association.

Tracy, K. (in press). Reconstructing communicative practices. In K. Fitch & R. Sanders (Eds.), *Handbook of language and social interaction.* Mahwah, NJ: Erlbaum.

Tracy, K., & Agne, R. R. (in press). "I just need to ask somebody some questions": Sensitivities in domestic dispute calls. In J. Cottrell (Ed.), *Language in the legal process.* Brunel, UK: Palgrave.

Tracy, K., & Anderson, D. L. (1999). Relational positioning strategies in calls to the police: A dilemma. *Discourse Studies, 1,* 201–226.

Tracy, K., & Ashcraft, C. (2001). Crafting polices about controversial values: How wording disputes manage a group dilemma. *Journal of Applied Communication Research, 29,* 297–316.

Tracy, K., & Baratz, S. (1993). Intellectual discussion in the academy as situated discourse. *Communication Monographs, 60,* 300–320.

Tracy, K., Craig, R. T., Smith, M., & Spisak, F. (1984). The discourse of requests: An assessment of a compliance-gaining approach. *Human Communication Research, 10,* 513–538.

Tracy, K., & Muller, H. (2001). Diagnosing a school board's interactional trouble: Theorizing problem formulating. *Communication Theory, 11,* 84–104.

Tracy, K., & Naughton, J. M. (1994). The identity work of questioning in intellectual discussion. *Communication Monographs, 61,* 281–302.

Tracy, K., & Naughton, J. M. (2000). Institutional identity-work: A better lens. In J. Coupland (Ed.), *Small talk* (pp. 62–83). Harlow, UK: Pearson.

Tracy, K., & Spradlin, A. (1994). "Talking like a mediator": Conversational moves of experienced divorce mediators. In J. Folger & T. Jones (Eds.), *New directions in mediation* (pp. 110–132). Thousand Oaks, CA: Sage.

Tracy, K., & Tracy, S. J. (1998). Rudeness at 911: Reconceptualizing face and face-attack. *Human Communication Research, 25,* 225–251.

Tracy, K., van Dusen, D., & Robinson, S. (1987). "Good" and "bad" criticism: A descriptive analysis. *Journal of Communication, 37,* 46–59.

Tracy, S. J., & Tracy, K. (1998). Emotion labor at 911: A case study and theoretical critique. *Journal of Applied Communication, 26,* 390–411.

Trudgill, P. (1974). *Sociolinguistics: An introduction.* Hammondsworth, UK: Penguin Books.

Tusing, K. J., & Dillard, J. P. (2000). The sounds of dominance: Vocal precursors of perceived dominance during interpersonal influence. *Human Communication Research, 26,* 148–171.

U.S. English, Inc. [Online]. (2002). Available: http://www.us-english.org/inc/official/states.asp [2002, March 3]

van Dijk, T. A. (1987). *Communicating racism: Ethnic prejudice in thought and talk.* Newbury Park, CA: Sage.

Wander, P. C., Martin, J. N., & Nakayama, T. K. (1999). Whiteness and beyond: Sociohistorical foundations of whiteness and contemporary challenges. In T. K. Nakayama & J. N. Martin (Eds.), *Whiteness: The communication of social identity* (pp. 13–26). Thousand Oaks, CA: Sage.

Watanabe, S. (1993) Cultural differences in framing: American and Japanese group discussions. In D. Tannen (Ed.), *Framing in discourse* (pp. 176–209). New York: Oxford University Press.

Watzlawick, P., Beavin, J. H., & Jackson, D. D. (1967). *Pragmatics of human communication.* New York: Norton.

Weatherall, A. (1998). Women and men in language: An analysis of seminaturalistic person descriptions. *Human Communication Research, 25,* 278–292.

Weinstein, E. A., & Deutschberger, P. (1963). Some dimensions of altercasting. *Sociometry, 26,* 456–466.

Wetherell, M., Taylor, S., & Yates, S. J. (Eds.). (2001a). *Discourse as data.* London: Sage.

Wetherell, M., Taylor, S., & Yates, S. J. (Eds.). (2001b). *Discourse theory and practice.* London: Sage.

Whorf, B. L. (1956). *Language, thought, and reality.* Cambridge, MA: MIT Press.

Why wives use husbands' names. (1994). *American Demographics, 16*(3), 9–11.

Wierzbicka, A. (1991). *Cross-cultural pragmatics: The semantics of human interaction.* Berlin: Mouton de Gruyter.

Williams, A. (1996). Young people's evaluations of intergenerational versus peer underaccommodation: Sometimes older is better? *Journal of Language and Social Psychology, 15,* 291–311.

Wilson, T. P., Wiemann, J. M., & Zimmerman, D. H. (1984). Models of turn taking in conversational interaction. *Journal of Language and Social Psychology, 3,* 159–184.

Winchatz, M. R. (2001). Social meanings in German interactions: An ethnographic analysis of the second-person pronoun *Sie. Research on Language and Social Interaction, 34,* 337–369.

Wood, L. A., & Kroger, R. O. (2000). *Doing discourse analysis: Methods for studying action in talk and text.* Thousand Oaks, CA: Sage.

Wooffitt, R. (1992). *Telling tales of the unexpected: Accounts of the paranormal.* Hemel Hempstead, UK: Harvester.

Yahya-Othman, S. (1995). Aren't you going to greet me?: Impoliteness in Swahili greetings. *Text, 15,* 209–227.

Yamada, H. (1992). *American and Japanese business discourse: A comparison of interactional styles.* Norwood, NJ: Ablex.

Ylänne-McEwen, V., & Coupland, N. (2000). Accommodation theory: A conceptual resource for intercultural sociolinguistics. In H. Spencer-Oatley (Ed.), *Culturally speaking: Managing rapport through talk across cultures* (pp. 191–214). London: Continuum.

de la Zerda, N., & Hopper, R. (1979). Employment interviewers' reactions to Mexican American speech. *Communication Monographs, 46,* 126–134.

Zimmerman, D. (1998). Identity, context, and interaction. In C. Antaki & S. Widdicombe (Eds.), *Identities in talk* (pp. 89–106). London: Sage.

Index

Page numbers followed by "e" indicate example, "f" indicate figure, and "t" indicate table.

226

About the Author

Karen Tracy, PhD, is Professor of Communication at the University of Colorado at Boulder, where she regularly teaches a course on how everyday talk builds and reflects identities. She also teaches classes on discourse analysis and ethnographic methods, as well as special topic seminars that examine communicative trouble in the justice system and in educational sites. Dr. Tracy is the author of *Colloquium: Dilemmas of Academic Discourse* (1997, Ablex) and more than 40 articles and book chapters. She is especially fond of writing methodological reflection pieces about how communication research ought to be conducted. Currently, she is at work on a book exploring the interactional challenges of democracy in school board meetings. Dr. Tracy received her PhD in communication from the University of Wisconsin and is past editor of the journal *Research on Language and Social Interaction*.